CRISIS IN THE KREMLIN

BY THE SAME AUTHOR:

LETTERS FROM MOSCOW

CRISIS IN THE KREMLIN

Soviet Succession and the Rise of Gorbachov

by

RICHARD OWEN

LONDON

VICTOR GOLLANCZ LTD

1986

First published in Great Britain 1986
by Victor Gollancz Ltd,
14 Henrietta Street, London WC2E 8QJ

British Library Cataloguing in Publication Data
Owen, Richard, *1947–*
   Crisis in the Kremlin: Soviet succession
   and the rise of Gorbachov.
   1. Soviet Union—Politics and government
   2. Political leadership—Soviet Union
   I. Title
   351.003' 4' 0947   JN6541

ISBN 0–575–03635–4

Photoset by CAS Typesetters, Southampton
and printed in Great Britain by
St Edmundsbury Press, Bury St Edmunds, Suffolk

Question: A new generation of Soviet leaders has risen to power with you, Mr Gorbachov. What can this new generation give your country, apart from style?

Gorbachov: I think that what is taking place is a normal process. There is nothing out of the ordinary in it.

—From an interview with French Television 30 September 1985

CONTENTS

PREFACE

AT ALMOST ANY time of the year a crowd of tourists can be seen standing on Red Square near the Spassky Gate into the Kremlin, gazing at the fantastic gaily-coloured bulbous domes of St Basil's Cathedral. Few if any are aware that just behind them, through the well guarded archway from which sleek black Zil limousines now and then emerge, is the private office of one of the two most powerful men in the world: the General Secretary of the Communist Party of the Soviet Union. From his office, situated in the Kremlin's Council of Ministers building, the General Secretary rules an apparatus which controls the lives of the Soviet Union's 278 million people, including a still backward and inefficient economy, and directs Russia's global role as a mighty armed superpower. The office is reached through double doors from an ante-room containing up-to-the-minute telecommunications equipment as well as a traditional print of Lenin and a square modern clock. Inside the office itself is a long T-shaped table covered with green baize, and paper and pens laid ready at each place. The walls are hung with ivory silk wallpaper separated by Karelian birch panelling; three glittering chandeliers hang from the ceiling. There is no decoration apart from another framed picture of Lenin facing a framed picture of Marx on the opposite wall. When Andropov used this office a portrait of Brezhnev looked down as well, but most Soviet leaders prefer not to lay stress on any of their predecessors except Lenin himself.

This book describes the process by which Brezhnev, Andropov, Chernenko and finally Mikhail Gorbachov came to reach the General Secretary's office, and thus supreme power, in the secretive and Byzantine world of Kremlin politics. As recorded in *Letters from Moscow*, I was fortunate to arrive in the Soviet capital as correspondent for *The Times* in the period before the death of Brezhnev, and left towards the end of Gorbachov's first year in power. These four years witnessed three presidential deaths and several other Red Square state funerals as the old Kremlin generation gradually made way for the new. I was therefore able to watch at first hand a dramatically compressed process of political transition. Because the Soviet Union is an authoritarian and closed society, no foreign observer has direct access to the corridors of power. Soviet officials do their utmost, with remarkable efficiency, to ensure that even the smallest detail of what goes on in the inner councils of the Kremlin is hidden from the inquisitive, including Soviet press colleagues, many of whom are only told as much as the authorities think they ought to know. In a system controlled by the KGB as well as by the Party, it goes without saying that official records and files are kept under lock and key, and the penalties for releasing even the most innocuous unauthorized information or statistic are severe.

It was nonetheless possible to chronicle the tortuous and ruthless power struggle in the Kremlin by carefully following Politburo appearances and speeches to which the press is admitted; by scrutinizing the Soviet press, radio and television, and by gleaning clues through conversations with contacts in the Soviet hierarchy as well as with Western diplomats in Moscow over a period of time. There were also occasions, such as receptions for visiting VIPs, when one came into contact with senior Party figures, including the General Secretary himself, although alas such contacts are no longer as frequent as they were in Khrushchev's day.

This book records and analyses events both in public and behind the scenes in Russia over the past four years: Andropov's manoeuvrings to succeed Brezhnev, his record in power after Brezhnev's death, Chernenko's successful bid for power when Andropov died with his reform programme barely begun, and Gorbachov's takeover when Chernenko, too, succumbed to illness and old age. But the three successions between 1982 and 1985 could not be discussed without an understanding of the three preceding Kremlin transitions: the death of Lenin in the 1920s, the death of Stalin in the 1950s, and the overthrow of Khrushchev by Brezhnev in the 1960s.

The result is not a history of the Soviet Union, nor a series of biographies of Soviet leaders: instead I have focused on the moments of transition from 1924 to 1985–6, while at the same time looking in detail at the personalities and issues involved. Full treatments of Stalin's or Brezhnev's records in office will be found elsewhere. Here I have dealt with Soviet history in so far as it throws light on the transition from Lenin to Stalin, from Stalin to Khrushchev, from Khrushchev to Brezhnev, from Brezhnev to Andropov, from Andropov to Chernenko, and from Chernenko to Gorbachov (Gorbachov is the correct pronunciation). In the final chapters I also offer reflections on what the future holds for Russia now that the Gorbachov generation is in command.

I have avoided footnotes, largely because much of my account is based on my own observations, notes and reports as a correspondent on the spot, coupled with conversations with officials or diplomats who asked not to be named. Where necessary references to newspaper articles are given in the text. For the earlier chapters I have drawn on biographies of Stalin by Isaac Deutscher and Ronald Hingley; of Khrushchev by Roy Medvedev, Mark Frankland and Edward Crankshaw; of Brezhnev by John Dornberg; and of Andropov by Zhores Medvedev and by Jonathan Steele and Eric Abraham. To my knowledge no biography exists of Chernenko. I acknowledge a debt to research papers by Radio Liberty in Munich, whose biographies of Chernenko (RL 69/84) and of Gorbachov (RL 102/85) offer useful material. The latter summarizes evidence about Gorbachov's university days from his former fellow students, including Professor Lev Yudovich (now in emigration). Christian Schmidt-Häuer's biography of Gorbachov also cites evidence from Zdenek Mlynar on the student years and discusses Raisa's academic work. Zhores Medvedev's Gorbachev was published too late for inclusion.

Article Six of the Soviet Constitution specifically gives the Party the leading role in Soviet society. I am conscious of the fact that the General Secretary of the Party is only the pinnacle of the Soviet élite, or nomenklatura, which numbers hundreds of thousands of officials at all levels and in reality runs the Soviet system. The Soviet Union is not a one-man dictatorship: it is an authoritarian one-party state with eighteen million Party members. The Party is represented at the top by the General Secretary's office in the Kremlin and the Central Committee building on Old Square about a mile away, just beyond the giant Rossiya Hotel. Apart from the Party institutions, from the Central Committee down to provincial committees and primary level organizations, other power centres also influence the course of events: the KGB on Dzerzhinsky Square, just up the hill from Old Square, housed in the yellow stone building of a former insurance company (and also in a brand new monolithic grey wing across the street); the Council of Ministers, headed by the Prime Minister, the council of which shares a building with GOSPLAN down in Prospekt Marx, just beyond the Bolshoi Theatre; the Ministries of Defence, the Interior and Foreign Affairs; and the military command.

I have not sought to give a profile of the new Gorbachov nomenklatura by, for example, analysing the careers of newly promoted provincial level (OBKOM) Party secretaries (it is in any case too early to do so); but I have given a broad picture of the Party system, and of the conflict-of-interest groups within the system at points of crisis in the Kremlin, including the most recent transitions. I have concentrated on the manoeuvres at the very top since it is the leader himself who sets the tone and sends instructions down through the pyramid of command. The most perceptive and informed guide to this system, in my view, remains the late Leonard Schapiro's *Communist Party of the Soviet Union*, coupled with his *The Government and Politics of the Soviet Union*. A bibliography of these and other recommended works (such as Michael Voslensky's *Nomenklatura*) is given at the end of the book. Transliteration of proper names is based on the system used by *The Times*.

I was fortunate to have the benefit of Professor Schapiro's guidance and wisdom when I was a graduate student at the London School of Economics, before I joined *The Times*, and indeed before I entered journalism. I can only hope he would have approved of my attempt to live up to the exacting standards he set for us and which he exemplified in his own teaching and writing. If there is any merit in this contribution to our understanding of the Soviet political scene, much of it is due to him. I am also grateful to colleagues in the Western press corps in Moscow who lived through some of the same events with me and gave me the benefit of their views, including Mark Frankland of the *Observer*, Dusko Doder of the *Washington Post* and Don Kimelman of the *Philadelphia Inquirer*. Archie Brown of St. Antony's College Oxford, who takes a more optimistic view of Gorbachov than I do, gave advice. Roy Medvedev, whose great services to his own countrymen as a historian and political observer must surely one day be acknowledged by the Russians themselves, was an ever valuable source of insight and comment. Anonymous thanks go also to several Western diplomatic observers of the Moscow scene, NATO analysts in Brussels, and to equally anonymous informants in the Soviet media and Party and government structure. As it is customary to observe, all errors of judgement or fact are entirely my own.

This book could not have been written if the late Charles Douglas-Home, editor of *The Times*, had not sent me to Moscow in 1982 and given me thoughtful advice and invaluable guidance in the extraordinary period that followed. Ivan Barnes was a sharp, thorough but understanding news editor, guiding day-to-day coverage of the events now given what he would call "a considered view" in this book. The present editor of *The Times*, Charles Wilson, has also taken a close interest in events in Moscow, and I am grateful to him for authorizing a brief but vital spell of sabbatical leave to enable me to complete this book as Gorbachov's first year in power draws to a close.

My wife, Julia, has been an unfailing and essential source of help and support, typing the first draft of the manuscript and much of the final version, saving me from some of the worst errors and infelicities, and sharing with me her perceptions of the remarkable years we spent in Moscow together, all while running our household, whether in Moscow, Brussels or Gloucestershire. *Crisis in the Kremlin* is the result of her efforts as well as mine. My thanks go also to Joan Sodro and Barbara Amilhat, who typed sections of the final draft, and to members of my family for their tolerance, patience and support.

NORTHLEACH   R. O.
MARCH 1986

CHAPTER ONE

Six Soviet Successions

THIS NOVEMBER, AS on every anniversary of the Russian Revolution, Mikhail Gorbachov will walk on stage at the Kremlin Palace of Congresses to preside over the traditional ceremonies on the eve of the annual military parade. The annual appearance by the Politburo is intended to celebrate the unstoppable march of progress since 1917, and to affirm faith in the national and Communist future. Gorbachov, who has inherited this system as Russia's youngest and most sophisticated leader for decades, can convincingly present himself as the embodiment of hopes in the ability of the Soviet state to redeem itself after nearly seventy years, even if—as I will suggest later—there is a very real danger that he will be unable to reform the Communist system to meet the challenges of the late twentieth century and so runs the risk of disappointing the high expectations to which his victory in the succession struggle gave rise after the death of Chernenko.

The succession process is now temporarily closed, hidden from the public eye for some time to come, assuming Gorbachov remains in good health and politically vigorous as well. But in the extraordinary period between 1982, Brezhnev's last year, and 1985–86, when Gorbachov came to power and began to tackle the Brezhnev legacy, I watched the process of Kremlin transition at close quarters as on each Revolution Day the kaleidoscope was shaken up and a different Soviet leadership paraded before us. In 1985 Gorbachov attended his first November gala meeting as leader. The year before, the ailing Chernenko walked unsteadily on stage, with Gorbachov as virtual crown prince, and Marshal Ustinov, the powerful Defence Minister, mysteriously absent (he was mortally ill and died the following month). Over the four-year period of almost continuous Kremlin transition a series of deaths, disgraces and retirements revealed a great deal about how the succession process works, even though the complete inside story will have to wait until the KGB and Party files are opened, if they ever are.

When the Politburo walked on to the platform in November 1983, there were muted gasps of astonishment, among the delegates in the hall, at the absence of Yuri Andropov, President and Party Leader. On to the platform in his place walked Konstantin Chernenko, dismissed as a political has-been the previous year following his defeat by Andropov in the struggle to succeed Brezhnev. The return of Chernenko from political oblivion put many of the received ideas about Soviet succession processes in doubt, and cast many minds back to the Kremlin revolution anniversary celebrations of the year before, just before the death of Leonid Brezhnev.

When the Politburo had walked on to the Kremlin platform in November 1982, most of us up in the press gallery knew we were looking at a provisional government. Leonid Brezhnev, almost an automaton by this stage, puffy and stiff with drugs, took his place to stormy applause, as if he were still the vigorous 58-year-old who had taken over from Nikita Khrushchev nearly twenty years before and who used to be photographed haranguing Party meetings with his sleeves rolled up, his eyes alight beneath the famous bushy eyebrows.

1982 and the decline of Brezhnev was the beginning of the prolonged crisis in the Kremlin. With his obvious disabilities came a subtle campaign by his enemies to undermine his aides, supporters and closest relatives. The Brezhnev régime had become soft, lax, stagnant and corrupt, much to the disgust of the military and the KGB, who thought it was time for a change. Andropov, the former head of the KGB, and now Party secretary for ideology, sat on Brezhnev's left on the Kremlin platform; a gaunt, almost waxen figure, motionless by contrast with the oversized Brezhnev, who fidgeted throughout the ceremonies marking the anniversary of the October Revolution. Yuri Andropov did not look like an heir apparent that November day; if anything he seemed part of the geriatric leadership which had learned its craft under Stalin, and whose time on earth was coming to an end.

The heir to Brezhnev, to all outward appearances, sat on Brezhnev's right, a stocky, animated man with high Siberian cheekbones and a shock of white hair. Konstantin Chernenko had been Brezhnev's chief assistant for a decade, and it showed, as he whispered in his dying chief's ear, turned to talk to Politburo members in the row behind, and at one point even got up from the platform to walk along the back, gripping elbows in the manner of a Western wheeler-dealer politician, and pausing for long exchanges with senior leaders such as Vladimir Dolgikh, the management expert from Siberia so often tipped (wrongly) as a future Prime Minister. Down in the hall, Viktor Grishin droned on at the podium, reading out a speech to largely inattentive listeners, all specially invited, and all used to routine Kremlin utterances.

Far more important than Grishin's remarks on the need to maintain "Bolshevik idealism" in Soviet public life was the drama going on before our eyes on the platform. At the end, Andropov, still deathly pale and still, walked purposefully off into the wings, while Chernenko continued his elbow gripping act among colleagues and potential supporters. Brezhnev moved stiffly off stage, holding on to the backs of the chairs as he did so. As soon as he disappeared from view the spectators departed, but a few of us stayed, looking directly through the door leading off the platform, and saw what the cameras did not record for that evening's state-controlled news: the sight of Brezhnev, a large, shambling figure, falling on the stairs and having to be manhandled by two hefty aides to regain his balance.

A few days later he was dead, and the wily and ruthless Andropov was named his successor. The Kremlin Revolution Day speech was not quite Brezhnev's last appearance: we gathered on Red Square shortly afterwards for the annual November 7th military parade, and watched Brezhnev slowly climb the steps to the top of the Lenin Mausoleum. Again we saw what the cameras did not record, at least not for public consumption: the stiff automaton's wave; Brezhnev's painful aim at a spittoon in the corner; and an aide carefully, almost tenderly placing spectacles on the leader's nose. On a brilliantly sunny day Brezhnev stood for two hours in sub-zero temperatures. A Moscow journalist subsequently revealed to me what many had suspected but could not prove, that the clouds had been seeded with chemicals to ensure a cloudless day, though whether this was merely stage management for the military parade—watched by the world—or a plot by the KGB to undermine Brezhnev's health fatally was never proved.

At all events, four days later news readers appeared on the evening television news dressed in black—although no announcement was made at this stage—light entertainment programmes were cancelled, and Brezhnev's name was left off a telegram to the leaders of Angola. Even then a nation which had not experienced the death of a leader for thirty years was taken by surprise, and many failed to read the signs. The following morning I was on Kutuzovsky Prospekt, near the Politburo apartment building, when radios began to play solemn music. At eleven o'clock the announcement finally came: Leonid Ilych Brezhnev was dead.

In a sense the succession, unlike previous leadership struggles in Russia, had already been decided. There had only been three precedents in Soviet history, one of them Brezhnev's own succession in 1964 involving a plot against the incumbent leader, Khrushchev, rather than a power struggle to succeed a dead one. But it was clear even from these few examples that the death of a Soviet leader was so powerful a shock that the struggle for succession could be traumatic, and was certainly unpredictable. The main drawback, or one of the main drawbacks of the political system bequeathed by Lenin is that although the institutions of Party and government are fairly well defined, with the Communist Party exercising a monopoly of power through a pyramid of Soviets or government councils, there is no built-in mechanism for the election of a new Party leader. For that matter there is no democratic mechanism for the election of officials at any level in either Party or government. Although in theory political office is elective in the Soviet Union, in practice officials are appointed by the Party through a system known as *nomenklatura*, under which the Central Committee decides who is politically reliable and who is not. This rather primitive system inevitably gave rise to a perpetual power struggle, not unlike the ambitious rivalry and ruthless jostling for leadership in the Mafia, New York Tammany Hall style politics or the boardrooms of great multinational corporations—all bodies in which the struggle to achieve power for power's sake can override accountability to electors, shareholders or the rank and file.

Lenin, who never seems to have given much thought to this problem, was obliged to watch helplessly in the last two years of his life, as the men who had made the Revolution with him manoeuvred to succeed him, each of them motivated by personal ambition as much as by a desire to carry through the social and political reforms in the Bolshevik programme. Had Lenin laid down a clear mechanism for the succession, or even acknowledged that the problem existed, things might have been different. As it was, Lenin almost ignored the question of leadership change, only turning his thoughts to the Party succession as he lay dying and even then dealing with it in the kind of vague, semi-anarchistic mood which occasionally took hold of him rather than with the cold-eyed logic which underlay much of his political thought. In his last political testament, a rambling document, he seemed to have no clear guidance at all for those who came after him, beyond noting Trotsky's strengths and weaknesses and warning the Comrades against the "crude" Stalin, and recommending that he be removed. In the event it took Stalin some six years finally to outmanoeuvre all his rivals, exiling Trotsky to Turkey and ultimately to Mexico and death at the hands of one of Stalin's agents in 1940.

Similarly, after Stalin's death in 1953, the succession was unclear. Although one man—Georgy Malenkov—seemed to have manoeuvred himself into the position of heir apparent, the shock at the death of the Soviet Union's second leader, a man who had wielded power in a terrible dictatorship for over twenty years, was so great that once again the leadership struggle was confused, protracted and bitter. It was two years before Nikita Khrushchev was able to eliminate Malenkov and his allies and become both First Secretary of the Party and Prime Minister.

When Brezhnev died in 1982, therefore, a similar drawn out and bloody struggle might have been expected. Brezhnev, like Stalin, had been in command of Russia's affairs for some twenty years, and the rivalry to succeed him was intense. And yet, to those of us who walked the streets of Moscow on the day of his death and talked to ordinary Russians in ships and parks, it was striking that there was no confusion or panic, no sense of cataclysm of the kind veterans remembered after the death of Lenin in 1924 or the death of Stalin in 1953. There was a sense of shock that a familiar figure Russians had lived with for two decades was no longer there, as if some part of the landscape had suddenly disappeared overnight. But the shock was muted, and the atmosphere was surprisingly relaxed. It was only two days later, when the Central Committee met, that the atmosphere changed. Suddenly the main avenues and sidestreets were full of troops and police checking identity cards in a show of strength and discipline to coincide with Andropov's swift and apparently unchallenged appointment as Brezhnev's successor at the Central Committee. It was an impressive and carefully prepared coup backed by the armed forces and the KGB, Andropov's former fief.

In retrospect it seems that the Andropov succession, smooth and swift as it was, amounted to an aberration rather than the political pattern of the future, and that Gorbachov is the real successor to Brezhnev. In the stimulating first days of the new leadership it seemed quite logical that the problem of the succession should have been solved not only by the Party but also by the two institutions which after 65 years of Soviet rule clearly wielded enormous power and to a great extent provided the glue which held the Soviet society together—the armed forces (coupled with nationalist and patriotic sentiment) and the KGB, with all its impressive machinery of internal discipline and control. The impression was confirmed when Andropov embarked not only on a series of initiatives in foreign affairs, including arms control, but also on tentative economic reform moves at home designed ultimately, as he put it, to transform the cumbersome Soviet administrative system "from top to bottom", and to bring it into line with the needs of a twentieth century super power.

Several factors played a key role in undermining Andropov and once again throwing the whole succession problem into the air. One was his own health, which in turn linked to the fact that his generation of Soviet leaders has been in positions of power since the 1930s, with some senior ministers and officials taking office at advanced age. Another was the reassertion of the institution which rules the country at all levels—the Communist Party of the Soviet Union. When the Politburo walked on to the Palace of Congresses stage in November 1983, a year after Brezhnev's death, it was not Andropov we saw leading them to their seats but the stocky white-haired figure of Konstantin Chernenko, apparently so decisively defeated twelve months before. What had kept Chernenko in the position of Kremlin Number Two was the same force which had given Stalin his victory in 1930 and enabled Khrushchev to outmanoeuvre all rivals in 1956, and for that matter had enabled Brezhnev to consolidate his power after the fall of Khrushchev in 1964: the Party apparatus, from the three hundred men of the Central Committee down through the regional and district Party officials to the crucial Prefects of the Communist system, the provincial Committee Secretaries—or OBKOM (from Oblast or province).

In February 1984, when Andropov finally succumbed to rapidly deteriorating heart and kidney complaints, Chernenko was not the most obvious choice for successor. He was 72, the oldest man ever to be elected General or First Secretary, a dismal public speaker and a man with no practical experience whatever of industry, agriculture, diplomacy or indeed any field of economic or political activity except the Party bureaucracy. Ultimately he was put in power partly by cautious fellow members of the old guard anxious to retain their forty-year-old monopoly of power, but also by the *apparatchiks* who had been disturbed by the upheavals of the brief Andropov era, just as they or their predecessors opted for Brezhnev after the erratic policies of the unpredictable Khrushchev and had earlier given Stalin supreme authority in Russia rather than the arrogant and mercurial Lev Trotsky. Gorbachov, too, though very different from Chernenko, is a Party *apparatchik* through and through. But he is the beneficiary of the Andropov revolution, and is carrying through his changes.

The question for the future is whether the mechanism for political succession in the Soviet Union—short of democratic reforms in the system, which are most unlikely—can settle down into a form of relatively smooth transition rather than the present almost continuous struggle for power, now subterranean, now on the surface, which makes the Soviet Union a difficult and unpredictable power to deal with. It is fairly well established, after several transitions, that the leader of the Soviet Union conforms to certain attributes. He is both a Politburo member and a Central Committee Secretary; he has the support of the armed forces and the KGB (although he is not solely their candidate); he works initially through a collective leadership, but swiftly becomes *primus inter pares* (although Gorbachov has broken this pattern); combining the jobs of Party leader and head of state, or possibly Party leader and Prime Minister, he is ruthless, having fought his way to the top in a political system which operates according to the laws of the jungle; and he will have earned the loyalty of the vast mass of uninspired middle and low ranking Party bureaucrats.

When Lenin was in power, in the early 1920s, most of the Bolsheviks in the Politburo of the time were in their early forties and were fired by the ideals for which they had made the Revolution. Khrushchev and Brezhnev came to power in their fifties, and between them took Russia into a period of peaceful coexistence with the Western world. The average age of the Politburo under Andropov and Chernenko was nearly seventy, and the fatigue and bitterness of the old men in the Kremlin was to some extent reflected in the isolationist and conservative policies of the Chernenko leadership. Gorbachov, the new leader, is a member of the younger generation; but will he be able to sweep away the cynicism, weariness and stagnation of recent years and give Russia a new sense of purpose and idealism?

The essential dilemma of the Soviet political system remains that posed by Lenin in the early 1920s as he came to grips with the problems of power and responsibility, as opposed to underground conspiracy. Seventy years on, Russia is a military superpower with a vast industrial base and a global reach. But, as in the 1920s, when it was a fledgling socialist state, Russia is unable to feed its own people properly (the Brezhnev food programme of May 1982 was a tacit admission of this, and so far Gorbachov has not altered the situation radically) or to meet consumer demands. The question which has occasionally been met head on by successive Soviet leaders but which has been equally often dodged is how—and whether—economic liberalization and concessions to popular demand can be combined with a political system which is essentially secretive, self-perpetuating and Jesuitical in its inner processes.

Of all the Soviet political processes, the most secretive remains the emergence of the General Secretary, who, until Gorbachov, was usually President (Chairman of the Praesidium of the Supreme Soviet) as well. A leader has to have the backing of the Central Committee, and a great deal of lobbying goes on in the Central Committee during a succession crisis, in particular during the critical month when it becomes obvious that the incumbent is dying or incapacitated. But new procedures adopted by the Communist Party in Italy following the death of Enrico Berlinguer are quite unthinkable in the Soviet Union itself. Berlinguer, who pioneered reformist Euro-Communism and independence from Moscow, insisted on taking the election of a leader out of the secret smoke-filled rooms and into the light of day or, at least, within the Party membership. Under the new rules in Italy an eight-man committee has to interview individually all members of the Party Central Committee, some 240 men and women, to sound out their opinions in advance of the vote.

It seemed doubtful whether Mikhail Gorbachov, who attended the Berlinguer funeral in Rome on behalf of the Politburo, found this semi-open system in the least attractive, let alone applicable to Soviet conditions. In Russia the process remains comparable to the election of a new Pope at the Vatican, except that no puff of white smoke emerges from the Kremlin roof, and no great crowd gathers on Red Square to shout joyously: "We have a General Secretary!" The Vatican is a sieve of leaks and revelations compared to the closed system operated by the Communist Party of the Soviet Union.

It is instructive to compare the succession crises of November 1982 and February 1984. In both cases what went on behind the Kremlin walls remained a strictly kept secret, but enough hints (possibly deliberately leaked) did reach the ears of those of us in Moscow to enable us to reconstruct what had taken place. When Brezhnev died, it was clear that the contest was between Yuri Andropov, the former head of the KGB who had taken the post of Secretary for Ideology six months before to secure his standing within the Party, and Konstantin Chernenko, also a Central Committee Secretary and for many years Brezhnev's chief assistant. To many Western observers it seemed a close-run thing, and surprisingly enough many Soviet observers also failed to see that Andropov had manoeuvred so skilfully over the previous year that he was able to present the Politburo with a *fait accompli*. When the Politburo met in advance of the Central Committee Plenum, Nikolai Tikhonov, the Prime Minister, got up to propose Chernenko, only to be told by Marshal Ustinov, the Defence Minister, that the decision had already been taken. It was in effect a coup by the military and the KGB to put the austere and intellectual Andropov in power.

When Andropov died in February 1984, Chernenko and Tikhonov made sure that their earlier mistakes were not repeated. Chernenko's election was not unopposed; on the contrary, the younger generation put in a firm bid in the form of Mikhail Gorbachov, Andropov's 53-year-old protégé and heir apparent. There was an unprecedented delay of four days between Andropov's death and the convening of the Central Committee Plenum which elected Chernenko. In between the Politburo met several times to thrash out the succession question, naming Chernenko to head the funeral commission in an obvious sign that his status as acting leader was to be confirmed. Rearguard action by Gorbachov and his allies kept the world in suspense for a few days, but the election of Chernenko showed once again that in moments of crisis the Central Committee, representing a vast body of Party bureaucrats, can play a critical role. A behind-the-scenes deal was struck between the generations, on the understanding that Gorbachov would not have long to wait—and he duly took over in March 1985. The drawback of this clandestine system of selection is that the struggle for power is a continuous one, especially when—as has happened in the past two or three years—one member of the older generation is succeeded by another. This in turn has the effect of making Soviet policy static or uncertain, as factions within the hierarchy manoeuvre for the next succession crisis, using policy issues as a political weapon.

New leaders have to take Russia into the future: they also have to deal with the past, including the recent past, by deciding how to present the last three succession struggles in the official Soviet history books. How the Gorbachov team do this will to some extent tell us what kind of men they are, and how they perceive the evolution of the Soviet system. Brezhnev, Andropov and Chernenko are buried on Red Square behind the Lenin mausoleum, and their memories have been kept alive by their followers as part of the continuing struggle for the soul of Russia. But Brezhnev and Andropov could easily find themselves joining Stalin and Khrushchev in the category of barely mentionable Soviet leaders, so could Konstantin Chernenko and so, ultimately, could Gorbachov. It cannot be very satisfying for a Soviet leader to know that the adulation he receives in his lifetime crumbles into dust the moment the Red Square funeral is over. It will take a courageous and farsighted man to change a system in which the only two leaders granted the virtues of political wisdom and achievement are Lenin and whoever happens to be the current occupant of Russia's supreme posts. The way in which Gorbachov approaches the history of his own country, and the role of his predecessors, will tell us much about whether the Kremlin transition process has begun to settle into an established pattern of change and continuity or whether the law of the political jungle still prevails.

CHAPTER TWO

The Struggle for Power after Lenin

WHEN LENIN DIED in 1924 the Bolsheviks had been in power for only six full years, and their grip on the country was still not secure. Civil war against the Whites was over and all opposition parties, including rival socialist ones, had been smashed. Yet to many in the West it seemed that the new régime was precarious, and the revolutionary order which Lenin had ushered in in October 1917 could not last long when it became clear that the Bolshevik Party was unable to fulfil its grandiose promises of social justice and economic plenty. At the Party's Tenth Congress, in 1921, Lenin had consolidated his power and had vowed to "put the lid on the opposition for once and for all", and with Lev Trotsky imposing iron discipline on the newly formed Red Army he was in a position to do so. But it was not long after the Tenth Congress had closed that Lenin fell seriously ill, and in the spring of 1922 he suffered a stroke. For the last two years of his life Lenin monitored the policies being carried out in his name by his lieutenants, including both Trotsky and Stalin, but was forced to watch helplessly from his country home at Leninsky Gorki while the struggle for control of Soviet Russia was fought out with no reference to his wishes.

Even if Lenin had not fallen ill in 1921 it seems likely that the power struggle for his mantle would have taken place in any case, and probably just as ruthlessly: for the fatal flaw in the system that Lenin had so confidently and ringingly proclaimed during "Great October" was its lack of any provision for a succession mechanism.

For centuries Russia had been ruled by a series of Tsarist dynasties, most recently by the Romanovs, under which the principle of succession to the throne was clearly laid down. When disputes arose—for example when the heir to the throne was mentally unstable—the succession was resolved by court intrigues as Byzantine and as ruthless as anything Soviet Russia was later to witness. But at least the monarchy provided a procedure for the transfer of power.

It could be violated, ignored and abused, but it existed. After the Bolshevik seizure of power, by contrast, the problem of political transition and the mortality of national leaders was simply brushed under the carpet, as if the doctrines of Marxism as elaborated by Lenin would somehow solve the problem of their own accord. The shortlived provisional government established after the abdication of Nicolas II in February 1917 had tried to operate along democratic lines copied from Western models, in particular the parliamentary systems of Britain and Germany. Many of the leading ministers in the successive provisional government cabinets from February to October were Liberal politicians and Anglophiles who deliberately set out to try to plant the seeds of parliamentary democracy in the thin and infertile soil of the Russian body politic.

Since the Middle Ages Russia had known nothing but a version of Asian despotism qualified only during the last years of Nicolas's reign, when the Tsar was obliged to concede a very restricted and watered down version of constitutional monarchy. But neither the revival of the Duma (National Assembly) between 1905 and the outbreak of the First World War, nor the provisional government headed by Alexander Kerensky in 1917, had taken root. Both were swept away by the burning desire of the Russian masses, the vast majority of them peasants, for extreme measures which would finally usher in the millennium of peace, plenty and social equality.

Lenin, seizing the day and sensing the mood of the time, leapt forward in October, manoeuvring skilfully to ensure majorities in the Soviets, as well as in the democratic workers' councils which had sprung up spontaneously after the fall of the monarchy; and he boldly mounted a coup against the provisional government despite the reservations of many fellow Bolsheviks, coupling this dramatic move with unqualified promises of peace and bread. He ruled initially with the support of the Left Socialist Revolutionaries, a radical splinter-group from Russia's main socialist party the SRs, who claimed to represent peasantry. The Bolsheviks, whose philosophy was based on the supposed class interests of the urban proletariat, were the self-proclaimed champions of the industrial working class, so that an alliance between the two socialist parties seems logical. But the political situation in Russia remained fluid and ambiguous after the October uprising. The Bolshevik victory, even in alliance with the Left SRs, was far from cut and dried.

Major opposition parties, including the mainstream SRs and the Mensheviks, continued to operate openly and indeed held a large number of seats in the workers' and soldiers' Soviets despite the Bolshevik majorities in those bodies. The Mensheviks were a particular threat to Lenin since they claimed to be the true social democrats and the real representatives of the Russian working class with a programme of gradual reform leading to a classless society once the industrial proletariat formed the majority of the population, which in 1917–18 it palpably did not (Russia was, after all, over 80 per cent agrarian based). Although the word Menshevik means minority in Russian, it was in fact the Bolsheviks who had been in the minority when the Russian Social Democratic party split at the London congress in 1903. Both wings of the party were avowedly Marxist but Lenin, together with Trotsky (who paradoxically was a Menshevik for some part of his career), came to the view that Russia could not wait for history to take its course. Lenin remarked rather wistfully, in exile in Switzerland during the First World War, that he and his generation would not live to see the revolution in Russia. But once the Tsarist system had crumbled Lenin became determined to "give history a push" by making the proletarian revolution rather than Marx had envisaged, and in a backward agrarian country rather than in the advanced industrial states of Western Europe. "*On s'engage et puis on voit*", was one of Lenin's favourite sayings, taken from Russia's arch enemy, Napoleon Bonaparte.

Lenin, after October 1917, was vulnerable to the Menshevik charge that he had acted precipitately and was taking Russia on the wrong tack, trying to introduce social and political changes for which the country was not ready. He was equally vulnerable to the charge put forward by the mainstream Socialist Revolutionary party, headed by Victor Chernov, that the Bolshevik-Left SR coalition government had not been voted into office by the Russian population, had not been democratically approved by any other popular mandate and was passing decree after decree without consulting the peasants, the majority of Russia's population and the class upon which the country depended for its very survival. Both the Mensheviks and the Social Revolutionaries argued that the true national forum would be the Constituent Assembly, which was elected in a remarkably fair and democratic poll after the Bolshevik seizure of power in the autumn of 1917. It convened in January 1918 with an SR and Menshevik majority under the chairmanship of Chernov, with a mandate for laying down the future form of government for post-Tsarist Russia.

Lenin's response was to disperse the Constituent Assembly by force with the help of revolutionary guards and to have Chernov arrested. There followed a period of intense political struggle from which the Bolsheviks were to emerge victorious thanks to their ruthless use of the Red Terror, spearheaded by the Cheka, the successor to the Tsarist Okhrana or secret police and the forerunner of the KGB. Under the intelligent command of its Polish-born chief, Felix Dzerzhinsky, known with reason as "Iron Felix", the Cheka had by the summer of 1918 used murder, torture and mass arrests to eliminate the last remnants of opposition to the Bolshevik monopoly of power, in a merciless campaign which in July of 1918 embraced and crushed the Left-SRs, Lenin's erstwhile peasant coalition partners. The Left-SRs had attempted a ragged military coup against the Bolsheviks following sharp disagreements over both Lenin's policy of appeasing Germany in order to win a costly peace at the Brest-Litovsk negotiations, and his cynical abuse of the peasantry, including grain requisitions by armed Bolshevik guards aimed at ensuring food supplies for Russia's shattered industries.

By the end of 1918 therefore Lenin and the Bolsheviks were in sole command, and had moved government headquarters from Petrograd (formerly St Petersburg, and, after 1924, Leningrad) to Moscow, the traditional heart of Russia. The newly formed Red Army was fighting the armies of the non-socialist opposition, the remnants of the Tsarist army, aristocracy and right wing parties known as the Whites. But Moscow itself was relatively safe and Lenin, ignoring the scorn of the outside world, set about establishing the new order he had so often dreamed and spoken about in the emigré cafés of Switzerland, France and Poland, in the wilderness years between the 1903 Party Congress and the cataclysm of August 1914.

The drawback of his Napoleonic dictum however, indeed the drawback of his revolutionary blueprint, was that it gave no clear guidance for the responsibilities of governmental power. Lenin's entire career, from his youth in Samara in the 1870s to his triumphant arrival from exile at the Finland station in April 1917, was bound up with the seemingly impossible task of overthrowing the corrupt, inefficient but firmly entrenched Tsarist régimes. Very little thought was given to what would be done with the machinery of the Russian state once the impossible had been achieved. Musing, in Finland, on the eve of the fall of the Romanovs, Lenin had mapped out the future in a pamphlet called "The State and Revolution". But in contrast to his other writings it was vague and Utopian, and boiled down to the naive proposition that any cook or factory worker could run a government office as easily as a trained administrator. Once in power Lenin found that he came to rely increasingly on those fellow Bolsheviks who had a strong practical streak and could impose some semblance of order on the chaos which followed the tremendous economic and social upheaval Russia had just experienced. Trotsky was put in charge first of the ramshackle revolutionary army and then of industry, to which he applied the same discipline and regimentation. In government affairs Lenin initially relied on the lean, capable and energetic figure of Yakov Sverdlov, chairman of the

Soviets. The Party itself was increasingly placed in the hands of a man regarded by most other Bolsheviks as a rather dull and plodding fellow ideally suited to the essential but unexciting work of managing the growing Party bureaucracy: Josef Vissarionovich Djugashvili, known by his Party nickname as Stalin.

Lenin gradually came to realize, as his grip slackened and he retreated more and more to Leninsky Gorki, that his vague blueprint for a socialist Russia had left many practical questions unanswered. But it was clear from 1921 onwards that factions in the Party were already manoeuvring to take advantage of the fact that neither in the Party rules nor in the newly adopted Soviet Constitution, or Fundamental Law, was there any mention of who should succeed the present leader or how the succession should be decided. Publicly it was unthinkable even to mention the fact that Lenin, who dominated the Party and the state and was hailed as a political genius, was mortal, let alone that someone would have to take his place. But under the surface the struggle began in earnest.

It was a confused struggle, especially since the very institutions of Party and State were not yet well defined. There were, as there are to this day, separate structures for the Communist Party, the only legally tolerated party in the system, the Government, operating through a council of Commissars (later renamed Ministers), and the State, exemplified in a structure of Soviets or workers' councils extending in pyramid form from local councils at the bottom to the Supreme Soviet at the very top.

Clearly, since the Communist Party exercised a monopoly of power by the end of 1918 in both Government and State, whoever headed the Party was theoretically in a position to act as virtual dictator. But so awesome was Lenin's authority that he overshadowed all three institutions, in effect running the machinery of government on a personal basis. Technically speaking, Lenin after the Revolution held the office of Chairman of the Council of Commissars (SOVNARKOM) making him Prime Minister. But did this mean that the office of Prime Minister was the crucial post in Soviet Russia, more powerful than that of General Secretary of the Party (Stalin) or President of the State (Sverdlov)? Clearly not; Lenin after all was not the Party Secretary nor the Head of the Soviets, yet he embodied the Party and he embodied the State just as he embodied the Government.

As his illness worsened between 1922 and 1924 it was an open question as to whether the next leader of the country would wield effective power through the office of Soviet President, Chairman of the Council of Ministers or General Secretary of the Party. To most Bolsheviks, including the brilliant Trotsky, the capable Sverdlov, and other leading lights such as Bukharin and Zinoviev, it seemed that General Secretary-ship of the Party was a rather humdrum post occupied by a humdrum man who posed little threat to their ambitions. One man knew that they were wrong; whoever held the threads of the Party structure in his hands, whoever had the power of patronage and appointment, whoever held the Party files and dispensed privilege and power had an unchallenge-able base from which to make a successful bid for supreme authority in revolutionary Russia.

The crucial event in the life of the Party following the Revolution and the Civil War was the Tenth Party Congress in 1921, which can be said to mark the beginning of the real succession crisis. Underneath what amounted to political consolidation and victory celebration by the Communist Party lay a challenge to Lenin's monopoly of power from the so-called Democratic or Left Wing Communist faction led by Nikolai Bukharin. Bukharin, widely regarded as the Party's leading intellectual, held views which in retrospect have earned him a reputation as an early champion of "socialism with a human face". In the early 1920s this amounted to a demand, also advanced by the Workers' Opposition led by Alexander Shaliapnikov, that officials should be elected not nomin-ated, that the Party should allow bourgeois specialists from the *ancien régime* to help run industry instead of insisting on the use of ideologically sound but incompetent Bolsheviks, and that the centralization and iron discipline imposed by Lenin and Trotsky should be relaxed now that the Civil War was over. Ranged against Bukharin in this debate were Trotsky, who wanted the economy under paramilitary control, and Dzerzhinsky, head of the Cheka, for whom internal discipline and security were prime considerations. With Bukharin in the Liberal faction was Grigory Zinoviev, the energetic Party leader in Petrograd. Lenin himself was above the battle, as, for the time being, for reasons of his own, was Stalin. The factional struggle might have been based purely on arguments for and against a more liberal and relaxed version of one-party socialism had it not been for the profound shock of the revolt at the naval base of Kronstadt only six days before the Congress opened.

Kronstadt, an island in the Gulf of Finland, not far from Petrograd, was considered a reliable stronghold of revolutionary sentiment, with the Baltic sailors Bolshevik almost to a man. It was therefore traumatic when the Kronstadt sailors suddenly mutinied and put out a list of demands which went even further than those of the Liberal Bukharin faction. They included new elections to the Soviets by free and secret ballot, the abolition of Party privilege, the release of political prisoners, the introduction of private enterprise and private ownership of land for peasants. It was a gut reaction, a rank and file vision of what socialism ought to be, but would have meant the end of Lenin and the Communist Party. In March Kronstadt sailors set up a provisional revolutionary committee, and support for their ideas began to spread in the Party in Petrograd. At this point Trotsky decided that the revolt had to be crushed at whatever cost, and ordered the Red Army to storm the island. The result was a terrible massacre which is still remembered to this day, but which left the Party's monopoly of power untouched. For Lenin himself the Kronstadt revolt meant a crisis of conscience; he knew that this was not a counter revolution, and that no "Outside forces" had instigated uprising. "We have failed to convince the broad masses", he said, when the Tenth Congress convened.

The revolt also brought Lenin face to face with the fact that his plans for the overthrow of the old government had left little room for planning the shape of the *new* government, and that his Utopian view that the State apparatus would somehow "wither away", once the classless society had arrived, had to be put to one side. But which way would Lenin now lean—toward the apparatus of class oppression advocated by Trotsky and Dzerzhinsky, or toward the economic and political relaxation favoured by Bukharin? Lenin's formula, which won the day at the Tenth Congress thanks to his unchallenged authority, managed to combine the two, rather as Yuri Andropov, some sixty years later, was to combine tight ideological and social discipline with cautious measures of economic liberalization.

Lenin's policy in 1921 was to "put the lid on opposition" while at the same time elaborating what became known as the New Economic Policy. Dealing with the opposition meant not only crushing the pitiful remnants of the other socialist parties but also clamping down on factionalism within the Party and attempts by the Workers' Opposition to establish free trade unions independent of Party control (a tendency which was to re-emerge in Poland in 1980 in the form of Solidarity). But Lenin combined this with new measures sanctioning limited private trading and a graduated tax system for the peasants which replaced the crude and oppressive system of grain requisitions. He also, despite Trotsky's reservations, relaxed the military-style regimentation of the country and tried to reinforce the rule that officials were elected and not appointed. Three of the more unimaginative members of the Party secretariat were removed from the Central Committee as a gesture to the Liberals.

Had he lived, Lenin might have been able to maintain this political balancing act indefinitely. But he was now visibly a dying man, and the contenders lining up to succeed him—albeit clandestinely, since no one could dare to manoeuvre openly to follow the great Lenin—used the debate between liberals and hardliners over the future of Russia in the struggle for power. When the Eleventh Party Congress was convened in March of the following year (1922), Lenin was absent except for the opening and closing sessions. It was by then clear to the Party that his successor must come from the five men who dominated the congress in his absence: Trotsky, Stalin, Bukharin, Zinoviev and Lev Kamenev. Between Lenin's first major stroke in May 1922 and his death on 21 January 1924, these five men manoeuvred skilfully. The most skilful was the former Georgian seminary student, valued by Lenin for his humdrum practical abilities rather than any political brilliance: Stalin.

Stalin was later to claim, when he was firmly in power and could not be contradicted, that he had always been Lenin's close comrade in arms, as well as his pupil and obvious successor. Faked photographs were released showing the two in an intimate father and son relationship. In fact, however, Lenin became increasingly critical of Stalin in his latter years, and one of the main causes of conflict was the question of Moscow's policy towards minority Soviet nationalities, a subject which has since preoccupied other Soviet leaders, notably Yuri Andropov, who on the sixtieth anniversary of the Soviet Union in December 1982 issued a stern warning to the Party not to ignore or trample on the sensitivities of non-Russian peoples. In 1922, when nationalities policies were still being formed, Stalin, a Georgian by birth, was a centralist and pro-Russian, possibly to prove that he was loyal to Moscow even though he was not a Great Russian. As Commissar for Nationalities Stalin took the view that the principles of self-determination and federalism enshrined in the constitution of the new Soviet state were only vehicles for imposing strict Communist Party rule from Moscow over all the constituent republics.

Lenin was acutely unhappy over Stalin's behaviour, and the crisis came to a head over the future of Stalin's own native Georgia. In 1919 free elections in Georgia had been won overwhelmingly by the Mensheviks, Lenin's Social Democratic rivals, who offered a programme of gradual Marxist reform and local nationalism. In 1920, to his credit, Lenin signed a treaty recognizing the independence of Georgia and promising not to interfere in Georgian affairs. Like many subsequent Soviet undertakings, this was cynically ignored in 1921 when the Red Army moved into Georgia on the pretext of restoring order after disturbances organized by the Bolsheviks themselves. But Lenin's role appears to have been a fairly honourable one. He was afraid that the

West would intervene to help the Georgians, even though Lloyd George had privately given assurances that Britain would not do so. A further reason for restraint, in Lenin's view, was that the Mensheviks were genuinely popular in Georgia and would not be easy to remove. But Lenin was a dying man, and it was Stalin who ruthlessly imposed central Moscow control over Tbilisi with the help of his associate Serge Ordzhonikidze, who was in charge of the Party's Caucasian Bureau.

When the news of the suppression and annexation of Georgia reached Lenin he exploded with anger. In a series of letters which remained secret until Khrushchev released them in 1956, Lenin accused Stalin and Ordzhonikidze of Great Russian chauvinism, and said that assimilated Russians were obviously worse than Russians themselves. Of course the central union had to be strengthened, but only for diplomatic and military purposes, Lenin raged. Local republics had to have some autonomy, otherwise the Party was simply taking over Tsarist Russia's imperialist attitudes, which in turn could only undermine Soviet prestige "on the eve of emergence of the East and its awakening". The newly established Soviet system, Lenin fumed, was riddled with corruption, hopeless bureaucracy and inefficiency, and run by self-serving *apparatchiks* who were just as bad if not worse than the administrators of the overthrown monarchy. "Our central apparatus is in fact nothing but the Tsarist apparatus anointed with a little Soviet holy oil", he wrote. But it was already too late.

CHAPTER THREE

How Stalin Won

STALIN'S SECRET WEAPON, and the weapon which most subsequent Soviet contenders for power were to learn to master and control, was the apparatus of Party and Government. Stalin was Commissar for Nationalities. He was also from 1919 onwards Head of the Workers and Peasants Control, known by the Russian acronym RABKRIN. RABKRIN was essentially an inspectorate, and running it was far too dull a job for the likes of Trotsky or Bukharin. But it gave Stalin an apparatus of control over the entire state machine, and was in effect a sort of super-commissariat or super-ministry, giving him what we would now describe as the powers of a government supremo or overlord.

As if this was not enough, Stalin in 1922 took over yet another humdrum job, which was also shunned by the Party luminaries, but which was to prove his real power base. This was the office of General Secretary of the Party, which previously had been held by Krestinsky and by Molotov, neither of whom had perceived its political possibilities. Stalin's peculiar genius was that he realized how to turn mastery of Party organization into personal mastery of the Soviet state.

The Party bodies which counted most at this stage, and which count most to this day, were the Politburo, the Party's top institution, and the Central Committee Secretariat which ran (and runs) Party affairs on a day-to-day basis. Another key institution, which still wields enormous influence, was the Supreme Defence Council, with overall control of defence allocations and national decisions in time of war. There was also a body which no longer has a modern day counterpart, the Organizations Bureau or ORGBURO, which tended to act in parallel with the Politburo (political bureau). Stalin was the only Bolshevik to be on all four key committees, although nobody at the time seems to have realized what a unique power base this gave him.

The Politburo had ceased to exist after the Bolshevik seizure of power, but continued to function informally as an inner circle of the Central Committee, and was formally reconstituted at the Eighth Party Congress in March 1919.

At this stage all Party bodies were much smaller than they are today. The Central Committee, which nowadays numbers over three hundred members, consisted in the early 1920s of a tightly knit group of some twenty men, and up to ten candidate members. The Politburo, or inner core, had only about half a dozen leading Bolsheviks. Its formal revival was opposed by the Left Wing Democratic Communists on the grounds, perfectly correct it turned out, that the Politburo rather than the Central Committee would actually take the key decisions. It did so in conjunction with the Organizational Bureau, which according to Lenin, was supposed to be an executive body where the Politburo was a political one.

To be one of the élite in the Politburo was itself a stepping stone to the top but Stalin, from 1922 onwards, was also on the ORGBURO, giving him a further advantage. Above all the Secretariat to the Central Committee was gradually expanding and widening its powers. Originally there had been only one Secretary (Sverdlov, subsequently Krestinsky when Sverdlov became Head of State), but within a relatively short space of time departments had proliferated in the Secretariat, each one headed by newly created Central Committee Secretaries. The Party which had led an uncertain underground existence in Russia for nearly two decades, with its leaders skulking from one émigré capital to another to avoid the long arm of the Okhrana, was now the party of power and administration, although not subject to democratic or popular control. The key figures in the new order were therefore the men who ran the Central Committee apparatus, all of them increasingly answerable to (and protégés of) Stalin. His nearest rivals in this sense were Zinoviev, the Party boss up in Petrograd, and Kamenev, Head of the Party organization in Moscow. Sverdlov had ceased to be an actor in the drama with his untimely death in 1919, a premature end which ensured him immortality in the Soviet system (one of Moscow's main squares was named after him, and the town of Ekaterinburg in the Urals was renamed Sverdlovsk). Aleksei Rykov—who survived to fall foul of Stalin and is therefore not commemorated—succeeded the dying Lenin as head of the Council of Commissars, the equivalent of Prime Minister, but (as it later transpired) was not in the position to succeed Lenin as effective leader of the country since the key to the power struggle lay not in the SOVNARKOM but in the Party apparatus.

Similarly Trotsky, although by far the most visible and most highly regarded of Lenin's comrades and rivals, had no Party department under his control, no protégés loyal to his policies and dependent on his career, in fact no real power base at all except the Commissariat of War and Transport. He had tremendous personal charisma and an ability, regarded by other Bolshevik leaders as demagogic, to sway a crowd with passionate revolutionary oratory. He was feared and even disliked by fellow Politburo members, especially when he was able to install an ally, Antonov-Ovseenko, as Head of the Political Directorate of the Soviet Armed forces. Antonov-Ovseenko was a colourful and well known figure who had led the Red Guards into the Winter Palace during the fall of the Provisional Government in 1917. But none of this compensated for the fact that when it came to the crunch Trotsky could count on very little support in the Secretariat, ORGBURO or Politburo.

In retrospect Stalin's rise to power therefore looks irresistible, if not inevitable. It did not appear so at the time. On the contrary, Lenin, who had already crossed swords with Stalin over Georgia and the national-ities question, increasingly came to realize that Stalin was a cunning and ambitious man. Ironically what finally brought Stalin's true character home to Lenin was not so much differences over policies as Stalin's behaviour towards Nadezhda Krupskaya, Lenin's wife. Krupskaya, a rather plain woman of great character and fortitude, had accompanied Lenin all through the years of exile and was now revered as a legendary figure in the pantheon of the Revolution. Stalin however had no patience with niceties such as respect for a comrade, let alone chivalry towards a woman, and roundly abused Krupskaya when she prevented Stalin from seeing Lenin as part of her policy of shielding him from unwelcome visitors. The incident, which was only revealed later by Trotsky, and subsequently confirmed by Khrushchev, became a political matter when Krupskaya complained to Kamenev about Stalin's outburst. Lenin, incensed by Stalin's rudeness, rebuked him in a stiff letter and demanded that Stalin apologize to Krupskaya, adding that he would break off relations with him if he failed to do so. To add insult to injury Lenin then summoned Trotsky, Stalin's deadliest rival, and asked him to take over Soviet Policy towards Georgia, hitherto Stalin's exclusive preserve.

This might have been the beginning of the end for Stalin, and the beginning of the beginning for Trotsky, especially since the question of Georgia was to be discussed at the Twelfth Party Congress in April 1923. But, on 10 March, a month before the Congress met, Lenin was incapacitated by a further stroke. He was in effect removed from the political scene altogether. When the Congress convened, Trotsky, characteristically if incomprehensibly, made no move at all to use Lenin's censure of Stalin, and indeed remained silent on the Georgian issue despite proliferating rumours in the corridors of the Kremlin that Stalin was out of favour. Stalin meanwhile used his extensive contacts to have key members of the Party in Georgia, who might otherwise have made use of the dispute, removed from their posts. Lenin's secretary gave the Politburo his dictated notes on the Georgian question and thus made plain to the Politburo, on the eve of the Congress, his support for Trotsky rather than Stalin. But she added that Lenin had not been able to revise them for publication, which gave Stalin the excuse to suggest that they should be quietly shelved. Trotsky—always his own worst enemy—did not disagree. Afterwards, in exile, he explained that he had avoided invoking Lenin's authority to challenge Stalin in case he was accused of trying to step into Lenin's shoes before Lenin was actually dead.

The Twelfth Congress was packed with Stalin's acolytes and supporters, and he was easily able to overturn a Georgian resolution complaining that the autonomy and right to secede granted to Soviet republics under the Constitution had been rendered meaningless by the stranglehold of the central apparatus. Sensing that his power was on the rise, Stalin allowed himself gently to mock his opponents. "I must say I have not seen a Party Congress so united for a long time," he said. "I regret that Comrade Lenin is not here. If he were, he would be able to say: I have been forging a Party for 25 years and now here it is, complete, great and strong."

This was in April 1923, barely six months after Lenin had dictated the document known to history as his last political testament, in which the dying man took a long hard look at each of his potential successors. Trotsky he characterized as the most able man in the Central Committee, but said he was too self-confident (most of the comrades would have said arrogant), and too attracted by theoretical and administrative matters. Bukharin, "the Party's favourite", was its most significant theoretician, although Lenin thought him too professional in manner. As for Stalin, Lenin noted from his sick bed that the General Secretary had concentrated enormous power in his hands "and is not always sufficiently cautious in using it". A few days later Lenin dictated a crucial postscript which was to echo down the years when his final testament, suppressed for so long, was revealed to the Party by Khrushchev in 1956. "Stalin is too rude (*slishkom grub*), and this is insupportable in a General Secretary . . . I therefore propose to the comrades to work out some way of removing Stalin from the post." If this was not done, Lenin said, there was serious danger of a leadership split.

Lenin was quite right, but he had diagnosed the disease too late. His antidote, in so far as he was still able to carry through decisions, was to purge and expand key Party bodies like the Central Committee, the Central Control Commission, and RABKRIN, to rid them of entrenched bureaucrats and bring in fresh proletarian blood. On the face of it this undermined Stalin, who however displayed political cunning by turning Lenin's move to his advantage. Of the 27-man Central Committee of 1923–4 a number were supporters of Stalin, but a number also owed their careers to Zinoviev or Trotsky. Stalin therefore agreed that the Central Committee should increase to forty full members and half as many Candidate members, secretly making sure that the new men owed allegiance to him. He took similar steps with regard to the Control Commission, which was merged with Stalin's own RABKRIN (Workers and Peasants Inspectorate). Hardly any of the new entrants were the rank and file workers and peasants Lenin had in mind. The majority were the new breed of Communist bureaucrat, and all owed their careers to Stalin, as did the three new Candidate members of the Politburo: Molotov, Kalinin and Rudzutak.

As in later succession crises, the country as a whole was kept in the dark about the failing health of the leader, although most people were aware that Lenin was in poor health and disappeared from public view for long stretches. The atmosphere was similar to that surrounding the death of Yuri Andropov, when senior Soviet officials repeatedly assured diplomats and correspondents that the leader was not seriously ill but merely had a cold and was working part-time at his desk prior to resuming full responsibilities for affairs of state. At the Twelfth Congress in 1923, Kamenev deliberately spread the word among delegates that Lenin was recovering from his illness (most people were aware that he had been weakened by an assassination attempt in 1918, when a bullet lodged in his neck), and would return to work in the Kremlin shortly.

It was difficult to disguise the true state of affairs however, especially since the struggle for succession was taking place against a background of fierce dispute over economic policy, with contenders for power advocating different roads to recovery and prosperity after the chaos of revolution and civil war. Trotsky took the view, to be reflected in later debates between Khrushchev and Malenkov, that heavy industry had to have priority. Thanks to the new economic policies, Trotsky argued, the peasants were prospering and agriculture was recovering, while industry was stagnating for lack of capital and investment. This, in Trotsky's analysis, led to a fall in agricultural prices at a time when industrial goods were increasingly scarce, a phenomenon he described in a famous image as the "scissors crisis", since when plotted on a graph the two sectors crossed dramatically. What the graph meant in practice was that the towns could no longer afford to pay the countryside for food, with the attendant danger of famine and the kind of grain requisitions which had met such fierce peasant resistance in 1918–19 and had led to the collapse of the Bolshevik-Left SR coalition government. With no socialist peasant party operating any longer in Russia, the role of defender of the countryside fell to Bukharin, who as a left-wing Bolshevik had in the past been allied with the now extinct Left-SRs. Bukharin took the view that in a predominantly agrarian country like Russia, agricultural prosperity was the most important priority since it provided the basis for industrial recovery and economic growth. Stalin, while waiting to see which way the argument would go, sided for the time being with Bukharin and the pro-peasant faction.

It was now becoming obvious to Trotsky, Zinoviev and Bukharin that, as Lenin had tried to warn them, Stalin's power base was becoming almost unassailable. After the Twelfth Congress Zinoviev met Bukharin secretly in the Caucasus to plot Stalin's removal, but Stalin, whose intelligence network was already well-developed, got wind of this. Characteristically, and with the Georgian political cunning his rivals could not match, Stalin did not react by denouncing the conspirators but said that if they felt he had accumulated too much power, then of course he was willing to resign. It was a gamble, but, as later in the 1930s when he used the same ploy, it paid off, and the Politburo asked him to stay on. In a masterly move Stalin then proposed that if Zinoviev, Trotsky and Bukharin wanted to make their voices better heard in the leadership they should be co-opted on to the Orgburo. In practice the three became swiftly bored with routine administrative matters and hardly ever attended meetings, just as Stalin had calculated.

Stalin's rise to power can therefore be explained not only as a result of his political genius and his use of the Party machine but also as a result of repeated mistakes by Stalin's opponents—especially Trotsky—and his ability to exploit them. When Trotsky called for more democracy in the Party and said a change of leaders was desirable, Stalin was able to persuade the Central Committee to condemn Trotsky's move as factionalism and a "grave political mistake". It was not that he was against democracy, Stalin assured the Party, only that unity was the top priority. It was the same story at the beginning of 1924, when Trotsky published an article entitled "The New Course" in *Pravda* (at that time leaders could use the Party press to argue out rival theories). Trotsky's theme once again was that the *apparatchiks* and bureaucrats had taken over the Party, and he appealed to the rising younger generation to clear out the dead wood and restore the original fervour and idealism of Bolshevism. But what Trotsky had forgotten, and was never entirely to come to terms with, was that the bureaucrats already controlled all the major levers of power—and the man behind the bureaucrats was Stalin.

On 21 January 1924, Lenin died at his country home. Stalin and the others (but not Trotsky) went out by sleigh to pay their last respects.

As in subsequent transitions in the Kremlin, rumours proliferated in an atmosphere of national shock and dismay. For some time after Lenin's death it was confidently rumoured that Lenin had discovered various conspiracies against his life when he made his last visit to Moscow from Leninsky Gorki in October 1923. Among these conspiracies, it was said, there was a plot to poison him, and there were many who firmly believed that the plot had succeeded, although it was never clear which of the contenders for power was supposed to have delivered the fatal dose. Given the atmosphere of Byzantine intrigue which surrounds Kremlin politics, it is hardly surprising that rumours also circulated in 1953 and again in 1982 that high officials had hastened the ends of both Stalin and Brezhnev.

Stalin proved abundantly throughout his career that he was fully capable of such an act. But all the evidence points to the fact that Lenin died of a series of strokes, and that by the beginning of 1924 Stalin was in a sufficiently confident position not to have to "give history a push". It was immediately obvious, at least to the inner circle of leaders, that Stalin held many of the threads of government in his hands, and Zinoviev and Kamenev were quick to associate themselves with his leadership. A sign of Stalin's ascendency was his prominence at Lenin's funeral, when he delivered a remarkable oration in liturgical form with every sentence beginning "We vow to thee O Lenin". No doubt thinking of his own personality cult to come, Stalin immediately deified the dead leader, ordering the construction of a mausoleum on Red Square and presenting Lenin as an almost icon-like figure of superhuman virtues, even though in his lifetime Lenin had been a man of personal modesty and austerity of a kind not to be witnessed again in the Kremlin until the rise of Yuri Andropov. The funeral of Lenin, as other state funerals were later to do, thus gave key pointers to the succession and likely future policies. Trotsky, who as a close comrade-in-arms of Lenin might have been in a position to counteract the Bolshevik leader's posthumous canonization, did not attend the funeral at all. He later claimed in his memoirs that he had been misled by Politburo colleagues as to the date of the ceremony.

It is a characteristic of Soviet transitions—or was until Gorbachov—that the leadership which emerges following the death of a leader is initially collective, with one man acting as *primus inter pares*, or first among equals, only later emerging as the unrivalled leader, demoting or neutralizing potential challengers. So it was in 1924 when Stalin began to purge the Trotskyists, removing Antonov-Ovseenko from the Army

Political Directorate, and ultimately depriving Trotsky himself of the post of Commissar for War, replacing him with a Stalin associate, Frunze. Stalin's weapon in the aftermath of Lenin's death was the overriding need for unity, and in a series of lectures called "The Foundation of Leninism"—his first main claim to fame as a theoretician—Stalin stressed the need for iron discipline to maintain the purity of the Party as the vanguard of the working classes.

The Thirteenth Congress of the Party, which met in May 1924, was dominated by a desire to demonstrate unity, a desire of which Stalin took full advantage. It was at this Congress that Trotsky made his celebrated capitulatory speech, saying "One cannot be right against the Party . . . it is my Party, right or wrong." But it was *not* his Party. Nor was it the Party of other old Bolsheviks who had fought in the underground with Lenin and had taken part in the risky uprising against the Provisional Government in 1917. It was Stalin's Party, because the growing apparatus of government was Stalin's, and he was able to argue convincingly that to attack the apparatus was to risk undermining the rule of the Party itself.

On the eve of the Congress, Nadezhda Krupskaya, Lenin's widow, made one final and desperate bid to stop Stalin by sending all members of the Politburo copies of Lenin's last testament, in which he had recommended Stalin's removal. Lenin, she said, had wanted the document made public after his death. In the event, under Stalin's influence, the testament was not put on the record at the Congress at all but only read out to selected leaders of delegations with a suitable commentary explaining why they should take no action. When the Central Committee convened, Stalin once again stood up to say that if the comrades did not want him he was ready to resign. To a man, the comrades asked him to stay. It was the beginning of a climb to absolute power which would usher in bloodshed comparable with the reign of Ivan the Terrible, and would virtually destroy the Party as an institution of rule for over twenty years, substituting for it a personal tyranny using socialist ideology as a vehicle for paranoia and terror.

CHAPTER FOUR

The Opposition to Stalin

WHEN STALIN'S AIDES went into the room where he had retired to sleep at his strictly guarded dacha at Kuntsevo on the outskirts of Moscow in March 1953 and found him lying on the floor "in an unusual kind of sleep", they were paralysed with fear and uncertainty. When the death was finally announced after a long gap, the Central Committee appealed to the Soviet people not to panic, a measure of the national trauma caused by the passing of a man who had exercised total personal sway over Russia for some twenty years. In his lifetime he was ritually eulogized as the great father of the nation, the beloved teacher, political and military genius, who was literally infallible. Nobody beyond the closed circle of the Politburo and Stalin's personal secretary knew that he was a short, pockmarked man given to paranoid rages, long-term vengeful plotting in the Caucasian manner and behaviour that was at once cruel, crude and cunning. Even the "inner circle" of Khrushchev, Malenkov and Beria, who attended his deathbed, were as much in awe of Stalin in death as they had been in life (although Beria managed a "triumphant smile"). For most Russians, Stalin was an almost God-like figure, ruthless, terrifying but also paternal and benevolent, who had dominated their lives through the upheavals, industrialization and purges of the 1930s and the sufferings of the war against Hitler known in Russia as the Great Patriotic War. Suddenly he was no longer there, and they did not know what to do.

Above all there was no one even remotely approaching Stalin's semi-divine status who could step into his apparently immortal shoes. As in the early 1920s before the death of Lenin, manoeuvring had been taking place for some time as Stalin became more obviously ill and more obviously paranoid. But such was the atmosphere created by Stalin's rule of terror that it was even more unthinkable for a leading Party member openly to make a bid for the succession than it had been for the old Bolsheviks to present themselves as heirs to Lenin. The old Bolsheviks had in any case been killed off by Stalin—"liquidated" was the official euphemism—as he systematically destroyed any conceivable challenge to his position. Nominally speaking, Russia was still governed by the structure which Lenin had created, a complex parallel system of

Communist Party institutions, government ministries and Soviets. But the Party, the ruling instrument, had been destroyed, purged and rebuilt so many times by 1953 that it had in effect become an empty shell in the hands of a man who ruled instead of the Party rather than through it. Stalin's dictatorship was a personal one, and his political achievement was to have dominated the apparatus to the point where his every whim was more important than Party resolutions or instructions, or indeed than the collective will of the Politburo, which by the mid 1930s was reduced to an inconsequential gathering of Stalin's yes-men. He did not even bother to convene Party congresses, as Khrushchev was later to complain, because they were of no relevance to his running of the Soviet state.

The seeds of Stalin's personal dictatorship lay in his increasingly vicelike grip on the apparatus in the late 1920s, following the failure of Stalin's opponents to use Lenin's last-minute warning to have him removed. Just as Andropov was later to do in his brief period of leadership following the death of Brezhnev, and as Gorbachov has done since Chernenko's death, Stalin brought a large number of loyal lieutenants into the Party machinery following Lenin's death in 1924, both to reward those who supported his bid for power and to ensure that it was his policies and his vision of the future of Russia which carried the day. One of the most prominent beneficiaries of Stalin's patronage was Lazar Kaganovich, who came from obscurity to a leading position in the Central Committee. Unlike other Stalin associates, who found to their cost that to be close to the dictator was to risk his wrath and therefore their lives, Kaganovich survived the Stalin era and played a key role in the Soviet Union's second succession crisis, eventually suffering defeat at the hands of Nikita Khrushchev.

Uppermost in the minds of Stalin's successors as they looked back through the long dark ages of his rule to the first succession crisis, was the realization that if the first struggle for power was anything to go by the transition was likely to be prolonged. It is sometimes forgotten that Stalin was not able to impose unchallenged rule over Russia until some ten years after the death of Lenin. In the late 1920s, as in the later transitions—for example the struggle to succeed Chernenko—the fight at the top had gone on, sometimes concealed and sometimes in the open, even after it was obvious that one man had reached the apex of the pyramid of power.

In the case of Stalin's succession to Lenin, it had been Zinoviev, the Leningrad Party boss, who continued to manoeuvre, sometimes siding with Stalin and sometimes with Trotsky. Formally speaking in the late

1920s Stalin ruled in a troika with Zinoviev and Kamenev, but he could not resist undermining them and making it clear on every occasion that they were his subordinates. The troika might well have split earlier than it did had Trotsky not helped Stalin to maintain the façade of collective rule by vociferously attacking Zinoviev and Kamenev for allegedly betraying the original revolutionary ideals of Bolshevism. With characteristic lack of political timing Trotsky condemned Zinoviev and Kamenev's "wavering" during the Revolution in his book *The Lessons of October*, a move which drove them firmly back into Stalin's embrace. Stalin perceived, no doubt correctly, that it was Trotsky who posed the greatest threat to his political ambition and that Zinoviev and Kamenev could be dealt with later. Throughout the 1920s Stalin rewrote Soviet history to play down Trotsky's role in the Revolution and the Civil War and to exaggerate his own importance as Lenin's disciple.

In the first succession crisis, the cardinal principle was that whoever rose to the top had to legitimize his power in terms of his adherence to the line followed by his predecessor, namely Lenin. After the death of Stalin, and in all subsequent crises, this principle was reversed, beginning with Khrushchev's denunciation of Stalin's aberrations from the true path. Similarly, Brezhnev was to justify his overthrow of Khrushchev by condemning the "deviant" policies he had followed, and Andropov in 1982 both implicitly and explicitly criticized Brezhnev's own record in office. Andropov's political legacy was jeopardized after his death in 1984 by Chernenko, while Chernenko was implicitly criticized by Gorbachov. In all cases Soviet leaders tend to hark back to what they hold to be the pure and unsullied teaching of Lenin rather than the policies carried out by any subsequent leader.

Even in the case of Stalin, however, it was far from clear what the true Leninist path was, and both Stalin and Trotsky used different elements of Lenin's complex legacy to justify their claims to the Kremlin. Trotsky, deriving his authority from a philosophy formulated by himself in 1905 and subsequently taken up by Lenin, put forward the theory of permanent revolution under which Communist parties, having overthrown the *ancien régime*, should force the pace of history by going straight from the "bourgeois period"—envisaged by Marx as a prolonged transition—to the all-out proletarian revolution. Trotsky's assumption, increasingly disproved in the course of the 1920s, was that the spark of the Bolshevik revolution would ignite revolutions in Western Europe and other industrialized countries, leading the world to the millennium in a cauldron of social and political upheaval. The harsh truth however was that the Bolshevik party, acting in the name of a proletariat which barely existed, had seized power in a predominantly peasant country in need of fundamental reform, whereas the industrial countries of the West were working their way through parliamentary and electoral processes to periods of relatively peaceful social change rather than revolution. Stalin, ever the practical and realistic politician, realized what was happening and formulated the policy of "socialism in one country", under which Russia would conduct its Marxist experiment regardless of conditions in the outside world. This was an astute move since it suited the mood of the country to turn inward after the deep wounds opened up by the Revolution, and could also be combined with old-fashioned Russian patriotism, on which Stalin increasingly came to rely, rather than Communist ideology as an instrument of rule. When the very existence of the Soviet state was threatened by the Nazi invasion in 1941, Stalin deliberately dropped ideological terminology and addressed Soviet citizens on the radio as "brothers and sisters" rather than "comrades". He also co-opted the patriotic support of the Russian Orthodox Church.

On the other hand Stalin's assumption of supreme power was gradual and deceptive, and few people realized that his manoeuvres against opponents were leading towards a dictatorship. At one point in 1925 Zinoviev suggested to Stalin that Trotsky should be expelled from the Party, but Stalin refused, remarking with breathtaking cynicism that once a purge had begun there was no knowing where it might stop. "You cut off one head today, another tomorrow and a third the day after, and what will then be left of the Party?" Stalin said. At the Fourteenth Party Congress in 1925 Kamenev, apparently realizing the way things were going, had publicly warned against one-man rule and the creation of a Leader. But his warning was lost in an ovation for Stalin, who responded by claiming that leadership was collective. The Party could not be led without Rykov, Molotov, Kalinin, Tomsky and Bukharin, he said. In fact it could, and was: Bukharin and Rykov were shot as traitors in the purges of the 1930s, while Tomsky was forced to commit suicide. Molotov and Kalinin, who joined the Politburo in 1925, survived, as did Voroshilov, who also entered the Politburo at this time, increasing its membership to nine, the majority Stalin's men. In 1926 came the fall of Zinoviev, who was removed as Party boss in Leningrad after Molotov had been sent by Stalin to Russia's second city to undermine him. Zinoviev now joined forces with Trotsky, who warned that Stalin was ushering in the Thermidor of the Russian Revolution, an analogy taken from the French Revolution of 1789, when the original ideals were lost in a welter of bureaucracy and state terror. But Stalin by now was packing the key institutions, removing Trotsky and Zinoviev from the Politburo and bringing in five candidate members of his own choosing: Mikoyan, Ordzhonikidze, Kaganovich, Andreev and a handsome, able young man brought in to head the Party apparatus in Leningrad: Sergei Kirov.

The expulsion of Trotsky and Zinoviev from the Central Committee met some resistance within the Politburo, according to Moscow rumours reported by Boris Souvarine, one of Stalin's biographers. The move was opposed in particular by Bukharin and Rykov, but Stalin was able to use his support in the larger Central Committee to outflank the Politburo, the first time this had been used as a political manoeuvre. He was also able to use foreign policy against Trotsky and Zinoviev. The British General Strike of 1926 had been a disappointment to Moscow, and when in 1927 the Soviet trade delegation in London was raided the police found proof of Soviet-supported subversive activities. The British government broke off relations. It was all too reminiscent of the Zinoviev Letter affair, when the *Daily Mail* published a letter allegedly signed by Zinoviev in his capacity as Head of the Communist International, the COMINTERN (a post from which he was later removed by Stalin), urging British Communists to acts of sedition on the eve of the 1924 British election. For a time there was even a threat of war between Britain and Russia.

Zinoviev and Trotsky used the occasion to allege that Stalin was not competent to lead Russia at a time of crisis, whereas Stalin argued— more successfully—that now was the time to close ranks against a common enemy with himself at the helm. The opposition's last gasp came at the Fifteenth Party Congress in December 1927, when Trotsky and Zinoviev demanded a new leadership close to the masses and independent of the Party apparatus. At a session of the Central Committee which preceded the Congress, Trotsky made a final speech in which he revealed Lenin's strictures on Stalin in his political testament. Stalin retorted that Trotsky had been among those who had dismissed the testament as a forgery when it was first rumoured. The Congress approved the expulsion of Trotsky and Zinoviev from the Party, despite their humiliating pleas for readmission, and in January 1928 Trotsky's exile was announced. He died twelve years later, an icepick in his skull, in Mexico.

With his grip on power almost complete Stalin continued to use the Central Committee rather than the smaller Politburo to push decisions through, since in the Central Committee he could count on an automatic majority. After 1927 the Politburo consisted of nine men, four of them— Molotov, Kuibyshev, Voroshilov and Rudzutak—close followers of

Stalin, with Kalinin a probable fifth. Stalin still faced an influential rival in Bukharin, allied with Rykov and Tomsky, who headed the trade union structure. On the other hand, Stalin had almost total control over the growing Party apparatus, which now employed some twenty thousand full-time officials. The Secretariat, which now absorbed the former Orgburo, and governed all Party administration and appointments (much as Chernenko's General Department was to do later) became the real decision making body, rather than the Party Congress or even the Politburo. Stalin moreover was able to use economic policy as a weapon against Bukharin, abandoning his support for the pro-agrarian policy Bukharin had advocated and cynically adopting the policy stressed by the defeated Trotsky and Zinoviev, namely an emphasis on heavy industry and defence.

Stalin did not yet abandon Lenin's New Economic Policy, but he did return to ruthless requisitions of peasant grain. By the end of the 1920s it became clear that what he had in mind was nothing less than the breakneck industrialization of Russia, combined with the enforced collectivization of agriculture, whatever the cost. Bukharin fought a rearguard action against this policy turn, predicting (correctly) that it would lead to terror and famine. Bukharin also objected to Stalin's new doctrine that Communist parties in the West should no longer collaborate with moderate Social Democrats. Bukharin predicted—again correctly—that a broad left front would be more effective against the growing threat of European fascism. These ructions in the Politburo filtered through the Party structure in the form of rumours, and were also reflected in articles by Bukharin in *Pravda*, of which he was still the editor.

Ironically Stalin, the future dictator, was widely seen in the West at this time as a solid and statesmanlike figure. His sensible and realistic policies were preferable to the revolutionary schemes of a firebrand Left. Within Russia itself his main weapon continued to be the fear that to strike against Stalin would be to strike against the Party's monopoly of power, since Stalin and the Party were increasingly identified. In 1928 Bukharin threatened to resign. The row was patched up in a compromised resolution at the Central Committee Plenum in November 1928. But Stalin then decreed that Russia needed rapid industrialization and strong defences if it was to catch up the capitalist world. The time for "pampering the peasants" was over. Again Bukharin replied in *Pravda*, in an article significantly entitled "Lenin's Political Testament", arguing that there was no need to intensify the class struggle against so called *kulaks* or rich peasants, and that non-Communists had to be persuaded that socialism worked better than subduing by force. For this heresy Bukharin was summoned to a meeting of the Control Commission in February 1929 and removed from all his posts. Tomsky was similarly disciplined, although Rykov, surprisingly, remained Prime Minister. Like Trotsky before him, Bukharin had been forced by Stalin into a position where his best course was to beg to be allowed to remain in the Party in the faint hope that he could still influence decisions.

In June 1929 Tomsky lost his post as Head of the Trade Unions, and the following month Bukharin was removed from the Comintern. In November Bukharin was expelled from the Politburo, making Stalin's victory complete. In January 1930 the Central Committee agreed that the majority of peasant holdings should be collectivized, not 20 per cent as previously suggested, and *kulaks* were to be "liquidated as a class", which in effect meant massacres in the countryside. The purges began, with "Trotskyites" going before the firing squad long after Trotsky and his followers had ceased to exist as a political force.

Russia now entered that long night of terror, backbreaking toil, fear and war from which it was only rescued by the death of the tyrant in 1953. Many old Bolsheviks, as Arthur Koestler later was vividly to describe in his novel *Darkness at Noon* through the character of Rubashov, submerged their personalities in the Party without realizing—or perhaps not wanting to realize—that the Party did not exist except as the will of one man, Stalin. One by one the old Bolsheviks went to their deaths, arrested on ridiculous treason charges, believing, like Kafka's Joseph K, that they must have done something wrong. Into their shoes stepped the men who had benefited from Stalin's ruthless methods, who had scarcely a trace of idealism left in their veins, and who were to form the band of Stalinist henchmen from which his successors would emerge. The Politburo elected at the Sixteenth Party Congress in July 1930 were all Stalin's men: Kaganovich, Kalinin, Kirov, Kuibyshev, Kosior, Molotov, Rudzutak, Voroshilov and Ordzhonikidze, who replaced Rykov. At the Seventeenth Congress, four years later, known as the Congress of Victors, Stalin was hailed as the undisputed master of Russia, with the lengthy ovations in his honour carefully timed and stage-managed by his sycophants.

Even as dictator Stalin faced the problem which has dogged all Soviet leaders: how to control their second in command, at once the leader's assistant and rival. In Stalin's case the challenge came from the youthful and good looking Leningrad Party boss Sergei Kirov, considered an alternative to Stalin by those who had still not reconciled themselves to one-man rule. In December 1934 Kirov was shot dead by a mysterious assailant in the Leningrad Party headquarters. It was rumoured at the time, and has often been suggested since, that the crime was Stalin's and that evidence linking him with Kirov's death was covered up. At all events Stalin used the panic which followed the assassination to introduce an anti-terrorism Act providing for summary executions with no appeal, and tens of thousands of innocent Russians were put to death as a result. He also used the Kirov affair to put Zinoviev and Kamenev on trial. They had no connection whatever with the murder of Kirov, but were nonetheless tried and shot in 1936 on the absurd charge of acting on orders from Trotsky in exile.

In 1937 Bukharin and Rykov were arrested, expelled from the Central Committee, and put on trial for their lives in March 1938, with Bukharin accused of having plotted to kill both Lenin and Stalin as far back as 1918. Both were executed. Tomsky committed suicide, as did Ordzhoni-kidze, who was officially said to have suffered a heart attack but in reality is thought to have joined the rest of Stalin's victims who opposed the bloodshed. As Khrushchev later revealed, no less than 98 of 139 full and candidate members of the Central Committee were tortured to confess to absurd crimes and then shot, despite their proven allegiance to Stalin. The dictator's bloody purge extended to the armed forces, where the flower of the military leadership was cut down for no reason at all, leaving Russia disastrously unprepared for the German onslaught in 1941.

Three of Stalin's henchmen managed to survive this holocaust: Lavrenty Beria, First Secretary of the Party in Georgia, who became Head of the Secret Police; Georgy Malenkov, the Head of Party Cadres who joined the Control Commission to help carry out the purges; and a rising young man from the Ukraine called Nikita Khrushchev. All three presented themselves as heirs to Stalin's mantle, with Malenkov emerging as the favourite in Stalin's final years. Yet it was Khrushchev, a man who no less than Malenkov and Beria was implicated in Stalin's crimes, who was to come to power by unexpectedly repudiating what Stalin had done in the name of the Party.

CHAPTER FIVE

Khrushchev versus Malenkov

GEORGY MALENKOV IS the Soviet Union's forgotten leader. So condensed does history become that we have the impression that Stalin was succeeded by Khrushchev, although in fact there was intense Kremlin manoeuvring from Stalin's death in 1953 until Khrushchev's Secret Speech in 1956, and even beyond. For that matter manoeuvring went on in conditions of strictest secrecy before Stalin died, and for a while the shadow of his tyranny was cast over all political activities. As it became clear that Stalin was not immortal, it was Malenkov who seemed best placed to succeed him either as Party Secretary or as Prime Minister, or possibly as both, since Stalin combined the two posts in 1941 on the eve of the Nazi invasion, to symbolize the unity of Party and government.

Malenkov had serious rivals, some of whom had as much access to Stalin as he did. Among them were Beria, who succeeded Yezhov as Head of the NKVD (Secret Police) in 1938; Molotov, Zhdanov and Khrushchev, who joined the Politburo in 1939. All benefited from the bloody purges, in which no less than four fifths of the Central Committee were replaced. There had been one obscure attempt to restrain Stalin in 1934, when he was mysteriously described in the press as "Secretary" rather than "General Secretary", an important distinction in Soviet political jargon. But after that he ruled through his personal apparatus unchallenged, and his would-be heirs jostled for power within the framework established by Stalin, a framework which for all of Khrushchev's reforms and subsequent modifications remains in place to this day.

Since the Central Committee had become a cipher, and since Stalin did not bother to hold a Party Congress between 1939 and 1952, the heart of the struggle for power in the years preceding Stalin's death was in the Secretariat and the Politburo. The pudgy-faced Malenkov was responsible for personnel ("cadres", in Soviet terminology) as well as for industry and transport, a range of responsibilities which gave him a powerful position not unlike that held by Mikhail Gorbachov after the death of Andropov in 1984. But just as Gorbachov had a powerful rival in Grigory Romanov, the former Leningrad Party boss, so Malenkov faced his main challenge initially not from Khrushchev or Molotov, but from Zhdanov, who was Party boss in Leningrad and also responsible for ideological matters. In Soviet politics the ideology portfolio is a key post, since the interpretation of Marxist doctrine is of overriding importance. At that time, of course, the only possible doctrine was that laid down by Stalin himself. But Zhdanov nonetheless acted as Stalin's voice, which to some extent compensated for the fact that he was not on the Supreme Defence Council whereas Malenkov, Beria, Molotov and Voroshilov all were. Zhdanov, in fact, was the third most important Central Committee Secretary after Stalin and Malenkov.

The struggle between Zhdanov and Malenkov in the years after the Second World War illustrates the way in which political issues can become instruments in a personal conflict of ambition in the Kremlin. One of the most burning issues after the sufferings of wartime was the question of German reparations to the Soviet Union, which largely involved the wholesale dismantling of German factories and industrial plants and their re-erection on Soviet soil. In post war conditions this was a somewhat disorganized, not to say chaotic, process and the disorder reflected badly on Malenkov, who was in charge of the relocation. Zhdanov, spotting this chink in Malenkov's armour, demanded a commission of inquiry, to which Stalin agreed. The inquiry, headed by Mikoyan, reversed Malenkov's policy and recommended that German industries should be left where they were but put under Soviet control, with their products sent directly to Russia. Malenkov suddenly ceased to be listed as a Central Committee Secretary, and for a time it looked as if Zhdanov, who had increased his grip on Leningrad by means of a vicious campaign against intellectuals and writers, was the heir apparent. Zhdanov was also prominent as Stalin's right-hand man on cultural matters, placing the arts in Russia in the grip of sternly orthodox "socialist realism", from which they have still not entirely escaped. (Konstantin Chernenko, indeed, was to try and revive Socialist Realism when he became Secretary for Ideology in 1983.)

But Malenkov was saved from oblivion and disgrace by the sudden death of Zhdanov in August 1948. It was inevitably said that Malenkov was behind Zhdanov's death, together with Beria and the NKVD. It is certainly true that Malenkov had begun his return to power before Zhdanov died, and that a number of Zhdanov's associates, especially in Leningrad, were falsely accused and shot by the Secret Police. At all events Malenkov sealed his victory over Zhdanov by overturning his dead rival's policy on the administration of the economy, a central issue in what Leonid Brezhnev—at this time a young Party official in the

Ukraine and Moldavia—was to describe in his memoirs as the Rebirth of Russia after wartime destruction.

Zhdanov had favoured a degree of decentralization, a theme which was to surface again in the Brezhnev years when decentralization was championed by Prime Minister Kosygin, and which reappeared in a different form under Yuri Andropov and Mikhail Gorbachov. Zhdanov, in all other respects, was a man of crudely dictatorial views. Malenkov perceived that the reconstruction of Russia required a firm central grip, with only some local autonomy in the matter of appointments. He also realized that central control was needed in agriculture, where the collectivized system was on the verge of collapse, partly because the Russian peasants—ever hopeful of a system which would acknowledge their rights to the land—had expected that the Soviet régime would be magnanimous in victory and take a more relaxed and less doctrinaire approach to the agricultural economy. The result was near-anarchy, with the peasants gradually increasing their private plots and some farms in danger of breaking up altogether. To counter this Malenkov set up a Central Council of Collective Farms and ruled through a network of provincial Party (OBKOM) Secretaries. Taxes on private plots were stepped up, and the state continued to buy agricultural products compulsorily at fixed prices.

The trouble was that these measures, although perhaps ideologically and even administratively justified, did not work. On the contrary they aroused tremendous peasant hostility, leading to a disastrous fall in agricultural production at a time when industry was expanding—the same problem Trotsky had identified in the 1920s as the scissors crisis. Malenkov tried to disguise this, claiming at the Nineteenth Party Congress, which finally convened in 1952, that Russia's grain problem had been "definitely and finally solved". But no figures were released, not surprisingly since when they were published after the death of Stalin the statistics revealed that agricultural output was below prewar levels. This brought Malenkov directly into conflict with a man who had some claim to expertise in agriculture and was to prove a more dangerous rival than Zhdanov: Nikita Khrushchev.

Malenkov had already perceived the Khrushchev threat, and had moved to head it off. From 1944 onwards Khrushchev was both Prime Minister and First Secretary in the Ukraine, the most important grain growing area. He was of peasant origin himself, and made no bones about it, knowing that many other Party leaders such as Molotov or Mikoyan were from comfortable middle-class intellectual backgrounds but pretended to have more humble origins. In 1946 Malenkov engineered a Central Committee censure of Khrushchev's personnel policy in the Ukraine, and the following year Khrushchev was replaced as First Secretary in Kiev by Kaganovich, while remaining Ukrainian Prime Minister. But Khrushchev was no simple peasant. He was, as the world was later to discover, a man who combined an earthy and unpolished manner with astute political cunning. By the end of 1947 Kaganovich was out, and Khrushchev was back in. By 1950 Khrushchev was a Secretary of the Central Committee in Moscow, and Secretary of the Moscow Provincial Committee. He began a determined battle with Malenkov and Beria, choosing as his proving ground the subject which he knew best: conditions in the countryside.

Khrushchev put forward an array of ideas, including the amalgamation of farms to form large-scale holdings, which was put into practice, and the quintessentially Khrushchevian idea of agricultural towns (AGROGORODs) which would overcome the gap between town and country by bringing urban conditions to the countryside, with peasants living in blocks of flats on their private plots on the outskirts. This was not implemented, at least not for the time being, but it was published as an idea for discussion by *Pravda* in 1951.

When the Nineteenth Congress met in October 1952, Malenkov still seemed to be the man to watch. Stalin did not take part in the Congress, rather as the unseen figure of Andropov was to dominate the crucial Party Plenum of December 1983. It was Malenkov who rose to give the main report at the Congress in place of Stalin. Beria was in charge of both the Secret Police and the Interior Ministry, and Khrushchev also manoeuvred to place his supporters in key positions, with one of his protégés, a young man called Leonid Brezhnev, becoming one of the ten Central Committee Secretaries. Another, A. B. Aristov, also joined the Secretariat, acquiring responsibility for Party cadres, trade unions and the Komsomol. As before it was the Secretariat which remained the key political institution, although there were signs, with only a year to go to Stalin's death, that the Party structure might revive once the old tyrant was gone. The Politburo was abolished at this time and replaced by a body called the Praesidium (the term Politburo was later reintroduced); the new Praesidium had 25 full members and eleven candidate members, most of whom had joined the Party after Lenin's death in 1924. They were a generation for which the central events and experiences were not the Revolution and the Civil War, in which the new men had not taken part, but the Second World War and Stalin's tyrannical personal rule. It was the generation which was to govern Russia for the next thirty years, and which is only now releasing its grip on power. SOVNARKOM, which Lenin had once headed, became the Council of Ministers in 1946, suggesting that Soviet Russia was no longer a young revolutionary power but an established and even conservative state with global responsibilities.

The Central Committee elected at the 1952 Congress numbered some 236 full and candidate members, twice as many as in 1939. In a final break with the past the Party itself was renamed the Communist Party of the Soviet Union, instead of the All Union Communist Party (Bolsheviks). In other words, formally speaking there was no longer any reminder of the nineteenth-century Social Democratic Party from which the Bolsheviks and Mensheviks had both sprung, or of the early struggle between Lenin's Bolsheviks and other socialist contenders for power. The Party was now an entrenched bureaucracy which was beginning to break free from the grip of one-man rule and to become the instrument of government in one of the world's greatest powers. In a move towards greater democracy it was decided that the Congresses should meet regularly every five years and the Central Committee Plenums should convene twice a year, rules which remain in force to this day.

Hope of a new era around the corner was however overshadowed by fear of a resurgence of Stalin's paranoia, together with the purges and arrests which Russians hoped belonged to a time before the national unity and comradeship of the war against Nazism. Stalin himself fuelled these fears by warning that the Soviet Union was at war with capitalism, and that there would be further restrictions on the peasantry. In one of the most bizarre displays of conspiracy theory, Stalin accused his own doctors in the Kremlin of a plot against the leadership, alleging that they had murdered Zhdanov and had plotted against Russia's military leaders in order to weaken Soviet defence during the war. In fact, of course, it was Stalin himself who had undermined Soviet defences by senselessly executing the élite of the armed forces. But nobody dared to say so. There was moreover a distinct anti-Semitic tinge to the so-called Doctors' Plot, since seven of the nine Kremlin doctors concerned were Jewish, and were said to have been agents of American Jewish organizations. The Kremlin surgeons were tortured to make false confessions and two of them perished in prison.

Their trial would have been the signal for another terrifying purge, just as the assassination of Kirov in the 1930s set off the first wave of Stalinist terror. Khrushchev later claimed that Stalin even intended to kill off all remaining members of the "old guard" in the Politburo (Praesidium) including Molotov, Mikoyan, Voroshilov and possibly Beria (the intended fate of Khrushchev and Malenkov is unknown). But on 5 March 1953, Stalin's bodyguards found him lying on the floor, dead from a haemorrhage of the brain. Malenkov was Russia's new leader.

Stalin's survivors moved swiftly to pre-empt any possible panic or disarray in the wake of the dictator's death, and on 7 March a new government was announced. Malenkov took over both of Stalin's posts as First Secretary of the Party and First Chairman of the Council of Ministers (Prime Minister). The other members of the Praesidium included Beria, Khrushchev, Molotov, Bulganin and Kaganovich. At the Council of Ministers Malenkov had four deputies: Beria, who was also Minister of the Interior, Molotov, the Foreign Minister, Bulganin, the Minister of Defence, and Kaganovich. There was no doubt that Malenkov was intended to be the unchallenged leader in the Stalin mould. *Pravda* even carried a faked photograph of Malenkov standing alongside Stalin and Mao Tse Tung, intended to show that he was a world leader of the same stature. (It was in fact a group photograph from which the others had been removed. The figure of Malenkov had been enlarged.) Malenkov indicated that he intended to be a Stalin-like leader in other respects as well, praising the "wisdom" of Stalin's policies, when everybody knew that the paranoid dictator had been about to launch yet another bloodbath.

In the event, perhaps because he had identified himself so closely with Stalin and had presumed to be his heir, Malenkov's rule lasted only one week. On 14 March Khrushchev, who had all the time been manoeuvring in the background, presented himself as candidate for the post of First Secretary at a Central Committee meeting. Malenkov resigned "at his own request", while remaining Prime Minister. The two structures of Party and government were thus separated again for the first time in over a decade, and each was headed by a powerful and ambitious politician. In retrospect it might seem obvious that Khrushchev was bound to emerge the winner in the end, since the post of Party leader was the more crucial one. But it did not appear so at the time. Stalin's dominance of Soviet politics had been so complete that it was not clear whether in the post-Stalin era power would lie more with the government than with the Party, or vice versa. Lenin, after all, had been Prime Minister while dominating both Party and government.

When Rykov was Prime Minister after the death of Lenin it was clear—or gradually became so—that the balance of power lay with the General Secretary, Stalin. The same was true from 1930 onwards when Molotov was Prime Minister. But by combining the two posts Stalin had reverted to the Leninist pattern of personal pre-eminence and had thus confused the issue. It seems possible, although this has never been conclusively proved, that, when making his coup against Malenkov in 1953, Khrushchev forced Malenkov to choose one post or the other, and that Malenkov opted for the position which appeared to carry with it the trappings of power, not least in Western eyes, to which the post of Prime Minister (at least in a multi-party system) appears the most important.

Khrushchev still had one major rival for power: Lavrenty Beria, the head of the Secret Police, a Georgian like Stalin and a man who had every intention of using the power he wielded as head of the feared Security Services to gain the supreme posts for himself. Khrushchev, characteristically, later gave so many versions of what happened next that it is difficult to say where the truth lies. But it is certain that both Khrushchev and other members of the Praesidium intensely disliked the malevolent and ambitious Beria and feared what he might do if he controlled the Kremlin. Beria seems to have made the tactical error of trying to mount a coup using NKVD troops and armour, which in the summer of 1953 suddenly appeared menacingly on the streets of Moscow. This was the first time since the days of the Revolution that the highly secretive struggle for power behind the walls of the Kremlin had spilled over on to the streets, with the use or threatened use of armed force. Khrushchev responded by using the power of the regular army to counter Beria's secret police troops, and Marshal Zhukov's soldiers and tanks surrounded Moscow in an impressive display of army support for the government.

According to Khrushchev, in his Memoirs, Beria was arrested at a meeting of the Praesidium before his bid for power could go any further. It was an extraordinary, almost Mafia-like event, with members of the Praesidium carrying guns in their briefcases. Beria was accused of having worked for the British intelligence for thirty years, an accusation as absurd as those he had so often levelled against others. His real crime was to have used secret police powers to try and revive Stalin's dictatorship. According to some sources, Beria was shot, at the time of his arrest, in the same building where the Praesidium meeting was taking place. According to others, he was executed later (his arrest was made public on 10 July 1953). There were even rumours that he had been strangled. More important than how Beria met his end—richly deserved in the view of most Russians—were the political consequences of his fall. The empire he had ruled at the Interior Ministry (MVD) was split into a ministry of internal affairs and a reformed security police organization, the Committee for State Security, known by its Russian initials as the KGB. Given the shudder of fears those initials still arouse, it is difficult to imagine that after the fall of Beria a deliberate attempt was made to cut the KGB down to size and to ensure that it was dominated by Party officials rather than established secret policemen whose ranks were thoroughly purged.

Khrushchev, who was officially confirmed as First Secretary at the Central Committee in September 1953, was determined that the KGB should no longer form a state within a state and so challenge the Party's monopoly of power. It was from this time on that it became conventional wisdom in Soviet politics that no head of the KGB should ever aspire to the post of Party leader, a convention that it took Yuri Andropov thirty years to overturn—although the subsequent "revenge of the Party" led by Konstantin Chernenko suggests that Andropov may have revived the fears which Beria—a quite different man in character and ambition—aroused in 1953.

The fall of Beria did not mean the end of the struggle, however, and Khrushchev was still not the unchallenged leader. He was at odds with Malenkov, the Prime Minister, on a number of issues, the most important of which, to the Soviet man on the street, was the question of economic priorities. Malenkov, courting popularity, took the part of the suffering Soviet consumer and promised a consumer-goods boom. Khrushchev took the view that in the unending battle for economic resources in Russia, heavy industry should have the priority. On the eve of the Central Committee Plenum in January 1955, *Pravda* supported this contention, attacking those who championed the consumer sector. Khrushchev and Malenkov were also at odds over foreign policy, with Malenkov taking the heretical view (which Khrushchev was later to adopt himself as if he had always held it) that a nuclear war was not winnable but would destroy the entire planet and not only the West. Malenkov also opposed Khrushchev's policy of giving China extensive military aid (presciently, as it turned out) but was powerless to stop Khrushchev going to Peking in a delegation that also included Bulganin and Mikoyan.

The fact that Malenkov's policies were in many ways reasonable, indeed later taken over by Khrushchev, did not save him from political disgrace. At the February session of the Supreme Soviet in 1955, he was obliged to resign from the premiership, again "at his own request", on the humiliating grounds that he lacked experience of administration (which had in fact been his forte). He was replaced as Prime Minister by Bulganin, who in turn was replaced as Minister of Defence by Marshal Zhukov, who had come to Khrushchev's aid during the Beria crisis. By 1956, when the historic Twentieth Party Congress convened, Khrushchev was able to purge the Provincial and District Party Committee of

Malenkov's supporters and replace them with his own men, a move which was eventually reflected in a pro-Khrushchev Central Committee.

Yet it was to be another year before Khrushchev, with the support of Marshal Zhukov and aspiring young politicians such as Leonid Brezhnev, was finally able to outmanoeuvre fellow members of the old guard who had survived with him the terrors and uncertainties of Stalin's dictatorship.

CHAPTER SIX

The Coup Against Khrushchev

BY THE TIME Khrushchev made his sensational Secret Speech in 1956, he was already firmly in control of Soviet policy at home and abroad. He had revealed the abysmal state of Soviet agriculture at the Central Committee Plenum of September 1953 which confirmed him as First Secretary. Brushing aside the world of agricultural make-believe created by Malenkov, Khrushchev adopted a down-to-earth and pragmatic approach to the eternal question of the Russian peasantry. He offered decentralized planning, a degree of local initiative and, above all, material incentives to the collective farmers to produce more, all coupled with a strengthening of Party control in the countryside. By 1958 Khrushchev had abolished the network of motor tractor stations (MTS) which Malenkov had tried to use as an instrument of control, and transferred the management of mechanized resources to the farms themselves. In the spring of 1954 Khrushchev launched his celebrated Virgin Lands campaign in Kazakhstan, a breathtakingly imaginative scheme intended to make maize and grain grow where no crop had grown before, making vast tracts of arid land fertile. It was later to be seen as one of Khrushchev's "harebrained schemes" and used by Brezhnev to undermine Khrushchev's leadership. But in the mid-1950s Brezhnev, by now a senior official in Kazakhstan, was directly involved in the Virgin Lands campaign, and took part in what amounted to a resurgence of enthusiasm and idealism after the dark age of Stalinist repression.

Khrushchev also increasingly took charge of industrial affairs following Mikoyan's resignation as Party leader. The fall of Mikoyan marked the beginning of the end for Lazar Kaganovich, who had been a kind of supremo of economic planning. In 1955 Kaganovich was demoted to the State Committee on Labour and Wages and later still to the Ministry of Building Materials. Mikoyan became Deputy Prime Minister with responsibility for industry. At the Central Committee Plenum of December 1956 a new State Economic Commission was set up to oversee the economy and improve the planning mechanism, a move accompanied by the downgrading of GOSPLAN to State Planning Agency. At the following Plenum, in February 1957, the officials of GOSPLAN made something of a comeback and the reform was adjusted so that GOSPLAN remained responsible for long term planning with the State Economic Commission taking the crucial short term decisions. In March Khrushchev submitted his thesis on industry to the Supreme Soviet, replacing the central industrial ministries in Moscow with a network of economic councils on a regional basis, each one responsible for the development of local industry and reporting to the SEC in Moscow.

In foreign affairs Vyacheslav Molotov, the Foreign Minister, lost influence at the same time that Malenkov's star was beginning to wane. The key policy issue was Russia's relationship with Eastern Europe, and in particular with Yugoslavia, where Tito had defied Stalin and had set up a heretical brand of socialism insisting on the right of East European countries to independence from Moscow. In May 1955 Khrushchev made his celebrated reconciliation trip to Belgrade, blaming the 1948 Soviet-Yugoslav split on the disgraced Beria. Tito would have none of this and there were disagreements, too, on other issues such as the Yugoslav concept of workers' control and self-management. But a rapprochement was achieved, and the trip ended with a joint declaration on the legitimacy of separate paths to socialism, a document which remains the basis of Soviet-Yugoslav relations to this day. Molotov, a thoroughly Cold War negotiator by instinct, strongly disapproved of Khrushchev's freewheeling liberal approach and refused to accompany the Soviet leader to Belgrade. In 1956 he was forced to step down as Foreign Minister and was succeeded by Alexander Shepilov, a Khrushchev protégé.

There was therefore an air of anticipation when the Twentieth Party Congress convened on 14 February 1956. Few of the delegates could have guessed quite how dramatic Khrushchev's Congress was to prove. He was now at the height of his power and was finally prepared to tackle the problem which had lain at the heart of the succession struggle but which nobody had so far dared to express openly—the legacy of the Stalin period.

Khrushchev had already adopted a more relaxed style and was known to Russians and Westerners alike as a refreshingly unpredictable politician who was ready to offer frank opinions peppered with peasant humour and wisdom at the drop of a hat. He had also made a number of liberal political moves, including restrictions on the power of the KGB and his tolerance for Yugoslav and East European independence. In his main address to the Congress Khrushchev advanced the thesis—later to become the basis of peaceful coexistence and subsequently détente—that war between socialism and capitalism was not inevitable and that the victory of world Communism would be achieved by peaceful means rather than by force. It was a view which did not please more militant elements in the Party, but it was to remain the basis of Soviet foreign policy for the next thirty years.

The bombshell came on the final day of the Congress, which met in secret session. The Secret Speech which Khrushchev made on that fateful day trickled out through foreign Communist observers and was eventually published by the American State Department. But so explosive were its contents that it was first greeted with scepticism and disbelief. In the open conference session Mikoyan had already caused a stir by referring critically to Stalin's theories and his abuse of the principle of collective leadership, noting that Stalin had built up an unacceptable personality cult. But in his Secret Speech Khrushchev went much further, holding his audience spellbound in horrified fascination as he gave a detailed exposé of the crimes perpetrated by the man who had sent untold millions to their deaths for daring so much as to whisper adverse comments.

Khrushchev told the delegates for the first time that Lenin himself had heartily disliked Stalin and had tried to have him removed from the post of General Secretary. One by one Khrushchev detailed the cases of innocent victims of the purges who had been forced by Stalin's evil secret police chiefs to make fabricated confessions of guilt under torture. Khrushchev was careful only to rehabilitate Party members who had been shot or imprisoned under Stalin, and he did not go so far as to rehabilitate either Trotsky or Bukharin, both of whom still remain non-persons in official Soviet histories. Equally, for obvious reasons, Khrushchev forbore to mention that he too was implicated in Stalin's crimes since he had spent over a decade at the dictator's side. But the deed was done, and Khrushchev had done the unthinkable by bringing the idol Stalin crashing down from his pedestal. His speech electrified both Russian and foreign Communists who had revered Stalin as the leader of world Communism and had not wanted to face the fact that he was one of the bloodiest tyrants known to history. Khrushchev's great merit was that he forced them to face this, at the risk of undermining the basis of Communism itself.

As the shock waves of Khrushchev's de-Stalinization campaign began to spread there was panic and alarm in the Kremlin, with Khrushchev's colleagues accusing him of having irresponsibly released a genie which could not easily be stuffed back into the bottle. The Secret Speech, and Khrushchev's tolerance of the Yugoslav heresy, helped to create the conditions for the uprising against Communist rule in Hungary in

October 1956, a rising which was ostensibly directed against Stalin and his Hungarian counterparts, but which threatened to take Hungary out of the Warsaw Pact altogether. The rising was only subdued with difficulty in a blaze of world publicity as Soviet tanks rolled in to restore order and maintain Communist power. Imre Nagy, the liberal Hungarian Prime Minister, was double-crossed and executed by the Russians, and Janos Kadar was installed in his place, largely thanks to astute political manoeuvring by the then Soviet Ambassador in Budapest, a rising young Party diplomat and official by the name of Yuri Andropov.

There were similar upheavals in Poland, where riots and demonstrations finally brought about the dismissal of Marshal Rokossovsky, who had in effect been acting as Soviet Governor General, and the rise to power of Wladyslaw Gomulka, a Polish Communist previously gaoled for his nationalist leanings.

The Kremlin confrontation came to a head in the Praesidium (Politburo) in June 1957 when Khrushchev, for the first time, found almost all his colleagues ranged against him. A vote of confidence in his leadership went against him and he was threatened with removal from the Secretariat. Khrushchev responded by using the broader Central Committee, in which he enjoyed majority support, to defeat his Politburo rivals. As First Secretary he was empowered to convene an Extraordinary Plenum of the Central Committee, which he duly did, and Central Committee members from both Moscow and the provinces were impressed by a show of strength and support for Khrushchev from the armed forces under the command of Marshal Zhukov. There were even reports that the Defence Minister had provided military transport to ensure that Central Committee Members reached the capital in time to vote for Khrushchev and thus to ensure his political survival. The result was a triumph for Khrushchev and a defeat for his opponents, who from now on were dubbed the "Anti-Party Group". It would have been more accurate to have described them as the Anti-Khrushchev Group, but like Stalin before him Khrushchev had now succeeded in identifying himself with the Party. The Anti-Party faction, consisting of Malenkov, Kaganovich, Molotov and Shepilov, was accused of breaking Party discipline on a range of issues, including agricultural policy, industrial reorganization, and attitudes to Eastern Europe. The four were expelled from the Praesidium and the Central Committee by unanimous vote with only one abstention—that of Molotov, the former Foreign Minister.

With the threat to his leadership averted, Khrushchev felt confident enough to purge the Praesidium, promoting six candidate members, all of them Khrushchev men, including Marshal Zhukov. Ironically, by the end of 1957 Zhukov had been stripped of his posts, accused of neglecting political indoctrination in the armed forces. The real reason, it seems, was that Khrushchev was highly suspicious of Marshal Zhukov, who not only enjoyed a high military reputation and was a war hero, but also had increasing political ambitions. The sacking of Zhukov was seen as an illustration of the fact that in the Soviet system services rendered do not always bring political rewards, and has often been cited as evidence of the pre-eminence of the Party, which relies heavily on the backing of the armed forces but will not tolerate a bid by the military for direct political power. In Marxist-Leninist ideology the military power is strictly subordinate to the civil power, and although in Poland the upheavals of 1980 and the Solidarity movement brought a military régime to power with only a thin coating of Communist ideology, in Russia itself suspicion of "the man on horseback" remains profound. Some 25 years later Yuri Andropov was to reach the pinnacle with the active backing of the armed forces led by Marshal Ustinov, the Defence Minister; but suggestions that Marshal Ustinov might be rewarded with the Presidency came to nothing, possibly because the Kremlin fears that to have a military man in one of the supreme posts would illustrate only too clearly that Communist power emerges, as Mao Tse Tung put it, from the barrel of a gun, rather than from popular consent.

The hapless Marshal Zhukov was replaced as Minister of Defence by Marshal Malinovsky, like Zhukov a military career officer, but one who had been close to Khrushchev during the war at Stalingrad and elsewhere. Zhukov was replaced on the Praesidium with a token representative from Uzbekistan. Of the fifteen Praesidium members, ten were Central Committee Secretaries and Khrushchev supporters. Of the remaining five, two—Frol Kozlov, the Leningrad boss, and Anastas Mikoyan—supported Khrushchev, leaving only three possible anti-Khrushchev members: Bulganin, Voroshilov, and Shvernik, none of whom wielded any clout. In 1958 Khrushchev set the seal on his personal ascendancy by combining the post of Party Secretary with that of Prime Minister, just as Stalin had done before him.

What Khrushchev did not foresee was that the threat to his rule would come not from his rivals, most of whom he had eliminated, but from those who claimed to be his protégés and political allies. Leonid Brezhnev, Alexei Kosygin, Nikolai Podgorny and the astute and sinister Mikhail Suslov became increasingly dismayed by what they saw as Khrushchev's erratic and unpredictable behaviour and his refusal to conciliate vested interests within the Party structure. One of the most startling of his reforms, and a measure which was to echo through the

Brezhnev years to the rise of Andropov and Gorbachov, was his insistence on a regular turnover of Party and government personnel, in an effort to ensure that unimaginative bureaucrats had no time to entrench themselves but were constantly replaced with fresh blood. Between 1960 and 1961 over half of the Party Secretaries at provincial committee (OBKOM) level were purged and replaced. The effect of this can hardly be underestimated, since Provincial Secretaries are the backbone of the Party structure. The upheaval caused by the policy of recurrent turnover, which Khrushchev even had written into the Party rules, caused tremendous resentment which continued to simmer throughout the early 1960s.

In 1962 Khrushchev went further still and took the dangerous step of trying to reduce the status of OBKOM and District Secretaries. The following year Khrushchev set up a new combined Party and State control system headed by Alexander Shelepin, a former head of the KGB, which not unnaturally aroused fears that Khrushchev's tampering with the Party structure was getting out of hand. Many years later, when Konstantin Chernenko came to power, he too was to present himself as a grass roots popularist who favoured more democracy within the Party. But Chernenko took care not to upset vested interests, and indeed came to power precisely because the Party *apparatchiks* knew that he would not endanger their sinecures but would preserve the status quo. Khrushchev, by contrast, aroused widespread apprehension, and also caused irritation by demanding that his subordinates fulfil impossibly grandiose schemes and then penalizing them when they failed.

The Pandora's Box of de-Stalinization which Khrushchev had opened still aroused anxiety at high levels despite the resounding defeat of the Anti-Party Group. It was under Khrushchev that devastatingly revealing accounts of the Stalinist era began to appear, including Alexander Solzhenitsyn's novel *One Day in the Life of Ivan Denisovich*. There was a persistent feeling that the exposé of Stalin's crimes had gone far enough, and indeed had already gone too far, with the attendant danger that it might come to embrace those who had been Stalin's accomplices and eventually cause fatal cracks in the Communist system itself. At the Twenty-Second Party Congress in 1961, there were indications that the power struggle was still continuing. How to deal with the legacy of Stalinism was still at the centre of the discussions at the Congress, which passed a resolution that Stalin should no longer lie alongside Lenin in the mausoleum on Red Square but should be removed to a more appropriate grave behind it. A young firebrand poet called Yevgeny Yevtushenko published a poem in *Pravda* calling on the Kremlin leaders to redouble the guard on the mausoleum in case the spirit of the dead tyrant still lingered there and might escape to terrorize Russia once more.

Behind the scenes, however, opposition to Khrushchev's determined course was gathering steam. As in the case of Gorbachov, it would be an error to suppose that Khrushchev was in any way a liberal in the Western sense. His rule was marked by an increase in suppression of religion in Russia, including the Orthodox Church, and by persecution of dissident writers and intellectuals. There were as yet no trials of dissident writers (that came later, under Brezhnev) but they were harassed and some were incarcerated in lunatic asylums. Nonetheless, Khrushchev's unpredictability included a tendency to sanction the publication of writings such as those of Solzhenitsyn, and it was under Khrushchev that the arts began to flow in Russia, with the literary magazine *New World (Novy Mir)*, edited by Alexander Tvardovsky enjoying its finest hour.

But above all fiascos in foreign policy ultimately led to Khrushchev's downfall. The most obvious of these was the confrontation with President Kennedy over the attempted installation of Soviet missiles in Cuba in 1962, an incident which brought the world to the brink of war and ended in humiliation for the Soviet Union. But Khrushchev also presided over the beginning of the great schism with China, which Malenkov had earlier foreseen, but he had not, and when the Twenty-Second Party Congress in 1961 bitterly attacked "Albania" everybody knew that this meant "Peking". Khrushchev further offended Kremlin hardliners by hinting that he was ready to talk about the possible reunification of Germany, and that he believed Soviet resources were over-stretched in the Third World, where it was not always necessary for Russia to lend total support to national liberation movements in countries like Viet Nam. He offended the generals, always a powerful interest group, by suggesting that the development of more sophisticated weaponry meant that armed forces manpower could be reduced. This was greatly resented, not only because the Army had supported Khrushchev in the 1957 internal crisis (the fate of Marshal Zhukov was not forgotten), but also because the split with China meant that extra Soviet forces were needed on the Sino-Soviet border.

Khrushchev, many Party leaders felt, was developing a personality cult not so different from the one created by Stalin, and was beginning to act in a dictatorial fashion, turning to the Praesidium only for approval of faits accomplis. Finally, Khrushchev's ambitious economic schemes were beginning to look unrealistic, and he came into direct conflict with leading economists and planners. He apparently believed, as Andropov later did, that his programme could be achieved if technocrats were placed in key positions in the apparatus, but this inevitably led to further resentment among the entrenched *apparatchiks*.

There had earlier been one attempt to mount a coup against Khrushchev, in 1960, when the rebels' candidate was Frol Kozlov, the Leningrad boss, who was seen by Khrushchev himself as his heir apparent. At the Central Committee Plenum of May 1960 Kozlov was named as Central Committee Secretary and at a further Plenum three months later Brezhnev, until then an obvious contender for power, was removed from his Party posts and made Chairman of the Praesidium of the Supreme Soviet, or President, a largely ceremonial post. Khrushchev reacted by packing the Central Committee with ten new Secretaries including Piotr Demichev (now Minister of Culture), Leonid Ilychov (now Negotiator with Peking), Boris Ponomaryov (later in charge of relations with Western left wing Parties), and Yuri Andropov, who joined the Secretariat at the November Central Committee Plenum in November 1962. All of these at the time were Khrushchev's men, which meant that Kozlov became one of several possible eventual successors rather than an immediate threat. He was in any case removed by a higher power when he died following a stroke in April 1963.

One clue to the fact that Khrushchev's grip was being loosened came in March 1963, when yet another planning body was announced, the Supreme Council of National Economy (SCNE). It had not been discussed at the November Plenum the previous year, which had specifically dealt with structures of industrial control. The new body, of which Khrushchev evidently did not approve, was headed by Dmitri Ustinov, who was later to play such a crucial role in Yuri Andropov's rise to power as Minister of Defence. Ustinov, who began his career as Stalin's Munitions Minister during the war, was a protégé of Alexei Kosygin rather than of Khrushchev. He nonetheless became First Deputy Prime Minister in 1963, together with Kosygin and Mikoyan. As a sign of Khrushchev's displeasure Ustinov was not made a member of the Politburo at the Central Committee Plenum in June 1963, as might have been expected.

The storm clouds were gathering, and in the course of 1964 the Politburo decided that the time had come for Khrushchev, the Soviet Union's third leader, to be removed. This was a bold stroke indeed, since both previous leaders had been removed by death rather than coup d'état. Since there was no machinery, such as a vote of no confidence, which could remove him from power in the Central Committee, the Politburo resorted to a dark plot worthy of the palace coups of Tsarist times.

Khrushchev had almost full control of the 175 Central Committee members, a majority of whom had either been directly or indirectly approved by Khrushchev personally by the appointment system known as *nomenklatura*, or were close associates and supporters. The plotters had to ensure therefore that Khrushchev did not repeat his 1957 manoeuvre and use the Central Committee to outflank the inner core of Party leaders. They also made sure that the KGB was firmly on their side, and co-opted the support both of Semichastny, the KGB chief, and his predecessor and close associate, Shelepin, who was duly rewarded with full Politburo membership after the coup had taken place (he had not previously even been a candidate member). On 13 October 1964 Khrushchev, who had earlier been seen off on the train to Pitsunda on the Black Sea by his smiling colleagues, was recalled suddenly to Moscow, to find them confronting him grim-faced and determined. With the Politburo solidly lined up against him, including those he had imagined to be his supporters, Khrushchev was left no choice but to step down.

He was replaced as First Secretary by Brezhnev on 15 October 1964, and as Prime Minister by Kosygin the following day. As in previous succession crises, the new era began with the structures of Party and government formally separated. Khrushchev himself was not tried or disgraced, but was simply sent into retirement and obscurity for the next six and a half years. When he died in 1970, *Pravda* recorded his passing in a very brief note, describing him as N. S. Khrushchev, a pensioner.

One by one most of Khrushchev's rivals also died off—except for Vyacheslav Molotov, who lived on as a recluse into his nineties. In July 1984 Molotov, who like Malenkov had been expelled from the Party at the 1961 Congress, received a telephone call from President Chernenko. At the age of 94, Stalin's Foreign Minister was to be re-admitted to the Party. It was a small, belated victory, but it must to some extent have compensated for his disgrace thirty years earlier at the hands of Khrushchev, his humiliating exile to Mongolia as Ambassador and later his appointment in Vienna as Soviet delegate to the International Atomic Energy Agency.

CHAPTER SEVEN

The Brezhnev Succession

IT IS A characteristic of the Soviet succession process—or at least it was until the Andropov era—that the new leader barely mentions his predecessors, who vanish from the public record as if they had never existed. Khrushchev's last public meeting was with Gaston Palewski, the French Minister of Space and Science, at Sochi on the Black Sea on 13 October 1964. But as soon as he had been recalled to Moscow and dismissed from the post of First Secretary his name disappeared from the press and his portrait vanished from Moscow streets and offices as if it had never been.

Another typical aspect of the succession mechanism in Russia is that the new leader represents himself as one of the collective leadership and only in the course of time emerges as *primus inter pares*. Brezhnev was not well known to most people except during his period as President of the Soviet Union, when he symbolically represented Russia and was often seen on television shaking the hands of foreign leaders. Otherwise he appeared to be a colourless *apparatchik*, something of an unknown quantity politically who had been Khrushchev's protégé and became his Number Two in 1960.

But Brezhnev did not make the same mistakes Khrushchev had made. One of Khrushchev's errors was to antagonize the armed forces. The army had supported Khrushchev during his first serious crisis in 1957, but by 1964 it had had enough of Khrushchev's antics and swung against him. Another error was to come into conflict with the country's chief planners and economists. Khrushchev's economic programme— ironically, in view of his clash with Malenkov after the death of Stalin— was avowedly pro-consumer, rather as Konstantin Chernenko's economic policy was to be during a later succession struggle. On the other hand the Party Programme which Khrushchev pushed through in 1961, which promised that Russia would achieve the fully abundant society and overtake the United States by 1980, was obviously unrealistic, not to say a fantasy, as Gorbachov was later tacitly to acknowledge when he presented a new and more modest (or realistic) programme to the Twenty-Seventh Party Congress in February 1986.

Khrushchev's third major error, which Brezhnev did not repeat until much later, was his development of a personality cult to rival that of Stalin, even though Khrushchev had himself spearheaded denunciations of the grandiose glorification of Stalin's name. After the fall of Malenkov in 1955 *Pravda* had pointedly remarked in an editorial that Lenin "taught us the collective nature of work". "He often reminded us that all members of the Politburo are equal, and the Secretary is chosen to execute the resolutions of the Central Committee." There were 175 full members of the Central Committee, of whom about 75 had been directly or indirectly approved by Khrushchev himself. Central Committee decisions are not necessarily unanimous, and only a two-thirds majority is required for important resolutions. Khrushchev, for most of the time, could count on a two-thirds majority, especially since a great many members of the Central Committee had been with him during the War or had climbed up with him through Stalin's apparatus, in addition to which he had supporters with close personal ties such as Adzhubei, the editor of *Izvestiya*.

Khrushchev had done his best, as all Soviet leaders do, to neutralize all potential challengers to his positions, but he failed. Once the coup had been mounted, with no apparent backlash of belated support for the disgraced Khrushchev, Brezhnev and Kosygin set out to reverse almost every policy move Khrushchev had made in his final years. His Supreme Council of the National Economy was abolished. In 1965 Kosygin masterminded a series of economic reforms, using the theories of the liberal economist Yevsei Lieberman, including a measure of autonomy for industrial enterprises, the relations of wages to output and of prices to demand. Like subsequent economic reforms with a similar thrust, the Kosygin 1965 reforms were overwhelmed by the tendency of the bureaucracy toward centralization, and by Soviet managers' dislike of initiative and enterprise and a preference for safety, predictability of instructions from above, regardless of whether or not the Plan handed down from Moscow meets either the needs of consumers or the production requirements of the factory concerned.

The Brezhnev-Kosygin leadership moved swiftly to repair some of the damage wrought by Khrushchev's determined de-Stalinization campaign. At the Twenty-Third Party Congress of 1966, Brezhnev's first Congress as First Secretary, Stalin was partially rehabilitated. The previous year celebrations marking the twentieth anniversary of the end of the Second World War had featured praise for Stalin's military genius, a pattern which was to be repeated during the thirtieth anniversary in 1975 and the fortieth anniversary in 1985. During the fiftieth anniversary of the Bolshevik Revolution in 1967, Stalinism came to be defined as a period of considerable achievement for the Soviet state marred by a number of "unfortunate and temporary errors", a definition which in essence still stands.

The early Brezhnev period also witnessed the beginning of a campaign against the emerging dissident movement, the first shot in the Kremlin's salvo being fired against the writers Sinyavsky and Daniel, who were put on trial. The trial did little to enhance the Soviet Union's reputation abroad, and in a sense encouraged the dissident movement among writers, intellectuals, and religious and nationalist activists which was to last for some ten years. But the campaign was a sign that the Brezhnev régime was settling in, and would brook no opposition. Military aid to North Viet Nam was increased at about the same time, despite the risk of worsening relations with the United States, and in a further reversal of Khrushchev's policies the Soviet military budget was considerably increased.

Nominally, the leadership was collective, just as Lenin and *Pravda* had decreed. In order to ensure that no one man ever again gathered all the reins of power together in his own hands, the Central Committee decided, in October 1964, immediately after Khrushchev's ouster, that the offices of First or General Secretary and Prime Minister should never again be combined—in other words, the top posts in Party and Government should from now on be kept separate. Khrushchev had not always been both Party Secretary and Prime Minister: Bulganin had been Premier for three years from 1955, and he and Khrushchev together had made a highly successful visit to Britain during those years. But it was always clear that Bulganin was essentially a second-rank figure, and that the real power resided in the dominant personality of Khrushchev. Kosygin, however, was no Bulganin. He was a weighty figure in his own right. With Kosygin as Prime Minister the new Soviet doctrine of separation of powers initially took on some reality. The Politburo regained its former name in 1966, and with the name it also regained its former position as the supreme decision-making body.

What the Politburo had overlooked was that the post of Party leader could be combined not only with that of Prime Minister but also with the third top position in the leadership, that of Chairman of the Praesidium of the Supreme Soviet or President. Eventually Brezhnev was to covet the symbolic power of the Presidency, which he felt conveyed to the world at large that he was a man able to speak for the entire Soviet nation and to sign international treaties and documents. But in the early Brezhnev years collectivity was the byword, and institutions and personalities undermined by Khrushchev were gradually restored.

Shelepin was thanked for his support of the anti-Khrushchev conspirators with abolition of his Party State Control Commission and loss of his seat on the Council of Ministers. On the other hand Ustinov became a Candidate Member of the Praesidium (Politburo) in March 1965, thus rising to power with his mentor, Alexei Kosygin.

The power of the KGB itself was reinforced, with Yuri Andropov becoming head of the KGB in 1967 and at the same time a Candidate Member of the Politburo—the first head of the security services to be in the Politburo since Lavrenty Beria. This was a new, "legalistic" KGB, with Andropov—not a secret policeman in career terms—placed in charge of the KGB in order to ensure strict Party control of its activities. There was no appeal to the Russian people, as there had been after the death of Stalin, to avoid "panic and disorder". But there was stress on order rather than anarchy, and on the need to appease the Soviet people by making economic concessions and promoting material improvements in their lives. The KGB was obliged to observe due legal process, and to operate (at least formally speaking) in accordance with law and regulations.

Brezhnev revived the Ministry of Internal Affairs which Khrushchev had abolished in 1962, and appointed as Interior Minister his old friend Nikolai Shcholokov, whom he had known in Dniepropetrovsk and Moldavia. Brezhnev's initial priority was to counteract the unpredictability, the muddleheadedness, the personality cult and the counterproductive policies of the Khrushchev years. The world that Khrushchev had left behind him, Brezhnev felt, was a world in which Soviet influence had not notably increased.

Who was the man who was to remain in power in Russia longer than any other Soviet leader except Stalin—longer than Lenin, Khrushchev, Andropov or Chernenko? Like Chernenko, and like Stalin, although in different times, Brezhnev came to power by appealing to the conservative majority in the apparatus, who thought of him as one of them rather than as a radical newcomer likely to challenge their sinecure. Brezhnev took many years to emerge as a man with any personality at all, and it was only when he encountered Western leaders in West Germany and the United States that he blossomed forth. He was not bumptious or flamboyant, as Khrushchev had been, but he was an outgoing personality, as the Americans discovered to their delight—a man who could grip elbows and bearhug with the best of them. Inside the Soviet Union, in the Party itself, he was seen above all as an able but modest servant of the Party rather than someone who wished to dominate it. Part of the secret of his success was that he tended to avoid taking sides in factional disputes. He was a man of broad experience in both industry and agriculture, with strong links to the armed forces. In other words, he was the ideal Party man of the 1960s and 1970s and he and his generation very largely forged the Soviet Union as we see it today; men of the new Gorbachov generation are now inheriting the system the Brezhnev generation created.

He ruled by consensus, even though he began his career under the Stalin dictatorship and climbed up the ladder when Stalin's one-man rule was at its height. Brezhnev, born in the Dnieper region of the Ukraine, did not join the Communist Party until he was 24 in 1931, just as Stalin was becoming unchallenged leader of the Soviet Union. It was in the Dnieper region that Brezhnev gathered the allies who were to serve him well later in his career and who formed the core of the "Dnieper Mafia". Another of Brezhnev's strengths lay in his links with the military, which took shape during the Second World War, when Brezhnev was a political commissar in the Eighteenth Army, and strengthened after the war, beginning in 1953 when he was named First Deputy Chief of the political administration of the Defence Ministry with the rank of Lieutenant General. In political terms this was something of an unpromising move for Brezhnev, but he made good use of it by forging ties with the military men who were to support him in his coup against Khrushchev and sustain him during his long career at the top.

Arguably, the anti-Khrushchev moves which took place around 1960 worked in the long run to Brezhnev's benefit. The immediate beneficiary of the manoeuvres was Frol Kozlov, who spearheaded demands for Khrushchev's resignation at the Praesidium meeting of February 1963. But in the spring of 1963 Kozlov had his fatal stroke following an agitated quarrel over the telephone with Khrushchev. Kozlov remained in the Secretariat and the Praesidium, but his power was at an end, and he died in February 1965. In 1963 Brezhnev retained the post of President while gaining re-election to the Secretariat along with Podgorny. The following year he passed the Presidency to Anastas Mikoyan and concentrated on bolstering his position within the Party leadership. Khrushchev's seventieth birthday in April 1964 appeared to mark the summit of his power and that of his protégés; but behind the impressive public celebrations, the protégés, Brezhnev included, were planning their coup.

Brezhnev's role in the fall of the man who had brought him to the pinnacle of power was not a central one. The key moves against Khrushchev were made by others, notably Mikhail Suslov, who throughout his career in the Politburo played the role of kingmaker without himself ever aspiring to the posts of First or General Secretary. Brezhnev was in East Germany at the beginning of October, for celebrations marking the fifteenth anniversary of the founding of the East German Republic, and, apart from the fact that he hardly mentioned Khrushchev at all in speeches in East Berlin, there is no evidence that he was masterminding the plot from a distance. He returned to Moscow on 11 October and was met by Suslov, who informed him of the plot against Khrushchev, who had gone to Sochi on holiday at the end of September. On 12 October Khrushchev telephoned the three man crew of a Voskhod spacecraft to wish them luck; in an unusual parallel move, Brezhnev did the same from Moscow.

On 13 October Khrushchev was summoned back to face the Praesidium, and found that his colleagues had prevented him from convening the Central Committee, as he had done in 1957 to foil the first attempt to remove him from power. When the Central Committee met in plenary session on 14 October it was already under the control of the plotters. Suslov read a list of Khrushchev's misdemeanours and policy errors, and the Central Committee accepted Khrushchev's "resignation"—"in view of his advanced age and the state of his health". On 16 October *Pravda* carried photographs of Brezhnev and Kosygin, and did not mention Khrushchev at all. The following day *Pravda* attacked "subjectivism, drift, wild schemes, half-baked conclusions, hasty decisions divorced from reality, bragging and bluster, rule by fiat, armchair methods, one-man decision making, and disregard for the practical experience of the masses." Brezhnev fully agreed with this list. When the cosmonauts returned to Moscow on 19 October it was Brezhnev, not Khrushchev, who met them, and the Soviet public accepted the change without a murmur. At the reception afterwards Brezhnev and Kosygin went out of their way to assure both Party officials and foreign diplomats that there was nothing to fear from the change of leadership, stressing continuity rather than change.

It took Brezhnev several years to achieve pre-eminence and become the unchallenged Number One in the Soviet leadership. Ironically, as he rose towards the top, Brezhnev came to adopt at least some of the policies for which Khrushchev had been criticized. He swiftly came to realize that Russia's priority was, as it remained throughout the 1970s and well into the 1980s, a sound relationship with the United States and Western Europe, the policy which was to become known as "détente", with which Brezhnev remains identified. His first public speech as Party leader during the reception for the Voskhod cosmonauts concerned the space race. "The spirit of reckless gambling in the great and serious matter of exploring and mastering space is deeply alien to us," he remarked.

Competition with the United States remained the priority, just as Khrushchev had been obsessed with both overtaking and achieving "peaceful coexistence" with the other superpowers. Attempts to restore relations with China had failed dismally, and despite a visit to Moscow by Premier Chou En Lai, Sino-Soviet relations worsened further, culminating in the bloody border-clashes on the Ussuri river in 1969. At this point Moscow began to turn to Viet Nam rather than China as its chief ally in Asia. At the same time Brezhnev began to speak openly of the need for rapprochement with both the United States and West Germany. Even the fact that President Johnson ordered the bombing of North Vietnamese ports at a time when Alexei Kosygin was visiting Hanoi did not stop Brezhnev from pursuing his aim.

Kosygin's standing was not exactly enhanced by the failure of his well-intentioned attempt in 1965 to make long-necessary changes in the economy. Kosygin's decentralization measures, adopted at the Central Committee Plenum of September 1965, were opposed almost unanimously by the entrenched Soviet bureaucracy, and by the time they came to be implemented they had been severely curtailed. The reforms were accompanied by the re-establishment of powerful central industrial ministries, so that the reformist effect of the Kosygin measures were more than counterbalanced by the reimposition of central control. (See *Pravda*, 28 February 1965.)

By the time the Twenty-Third Party Congress met in March and April 1966, Brezhnev's position was well established, symbolized by the fact that he was named General Secretary (rather than First Secretary), a title which harked back to the Stalin era. It was at this point that the Praesidium was renamed the Politburo. *Pravda*'s stress on collective leadership as "one of the greatest political inheritances of our Party" began to look a little irrelevant. Brezhnev was fulsomely praised by provincial party officials – including Gorbachov in Stavropol.

The struggle for supremacy which had taken place after the death of Lenin and Stalin now took place after the political death of Khrushchev, although in the conditions of the 1960s rather than those of the 1920s or 1950s. Brezhnev's technique was to try and bring his proven allies into the Politburo with him, without indulging in extensive purges. After all, he had risen to power on the understanding that he would not challenge vested interests. Frol Kozlov was ousted, but he was already a sick man. Nikolai Shvernik and Anastas Mikoyan both retired at the Twenty-Third Congress, but they too were old men. It was all what might be called, in modern management terms, "natural wastage". One of the few genuine political victims was Leonid Ilychov, who later made a comeback as Russia's chief negotiator with the Chinese. It was not until 1972, nearly ten years after the coup against Khrushchev, that Brezhnev began to remove Politburo members for purely political reasons. His management style was cautious rather than radical, conciliatory rather than challenging. Perhaps having in mind both the experience of Stalin as well as the Khrushchev years, he avoided choosing an obvious Number Two or heir apparent, although for a while Andrei Kirilenko appeared to have this role. Brezhnev repaid old political debts, rewarding Kunayev with the First Secretaryship in Alma-Ata, and renaming Vladimir Matzkevitch as Agriculture Minister (he was later sacked, as all Russian Agriculture Ministers tend to be). He brought in as agriculture secretary on the Central Committee a young man called Feodor Kulakov, who was to remain in that position until his death in 1978, when he was succeeded by an even younger man: Mikhail Gorbachov. Vladimir Shcherbitsky was given back his old position as Ukrainian Prime Minister, a post from which he had been dismissed by Khrushchev.

Another of Brezhnev's few victims was Piotr Shelest, who was sacked from the Politburo in April 1973, although he had earlier succeeded Podgorny as Party leader in the Ukraine. Shelest was a notorious hardliner, vehemently opposed to the policy of détente with the United States. But Brezhnev clearly had to accept as fellow members of the leadership other powerful men who did not necessarily support him body and soul. These included Alexander Shelepin; Shelepin's successor at the KGB, Vladimir Semichastny; Kyril Mazurov, the Byelorussian Party leader, who rose to Politburo membership in 1965; and Dmitri Ustinov, whose Party and government career took off during Brezhnev's period in office.

Ustinov was a protégé of Kosygin, who despite the debacle of the 1965 reforms remained a man to be reckoned with. He had after all been Deputy Prime Minister at the age of 36, Prime Minister of the Russian Federation at the age of 39, and a full member of the Politburo at the age of 42. Part of the problem was that although there appears to have been no great personal animosity between the two men, Kosygin's 1965 reforms were very largely elaborated without reference to Brezhnev. Their debate was, as is often the case, conducted through proxies in the Soviet press in Aesopian language. The editor of *Kommunist* observed in *Pravda* that the Kosygin reforms would spell the end of strict Marxist-Leninist ideology. *Izvestiya*, the government newspaper, replied, in an indirect slur on Brezhnev, that an engineering diploma was not everything, and that a real leader was "one who supplemented specialist knowledge with a talent for organization and an ability to motivate people".

Brezhnev also had to contend with the third member of the collective leadership, which was initially a triumvirate or troika. Nikolai Podgorny, the Head of State, nowadays thought of (if at all) as a political lightweight from the beginning, was in fact a dominant force at the November 1964 Plenum which followed Khrushchev's fall. Podgorny's main political error was to express outright support for the Kosygin reforms in a speech in Baku, insisting on the need for a profit principle in the Soviet economy and stressing consumer needs. In a curious incident Podgorny then disappeared for two months and was said by officials to be ill and confined to his home. In December 1965 he was moved sideways to the post of President, replacing Mikoyan, and at the Twenty-Third Congress was sacked as Central Committee Secretary. Brezhnev also felt strong enough in his first two years to begin to move against Shelepin, who had become head of the KGB under Khrushchev in 1958. Although he entered the Politburo after Khrushchev's disgrace, Shelepin's main power base was within the Party State Control Commission, which Brezhnev promptly abolished, at the same time sacking Shelepin as deputy Prime Minister.

Consequently by the time of the Twenty-Third Congress, in 1966, Brezhnev was already in a strong position, even though he was not strong enough to remove all potential rivals and enemies and had to rule through consensus. The Congress was dominated by a speech by Brezhnev lasting no less than eight hours which was noteworthy for its dullness as well as its length. This was safe rather than revolutionary leadership. The Central Committee was increased to 195 full members, with 165 Candidate Members. Arvid Pelshe, Latvian by origin, moved in as a full member of the Politburo and became head of the Party State Control Commission, a post he occupied until his death in 1983, when he was succeeded by Mikhail Solomentsev.

Once again *Pravda* sought to reassert the principle of collective leadership, as it tends to do in the initial period following a change at the top. "The Secretary of a Party committee is not its boss (*Nachalnik*), and is not invested with the right to give orders," *Pravda* pronounced. "He is merely the senior man in the collective." *Pravda* added, rather as *Izvestiya* had done during the dispute with Kosygin, that leaders had to show tact and be self-critical. On the other hand, the reality was that Brezhnev was acting like an unrivalled Number One, taking advantage of the natural tendency of the Russian political system, both during the Tsarist and Soviet years, to produce a strong man at the top who can set the tone and from whom all policy instructions in the end must flow. When De Gaulle came to Russia in June 1966 it was Brezhnev who dominated the conversations, even though Kosygin had shortly before won international acclaim for his mediation between India and Pakistan at the Peace Conference in Tashkent. In November 1966 Brezhnev was applauded on his sixtieth birthday in terms which would not have shamed either Stalin or Khrushchev before him, and he attended the winter session of the Supreme Soviet that year as the unchallenged Number One. He replied to extravagant speeches of praise in the manner of Soviet leaders before him, by stressing his modesty and vowing to justify the faith which had been placed in him.

The appointment of his close friend Shcholokov as Interior Minister secured for Brezhnev the support of the police and judiciary. The replacement of Shelepin's crude associate Semichastny by Andropov as head of the KGB in May 1967 also worked in Brezhnev's favour, even though Andropov, despite his early links with Brezhnev in the 1950s, was not a Brezhnev man. (Far from it, as later events were to prove.) Just to make sure that the KGB answered to him, Brezhnev installed two of his undoubted followers as Andropov's deputies: Simeon Tsvigun, who was related to him by marriage, and Viktor Chebrikov (the present KGB chairman), who had been associated with Brezhnev in Dniepropetrovsk. As for the armed forces, after the death of Marshal Rodion Malinovsky in March 1967, Brezhnev appointed Marshal Andrei Grechko as his successor at the Ministry of Defence, thus ensuring that the Army, too, was on his side. The twelve day delay between the death of Malinovsky and the appointment of Grechko has still not been satisfactorily explained, but it is thought to be because some members of the Politburo favoured a civilian candidate for the post of Defence Minister, probably Dmitri Ustinov, who indeed later succeeded to that post. The pattern whereby the Defence Ministry went to a civilian rather than a military figure did not survive Ustinov, however, and he in turn was succeeded by a career officer, Marshal Sokolov, in December 1984.

Shelepin, meanwhile, moved to a post as head of the trade unions, and relative obscurity. Brezhnev gradually began to ease out anyone in the apparatus likely to have owed allegiance to Shelepin. These included the head of the Party organization in Moscow, Nikolai Yegorychev, who was succeeded by the former trade union chief, Viktor Grishin.

Perhaps the most remarkable aspect of Brezhnev's rule is that it was only towards the end of his eighteen years in office that fellow members of the leadership began to manoeuvre against him, and this largely because he was visibly ill and deteriorating fast. In 1977, a full thirteen years after he succeeded Khrushchev, Brezhnev manoeuvred Nikolai Podgorny out of the post of President so that he himself could combine the jobs of Party leader and Head of State. He achieved this with the consent of his colleagues in the Politburo, rather than by trying to outflank them or undermine them politically. The talents which brought him to the top were the same which enabled him to preside over Soviet policy in the 1970s as the Soviet Union struggled with the responsibilities of being a superpower; practical ability and managerial caution.

CHAPTER EIGHT

Brezhnev in Decline

THE BREZHNEV ERA is likely to be remembered—to some extent is already remembered—as a period of modest economic progress coupled with dull authoritarianism. Neither of the twin problems of the cumbersome centralized industry or the chronically bad harvest was effectively tackled, let alone solved. On the other hand the majority of Russians could claim with some justification that at the end of the Brezhnev era they were a good deal better housed, clothed and fed than the previous generation had been. Most Russians would probably accept that the Brezhnev policy towards dissidents, although it caused outrage in the West, was restrained and possibly justified. The process, which began with the imprisonment of Sinyavsky and Daniel in 1965 for publishing their works abroad, continued through the sixties and seventies under the icy and subtle direction of Yuri Andropov as head of the KGB. A number of distinguished dissidents were forced to leave Russia, among them Alexander Solzhenitsyn, Vladimir Bukovsky (exchanged for a Chilean Communist), and Andrei Amalrik, who later died tragically in Spain. Thousands more were repressed or harassed. On the other hand over a hundred thousand Jews were able to emigrate during the Brezhnev years, a development due above all to the policy of détente which Brezhnev took up where Khrushchev had let it fall, and which he developed into the central plank of Soviet policy.

It was a policy based openly on the assumption that while Russia could benefit from co-operation with the West, and even make concessions in the field of human rights, it would never cease to gain influence wherever possible, if necessary by stirring up trouble in areas where the West had legitimate security or economic interests. By the time Brezhnev signed the Salt I treaty on strategic arms limitations with the United States in 1970, few qualified observers would contest the fact that the Soviet Union had achieved military parity with the United States and could be considered an equal, with full superpower status.

The policy of détente, which Brezhnev declared in 1977 to mean the overcoming of the Cold War and the resolution of differences by peaceful means at the conference table, became so central to Brezhnev's thought that at one point in 1974, at his last meeting with Richard Nixon, he declared it to be "irreversible". Détente meant not only trust and co-operation between the Soviet Union and the United States, it also meant peaceful coexistence with Western Europe, including Russia's former German enemy. Indeed it was the opening to Bonn which Khrushchev had foreshadowed which began the détente process, and the Soviet treaty with West Germany preceded and underpinned Moscow's over-tures in the 1970s to the United States. Détente was *not* irreversible, however, and by the time Brezhnev's health began to show signs of strain, in 1977, when he suffered his first serious heart attack, the foreign policy on which he had built his career as leader was beginning to become unstuck. 1977 saw the inauguration of President Carter, and the Carter era was to prove a great disappointment to the Kremlin. There was only limited progress in the sphere of arms control. Salt II, the second treaty on strategic arms limitation, ran into considerable opposition in Amer-ica, where it was argued that despite the six years of hard negotiation on Salt I, the resulting agreement did not actually control nuclear weapons—specifically intercontinental ballistic missiles—but rather allowed the Soviet Union to enhance its arsenal. The treaty was withdrawn from the United States Senate, where it had been submitted for ratification, not only because of the shortcomings of the treaty itself but also because of the Soviet invasion of Afghanistan in December 1979. The Carter administration's emphasis on human rights, with a strong moral bias, and its opposition to Soviet interference in the Third World, led to an atmosphere of mutual recrimination. Both the embargo on imports of Soviet grain imposed by the Carter administration and the American boycott of the 1980 Olympic games in Moscow were the direct result of this recriminatory atmosphere, and were to have repercussions well into the ensuing Reagan administration of the 1980s.

The Chinese problem also continued to exercise Brezhnev's mind. Throughout his eighteen years at the helm he proved unable to heal the rift which had begun to open up in Khrushchev's time. The tensions with Peking which had erupted in the border clashes of 1969 continued, although on the whole without the direct confrontation, and there was no reconciliation between the two Communist powers following the death of Mao Tse Tung.

It was probably the invasion of Czechoslovakia in 1968, four years after Brezhnev had taken power, which most fundamentally affected Russia's relations with the outside world. Although the Czechoslovak events did not prevent the Soviet Union from pursuing détente in the 1970s, the effects of the invasion lingered on, and to some extent underlay later anti-Soviet feeling which centred on the invasion of

Afghanistan and other Soviet acts considered reprehensible by the Western world. The invasion of Czechoslovakia was indelibly associated with Brezhnev, not only because he was unchallenged leader at the time the fateful decision was taken to suppress the Dubcek experiment by force, but also because, only a few weeks after the invasion, Brezhnev promulgated what has become known as the Brezhnev Doctrine: while Russia's allies in Eastern Europe had the freedom to determine their own path of development, any decision of theirs "must not damage either socialism in their own country or the fundamental interests of other socialist countries, or the world-wide workers' movement. Every Communist party is responsible not only to its own people but also to all socialist countries and the entire Communist movement." Later, towards the end of the Brezhnev period, the rise of Solidarity in Poland provided a further test case of the limits of Soviet tolerance. The imposition of martial law in Poland in 1981, and the suppression of Lech Walesa's Solidarity movement, constituted an internal move by the Polish military authorities under General Jaruzelski. But few Poles, and for that matter few Russians, had much doubt that the "internal invasion" of Poland had been sanctioned if not organized by the Brezhnev leadership, which by 1981 was in a process of political decline and determined to shore up its own position and that of its allies even as it tried to salvage something from the remains of détente with the West.

In his memoirs Henry Kissinger recalls his attempts to forge an understanding with Brezhnev's Soviet Union on the principle that Russia could be drawn into a network of economic and political links which would encourage it if not force it to modify its behaviour and reduce its adventurism in the Third World. By the end of the Brezhnev era, the Kremlin could draw relatively little satisfaction from its policy in the Third World, with a relatively poor record in Africa (despite the victory of the Soviet-backed faction, with the help of Cuban troops, in Angola in 1976) and a series of setbacks in the Middle East, beginning with the Six Day War of 1967. The 1973 Arab-Israeli War provided Russia with some comfort, especially since it emerged as co-chairman, with Britain, of the Geneva Peace Conference which followed the war. But the main Middle Eastern event of the late 1970s was the achievement, with American mediation, of the Camp David agreement between Egypt and Israel. The Brezhnev leadership poured scorn on Camp David, but it nonetheless put the United States firmly in the centre of the Middle Eastern stage. In the summer of 1982 an ailing President Brezhnev was reduced to warning the United States not to become involved militarily in Lebanon without being able to offer a realistic alternative. In a series of messages to Washington from his holiday retreat in the Crimea, Brezhnev warned President Reagan to stay out of Lebanon "or else"—but the "or else" never materialized, and the United States remained the dominant force in the region.

On the face of it Brezhnev remained a powerful figure. In July 1980 he fulfilled one of his major ambitions by opening the Olympic Games in Moscow. But already his health was failing fast. The portraits lining the streets of Moscow showed a youthful and energetic Brezhnev; yet the man who opened the Games could scarcely muster more than a few lines, and hardly smiled at all. This was not the ebullient leader who had met Nixon and Kissinger, or for that matter who had confronted President Carter in Vienna in 1979. His speech and his physical movements were slow, and it was often difficult to make out what he was saying. Comic imitations of this rather painful spectacle became common in Moscow, at least in private. There were rumours, which turned out to be well founded, that he was seeking treatment from a faith healer, and for a while in March of 1980 he emerged from a rest period—officially described as a "holiday"—with something of his former vigour. In May 1980 he even went to Belgrade for the funeral of President Tito, and stood up to a taxing schedule of talks with other world leaders in Yugoslavia. Yet by October 1980 rumours of ill health were again rife, and increased when Brezhnev failed to attend a dinner in his honour given by the visiting President of India.

By the beginning of 1982 it was clear that we were watching the decline of a once vigorous figure. Soviet officials maintained a brave front, and insisted that Brezhnev was recovering, a front they were to maintain through subsequent succession crises, when Presidents Andropov and Chernenko also began to show the combined effects of age and the strains of high office. There was a revealing incident in February 1982, when one of Brezhnev's former companions-at-arms, General Konstantin Grushevoi, died, and Brezhnev was shown on television weeping at his lying in state at the Red Army Hall in Moscow. Grushevoi, head of the political administration of the Moscow military district, had been a close friend of Brezhnev in the Ukraine in the late 1930s and was the same age as the Soviet leader. Only a month before Mikhail Suslov, the *eminence grise* of the Politburo, had died at the age of 79. Suslov, widely considered the most powerful man in the country after Brezhnev himself, had left a gap that nobody else could fill, and his death had an enormous impact on the Soviet political process. The evidence suggests that Suslov was instrumental in organizing the anti-Khrushchev coup in 1964 which put Brezhnev into power. One by one the Kremlin Old Guard, the generation which had grown up together and made its careers in the ruthless atmosphere of the Stalin era, was passing away.

In March 1982 Brezhnev flew to Tashkent in Uzbekistan for a four day visit and launched a major policy initiative, making an overture to the Chinese by offering to restore good relations with Peking. But it was an initiative which his successors would have to follow up. In Tashkent Brezhnev looked haggard and drawn, and his return to Moscow was not shown on Soviet television, as is the normal custom, for a very good reason: he had suffered a stroke. He dropped out of sight, allegedly because he was on holiday, but in fact because he was receiving medical treatment.

In retrospect the high spot of the final Brezhnev years was the Twenty-Sixth Party Congress of 1981, Brezhnev's last Congress as Party leader. But it was on the other hand a no-change Congress, in which both the Kremlin Old Guard and Russia itself simply marked time. Brezhnev was applauded at length when he announced that the Politburo had been re-elected unanimously with no changes, but the applause masked a deep malaise and stagnation underlying apparent stability. The Congress was a ritual in which Brezhnev and Tikhonov, the Prime Minister, assured the five thousand delegates that the Soviet Union remained on course, but that, because of internal problems, the world economic situation and the intrigues of the capitalists abroad, Communism might take a little longer to achieve than anticipated. Both Afghanistan and the crisis in Poland were very much on the minds of Congress delegates, but were not once mentioned in public.

Brezhnev was perhaps more honest when discussing the shortcomings of the Soviet economy, which after all is what concerns the Soviet people most of all. He offered a catalogue of failings which did no credit to his long stewardship at the Kremlin: shortages of consumer goods, shortages of foodstuffs, inefficient distribution systems, a dismal national health service (often presented to the world as second to none), growing alcoholism among Russians of all ages, a breakdown of the values of family life, increasing hooliganism and frustration on the part of young Russians, and the apparently unstoppable rise of the black market to fill the gaps left by the cumbersome, centrally-controlled economy. On the other hand Brezhnev offered no recipes to solve these problems; indeed it would have been surprising if he had done so, considering that he had offered no radical solutions during a period of nearly twenty years in office and was most unlikely to embark on fresh thinking now that the end was so obviously in sight.

As if these problems were not enough, there was growing cynicism about Soviet public life, and in particular about the grandiose self-congratulation which marked the Brezhnev style. On his 74th birthday, in December 1980, Brezhnev awarded himself yet another medal, the second Order of the October Revolution, to accompany those he already had—four Orders of Lenin, a medal of Victory, Hero of the Soviet Union, and the Lenin Peace Prize. He was shortly to collect the Prize for literature, awarded for his reminiscences, a move many people in the literary world considered ridiculous and disgraceful. Nor were they alone; many operatives of the state security services, ever conscious of Russia's image abroad, also felt that this state of affairs could not continue. Nonetheless on his 75th birthday, in 1981, Brezhnev received his fourth Hero of the Soviet Union and his seventh Order of Lenin. Exhibitions devoted to Brezhnev's life and work opened in Moscow, Leningrad and other cities, and the fourth volume of his memoirs appeared to universal acclaim. Books, films, television programmes and even gramophone records praising Brezhnev in extravagant terms poured out in large numbers. It was all rather reminiscent of the extraordinary personality cult surrounding Khrushchev, which reached its climax on Khrushchev's 70th birthday in April 1964, just months before his colleagues decided they had had enough and moved to oust him.

Brezhnev showed no signs at all of wanting to relinquish his hold on the Kremlin in his final days, although in the course of 1982 there were persistent reports that he was planning to retire, undoubtedly circulated by the KGB on the personal instructions of Yuri Andropov. The retirement rumours continued after Andropov, skilfully manoeuvring for the succession, had left the KGB in May 1982 and been elected as a Central Committee Secretary, taking the ideology portfolio vacated by Suslov. Although he was no longer formally head of the KGB, Andropov still orchestrated the anti-Brezhnev campaign, and the new head of the KGB, General Vitaly Fedorchuk, was Andropov's protégé and former deputy. Andropov's principal aim was to cut the ground from under the feet of Konstantin Chernenko, Brezhnev's seventy-year-old personal assistant, and his obvious choice for heir. Andropov managed to give the impression that Chernenko was associated with a declining personality who was not even able to leave the Soviet Union for a summit with the American President. The last Soviet-American summit had been the Brezhnev-Carter meeting in Vienna of 1979. Brezhnev's mysterious disappearance for four weeks in March and April of 1982 was also used as part of the Andropov campaign to prove that "the old man" was no longer capable of running the country. So too was the fact that during his holiday in the Crimea in the summer of 1982 Brezhnev was unable to receive all the Warsaw Pact leaders, as he had done for years.

In the spring of 1982 *Newsweek* magazine carried a cover story entitled "Brezhnev's final days", showing a bust of the Soviet leader with large cracks appearing in it. Despite Kremlin anger, the story was substantially correct, if premature. When Brezhnev went to Baku in Azerbaijan in September 1982 it was clear that he could hardly speak or walk, and even extravagant praise from Geidar Aliyev, the local Party leader, could not compensate. It took all the skills of the Kremlin propagandists to disguise the fact that Brezhnev was on his last legs, and at times did not even know where he was (he at one point said he was glad to be in "Afghanistan", not "Azerbaijan", a slip which was cleverly corrected when his speech, initially delivered live for television, was re-broadcast).

The old man was not finished yet. On 27 October, in a remarkable speech to top military leaders in the Kremlin, he spoke again of a possible improvement in relations with Peking and bitterly attacked the United States, suggesting that arms control agreement was no longer possible. Showing that he was fully aware that Russia was in danger of falling behind both military and technologically, Brezhnev lashed out at Washington for "launching a political, ideological and economic offensive against Socialism" at an unprecedented level. But his tone was defensive, and he was clearly responding to criticism from the generals on all fronts—criticism over arms control, criticism over the overture to Peking (Brezhnev spoke rather vaguely of "new things" in the Chinese attitude), and above all criticism of failings in the Soviet defence programme. Although he must have known he did not have much time left, Brezhnev looked ahead to the following year and assured the military leaders that the Politburo would provide them with everything they needed in the way of military hardware, and that he himself was closely in touch with military affairs. In November, with only days left to live, Brezhnev climbed painfully to the top of the mausoleum on Red Square and watched the might of Russia's army parade before him. He stood for a full two hours in bitter sub-zero temperatures and a biting wind, wearing sunglasses against the glare of the winter sun. His thoughts as he surveyed the largely obsolete tanks and rockets that rumbled over the ancient stones of Red Square have not been recorded. But what he said publicly, clearly with the self-confident attitude of the new Reagan administration in mind, was that the Soviet Union would deal a "crushing retaliatory strike" to any aggressor, adding that Russian might and vigilance "will, I think, cool the hot heads of some imperialist politicians." He was, in a way, setting the tone for the next few years, even though he would not himself be guiding Soviet policy. "We will do our utmost to see to it that those who like military adventures will never take the land of the Soviets unawares," he declared.

CHAPTER NINE

Andropov Undermines Brezhnev

YURI ANDROPOV'S MANOEUVRING for the succession began long before he made the Lenin Birthday Speech in the Kremlin in April 1982, and long before he left the KGB for the Central Committee Secretariat in May. Like other contenders for power in previous transitions, Andropov had already laid the groundwork. But it was these public events in the spring of 1982 which in effect announced his candidacy.

In many ways Andropov was and remained the great exception in the history of Soviet political successions. He was a Party man *par excellence*, and had made his early career in the Party. But he had also been head of the KGB since 1967, and conventional wisdom held that no head of the KGB could ever become General Secretary of the Party. Andropov did not conform to type; he broke all the taboos. He was by far the most intelligent and most intellectually aware of all Soviet leaders since Lenin, and had a far-reaching vision of the kind of Russia he wished to create for the latter half of the twentieth century. His tragedy was that, by the time he was able to manoeuvre to succeed the by now ponderous and deteriorating Brezhnev, it was almost too late. While Brezhnev was a very public man, or became so over his two decades in power, much as Lenin, Stalin and Khrushchev had been well known figures, Andropov remained something of an enigma, a very private man whose motives and personality were a mystery. Many Russians preferred it that way; the steely-minded and steely-eyed Andropov had controlled their destinies as head of the security services, but it was another matter for this austere disciplinarian to come to the fore as the public face of the Soviet Union. As he manoeuvred for the succession in 1981 and 1982, Andropov made no move to correct this impression. Even when he came to power he remained an essentially private man, releasing very few details of his family life for public consumption. Until his funeral in 1984 it was not even certain whether or not he had a wife.

In a way Andropov, described by foreign leaders when he came to power as a man with the "swift, dispassionate brain of a computer", had been preparing for supreme power all his life. When he moved to displace the grotesque figure of Brezhnev in 1982, and take charge of Soviet foreign policy, Andropov was already fully in command of all the details of Soviet public life. He was a gaunt, stooping figure, tall and bespectacled, shuffling slowly along rather like some spectral bird with his beady eye firmly fixed on the future of Russia. Although like Brezhnev before him, and Chernenko after him, a product of the Party bureaucracy, Andropov was no ordinary *apparatchik*. He was a man with a razor sharp mind who saw with extraordinary clarity all the failings of the Soviet economy and body politic, and was determined to do something about them. As head of the KGB for thirteen years, he had received daily detailed reports of the true situation around the country, and of the true state of Russia's relations with foreign nations, and thus enjoyed an advantage over those who had gone before him. He was austere, punctilious, modest, and a disciplinarian. He was unlike any other leader the Russian people had known since Lenin. When Chancellor Kohl of West Germany came to Russia in 1983 he described Andropov, not without admiration, as a man who had at his command "every detailed statistic".

It was not true, as KGB disinformation experts tried to make us believe, that Andropov was a closet liberal who enjoyed Western modern art or modern jazz. But he did like music, and he did like art. His daughter, a journalist and musicologist, and his son-in-law, an actor, saw to it that he had at least some connection with the world of artists and intellectuals. He was a thoughtful and intellectual Marxist himself, unlike most officials in the Soviet leadership, whose main contribution to Marxist thought was to repeat the clichés of Party propagandists. Andropov was a man who knew his Marx and his Lenin, who had studied and thought deeply, who had seen the effects of Marxism in action in Eastern Europe during his time as Soviet Ambassador in Budapest during the 1956 uprising and who had maintained his links with the liberal Hungarian experiment in subsequent years.

There was little hint of this future master of Russia in Andropov's early career. Born at a small railway town in the Northern Caucasus, where his father was a railway employee (possibly the station master), Andropov left school at the age of 16 in 1930. His initial academic career was hardly auspicious: he entered the Rybinsk Water Transport College in 1932, and stayed for five years. At the Water Transport College (photographs of his class at the college did not appear until after his death) Andropov is said to have met his first wife. On the eve of Russia's participation in the war, in 1940, Andropov attended university at Petrozavodsk, returning once the war had ended. But his chief educational experience was in the Higher Party School in Moscow in 1951 as an up and coming member of the Central Committee apparatus in his late thirties. Andropov's formative experiences were thus as a junior functionary of the Communist Party, rather than as a student. He was a Komsomol leader in the northern Caucasus and in Yaroslavl, and subsequently served in Karelia on the Finnish border, where he directed the activities of anti-Finnish partisans. After the war he moved up in the Party hierarchy in Karelia, and in 1951 was moved to Moscow.

In 1953 Andropov abandoned the Party apparatus for the world of diplomacy and was appointed Soviet Ambassador in Hungary, playing a significant role during the events of 1956. By 1957, however, he was back in the Central Committee, heading the department responsible for liaison with ruling Communist and workers' parties, which in effect meant that he kept a watching brief on Eastern Europe—Hungary included—on South East Asia, especially Viet Nam, and on Peking. Ten years later he was head of the KGB, not as a professional secret police-man, but rather to impose strict Party control over the security apparatus.

Andropov was an *apparatchik* of the Stalin era—yet he proved that the Soviet system can throw up men who, while conforming to the conventions of Soviet society, can nonetheless clearly see the need for change, and can even begin to take the first steps towards bringing that change about. Andropov's early newspaper articles during the Karelia days were fairly routine accounts of the activities of the partisans, plus appeals to patriotism. But like Brezhnev, Andropov was fortunate in his mentors: when he became Second Secretary at Petrozavodsk in 1947, with the job of reconstructing a war-ravaged region and incorporating it into Russia, the First Secretary was Otto Kuusinen, an old Bolshevik of Finnish origin with influence at the top at the Kremlin. When a corruption scandal erupted in Petrozavodsk in 1950, Andropov was accused of being too far removed from ordinary workers and their needs—an ironic charge against a man who was later to make much of his populist rapport with the working class—yet he was not sacked. The following year Andropov moved up to the Central Committee, first as an inspector, then as a head of department, and finally as head of the Foreign Ministry's Fourth European Department, dealing with Eastern Europe. Kuusinen was also evidently instrumental in having Andropov appointed Ambassador to Hungary, a post in which his true political calibre soon became apparent.

Andropov's role in the tragic events of the Hungarian uprising is still a subject of controversy. But one remarkable aspect of the affair is that even though he was directly involved in the brutal Soviet suppression of the revolt, many Hungarians regarded him as an honourable man, and some still do. It is sometimes forgotten that there were two Soviet military interventions in Budapest, not one. The first took place in the early autumn, when Hungarians took to the streets in large numbers, the statues of Stalin came crashing down, and it looked for a while as if the liberal Hungarian Prime Minister, Imre Nagy, might take the country out of the Warsaw Pact. For the Kremlin this was an intolerable threat to the Russian domination of Eastern Europe, and Soviet tanks moved in to surround Parliament and other public buildings. They then withdrew, to premature Hungarian jubilation, but reformed on the outskirts, reinforced by Soviet troops from the Ukrainian border.

Nagy called in Andropov for an explanation, one of the most testing moments in Andropov's career. He was now 42, and had arrived in the Hungarian capital three years earlier as Deputy Ambassador, taking over within a few months. Andropov realized that Stalin's death and Khrushchev's de-Stalinization campaign had set in train an impulse towards liberalization throughout Eastern Europe, and that Nagy was a better bet to keep Communism from collapse than Mateus Rakosi, the detested Stalinist leader he had replaced. But Andropov's function was to tolerate reformism without allowing it to undermine the Communist system as such. In extreme circumstances, such as those which arose in 1956, his job was to maintain Soviet control at all costs, if possible with the least upheaval and loss of life. Andropov is credited with recommending to Moscow, after the second Soviet intervention and the collapse of the uprising, that Hungary's new leader should be Janos Kadar, who was by no means a hardliner and had been imprisoned by the Stalinists. This was the beginning of a long relationship between Kadar and Andropov, which in turn was to have an important influence on Andropov's economic and political thinking as he followed closely the twists and turns of Kadar's uniquely successful attempt to heal the scars of 1956 with a system of economic reform, giving Hungary one of the highest living standards in the Soviet bloc.

Andropov's role in 1956 has its share of deception and dishonour. He assured Nagy that new Soviet troop movements were simply intended to cover the withdrawal of other Soviet forces from Budapest, which was untrue. He also pretended to engage in negotiations with the Hungarian authorities, lulling them into a sense of false security so that Soviet troops would meet no resistance when they moved in. It is not clear whether Andropov later was involved in the murder of Nagy, who had taken refuge in the Yugoslav embassy but emerged when he was given guarantees, only to be arrested and executed.

At all events Andropov's stock was high by the time he returned to Moscow and the Central Committee in 1957. To some extent he was a beneficiary of the administrative purges which followed Khrushchev's rout of the Anti-Party group. In Budapest Andropov had come to the attention of Mikoyan and Suslov, both of whom visited Hungary during the crisis, and Suslov, in particular, was now becoming a major force in the Kremlin. Suslov, austere and powerful, had a particular talent for placing able protégés in positions of power. His last major act before his death in January 1982 was to engineer the appointment to the Politburo of Mikhail Gorbachov. In the 1960s he took Andropov under his wing, despite differences between the two men over both China and Yugoslavia. Andropov continued to make efforts to keep China within the socialist camp despite the growing split with Peking, and supported Khrushchev's rapprochement with Tito despite the grave doubts of hardliners such as Suslov. Andropov also began to gather around him his own circle of associates and protégés, most of them young and liberal minded. The Andropov circle at this time included figures who were to become significant voices in Soviet political life—men like Feodor Burlatsky, an unorthodox intellectual who became a *Pravda* commentator, the rotund Alexander Bovin, now on *Izvestiya*, Georgy Arbatov, head of the USA and Canada Institute, and Oleg Bogomolov, the economist, who like Andropov advocated applying the lessons of Eastern European reforms to the Soviet economy.

Andropov gained promotion because of Brezhnev's successful campaign to undermine Shelepin after the overthrow of Khrushchev in 1964. Shelepin, the former Komosomol chief who had become head of the KGB in 1958, was an obvious rival of Brezhnev in the power struggle and enjoyed the support of Vladimir Semichastny, his successor at the KGB. In 1967 Brezhnev moved against them both, putting Shelepin in charge of the trade unions and sending Semichastny to the Ukraine as first deputy Prime Minister. Semichastny's record was appalling: even when head of the Komsomol he had managed to shock Western opinion with crude and offensive remarks about the writer Boris Pasternak ("even pigs do not eat in the place they have fouled"). Semichastny's period as head of the KGB was marked by such inglorious blunders as the defection to the West of Svetlana Alliluyeva, Stalin's daughter, and the trial of the writers Sinyavsky and Daniel, which confirmed the world's worst fears about Russia as a police state. Brezhnev decided to instal Andropov at Dzerzhinsky Square, making him a candidate member of the Politburo at the same time. He was not crude like Semichastny—on the contrary, he was subtle and sharp. Nor was Andropov a perverse or twisted soul like the infamous Beria, whose role in the succession struggle which followed the death of Stalin had not been forgotten. Beria had left a lingering fear of secret police chiefs whose aim was to build a "state within a state" and usurp the power which rightfully belonged to the Party alone.

Andropov posed no such dangers, and in an early speech in December 1967 he condemned unknown "political adventurists" who had tried to use the KGB for their own aims. The answer, he said, lay in strict Party control of the security services. He also outlined what was to become the basis of his policy toward the growing problem of Soviet dissidents: they had to be persuaded to perceive that their actions were harmful to the Soviet state. In 1968, the year of the brief but electrifying demonstration on Red Square against the invasion of Czechoslovakia, Andropov formed the Fifth Directorate at the KGB to analyse and crack down on political, nationalist and religious dissent. Behind the Andropov policy lay the widespread Communist Party assumption that the only legitimate values are Communist values, and those who disagree—as Vitaly Fedorchuk, a later KGB chief, put it in the *Literary Gazette*—must have "abnormal psyches" and need to be "re-educated". The hallmark of Andropov's KGB career was the evolution of a new breed of secret policemen, educated and sophisticated rather than merely thugs, with the emphasis on legal procedures rather than the midnight knock on the door and torture in the dungeons.

In all of this Andropov, although rarely seen on the international scene, was aware of the impact on foreign opinion of the way in which the Soviet Union handled internal security matters, including the neutralizing of dissent. As befitted the head of the secret police he kept a low profile. But he was nonetheless working his way towards a challenge for the leadership, watching the progress of Brezhnev's détente policy as well as the state of Brezhnev's health. Andropov became a full member of the Politburo in 1973, at the same time as Andrei Gromyko, the foreign minister, and Marshal Grechko, the defence minister; a move which neatly symbolized the importance of the triple alliance of foreign affairs, defence and internal security at a time of détente with the West, but which also underlined Andropov's personal status. In 1976, the year he was awarded the rank of army general, Andropov was chosen to make the traditional Lenin Birthday Speech, in which he strongly supported détente and attacked the arrogance and incompetence of Soviet bureaucrats. Like other Soviet leaders, Andropov always made it clear that détente did not mean an end to the ideological struggle with the west or an end to Soviet attempts to gain influence around the world by all means possible, including subversion. But he presided over the KGB in an era when the Kremlin was obliged to respond to world opinion over human rights, occasionally moderating its policies, and in the case of Soviet Jews allowing an unprecedented degree of emigration. In August 1979, when Andropov was awarded the Order of the October Revolution, Brezhnev praised his honesty and skill, and remarked that the security apparatus was in "clean and unimpeachable hands".

It is not clear what stand Andropov took over the decision to invade Afghanistan in 1979, the move which more than any other marked the formal end to détente and the beginning of the deterioration of East–West relations which gathered pace in the final Brezhnev years. Some KGB defectors have suggested Andropov foresaw the appalling drawbacks of intervention and argued against a military commitment, but was overruled. This may be true, although on the other hand Andropov also contributed to the souring of détente by exiling the dissident physicist, Andrei Sakharov, to the closed town of Gorky, in 1980, and possibly— although this has yet to be proved—by sanctioning the attempt on the life of the "Polish Pope", John Paul II, on 13 May 1981. Nonetheless he realized that Russia under Brezhnev was a stricken vessel, listing badly in both domestic and foreign waters, and was keen to take the helm. At the Twenty-Sixth Party Congress, in February 1981, Andropov was still playing a background role, and it was Chernenko who was prominent alongside the leader. But within the Party Andropov was seen as a far more impressive figure than Chernenko. As we have seen, he combined wartime experience with the partisans in Karelia with ten years' work in the Central Committee apparatus, distinguished service in the diplomatic corps at a time of crisis, and a successful period riding the tiger of the KGB, all without becoming indelibly associated with the obvious failures of the final Brezhnev years.

In December 1981 a curious story appeared in the Leningrad literary magazine *Aurora* about an old writer—clearly meant to be Brezhnev— who was mistakenly thought to have died. "My delight was premature", the anonymous author said, "but I don't think we will have long to wait". It was the opening shot in the final campaign to undermine both Brezhnev and Chernenko and install Andropov in the Kremlin.

Perhaps the most remarkable aspect of this campaign was the affair of Galina Brezhnev, Boris the Gypsy, and the Great Circus Scandal. Galina's association with devious characters was well known, but rumours of her involvement in a sensational corruption scandal began to circulate early in 1982, at about the time of the death of Mikhail Suslov, the *eminence grise* of the Politburo and the guardian of pure Marxist–Leninist ideology. The scandal began to emerge at another funeral in December 1981, when a former director of the Soviet circus died. After the funeral a female lion tamer went back to her flat to find that she had been robbed of some of her noted collection of jewels (in itself a sign that Moscow circus people were unusually well off). Police traced the missing jewels to a flamboyant character called Boris the Gypsy, who held a minor post at the Bolshoi, thanks to the influence of Galina Brezhnev, strongly rumoured to be his mistress. A swaggering character given to wearing expensive furs, Boris the Gypsy had originally been an obscure member of the Moscow Gypsy Theatre. His liaison with Galina was a godsend to him not only because she was Brezhnev's daughter but also because she was married to Lieutenant General Yuri Churbanov, Deputy Minister of Internal Affairs. In addition, her own official duties at the Foreign Ministry brought her in to contact with visiting foreigners, giving Galina a highly privileged position which she used to obtain goods and services for her unsavoury friends in the underworld.

As Head of the KGB Andropov knew every detail of the case and could have chosen to turn a blind eye to it. Instead he decided to use it for his own ends. His deputy at the KGB was General Simeon Tsvigun, who happened to be Brezhnev's son-in-law. Whether Andropov meant to use the circus scandal to drive Tsvigun to suicide, and thus get rid of a Brezhnev associate within the KGB as well as undermining Brezhnev himself, is not clear. At all events Andropov gathered voluminous material on Galina and her friends, put it into the hands of Tsvigun and left him to follow up the investigation of his own relatives in high places. Possibly Tsvigun was himself implicated in high level corruption surrounding the Brezhnev family, or possibly he fell into despair when asked to do the impossible and reconcile his duty as a security chief with his political and family links to Brezhnev. On 19 January he died by his own hand, and, as happens in Russia with high level suicides in embarrassing circumstances, was quietly and quickly buried at a second-rank Moscow cemetery rather than given a ceremonial funeral at the graveyard at Novodevichy Monastery, where members of Russia's élite are normally laid to rest. Brezhnev did not sign Tsvigun's obituary, a most unusual move, and neither did Mikhail Suslov, who according to Moscow rumour was profoundly shocked by the whole imbroglio and suffered a stroke when Andropov revealed to him the extent of the scandal. Six days later, on 25 January, it was announced that Suslov had also died, leaving a crucial gap in the leadership of which Andropov was able to make good use in the succession manoeuvring. Moscow police arrested Boris the Gypsy, and in February the scandal engulfed the head of the Moscow Circus, Anatoly Kolevatov, who was charged with having abused his position to obtain bribes from circus members who wanted to go on foreign tours. Kolevatov had amassed a personal fortune in diamonds and foreign currency amounting to 1.4 million dollars, a truly astronomical sum by Soviet standards. It subsequently emerged, after a raid on Kolyvatov's flat, that he had also accumulated an astonishing collection of jewels given to him by grateful circus performers whom he allowed out to the West.

Andropov, who was masterminding this operation, spared Galina herself from public shame, but insisted that she would have to leave Moscow. Her husband, General Churbanov, was exiled to Murmansk in northern Russia. Galina herself lived just outside Moscow in fairly comfortable surroundings, until eventually Andropov allowed her to return to the capital—a rather less self-confident figure—once he was safely installed in power. Kolevatov, the circus director, was not so lucky, and in September 1984 was sentenced to thirteen years in prison.

Another underworld associate of Galina's, Yuri Sokolov, was executed in August 1984 for extensive bribery and embezzlement at Gastronom Number One, the elaborately decorated food store on Gorky Street of which he was Director. Together with one of the department heads at G.U.M., the state department store on Red Square, Sokolov was unofficial purveyor of under-the-counter goods to the Soviet élite, and Galina was one of his prime "back door" customers. Sokolov was put to death for having been "an extremely cynical and pathologically greedy trickster, a large scale thief and bribe-taker who systematically misused his position to steal over one and a half million roubles."

It is striking that even after Andropov's death, when Chernenko had achieved the position of which he was cheated in November 1982, the impact of Andropov's campaign against Brezhnev's circle of corruption was still being felt. In December 1984, long after the ripples of the circus scandal had receded, General Churbanov was sacked as Deputy Interior Minister. At about the same time his boss, Interior Minister Nikolai Shcholokov, committed suicide, unable to stand the disgrace of having been sacked by the Andropov régime. Churbanov was replaced by Vasily Trushin, a close aide of Viktor Grishin, the Moscow city leader.

Given that the echoes of his anti-corruption sweep were still being felt long after his death, it must have been unnerving to have been at the epicentre of Andropov's manoeuvring as Brezhnev visibly weakened. While Brezhnev was still alive, in the summer of 1982, Andropov began to act as if he were already in charge. He summoned back from Havana a prominent protégé, Vitaly Vorotnikov, who had been banished by Brezhnev as Soviet Ambassador to Cuba, to clean up official corruption on the Black Sea coast. Vorotnikov was shortly promoted into the

Politburo. As Brezhnev lay dying, Andropov was already moving his pieces into place on the chessboard.

In March 1982 almost the entire Politburo went to see the play "Thus we Shall Win" (*Tak Pobedim*) by Mikhail Shatrov at the Moscow Arts Theatre. It was a play notable not so much for its dramatic originality as for the fact that it tackled a highly sensitive historical theme: what political succession the dying Lenin would have preferred, and what he really thought about Stalin, as expressed in his political testament. Brezhnev, Andropov and Chernenko sat in a row watching this controversial re-enactment of the first Soviet succession crisis. If Brezhnev had written his own last testament—and some claim he did— he would undoubtedly have asked the Party to name Chernenko as leader. But before the year was out, Brezhnev was dead.

CHAPTER TEN

The Death of Brezhnev

WHEN THE END came, and it had been coming for a long time, the leadership seemed temporarily paralysed. A sense of anti-climax seized Moscow when it was announced on 11 November 1982 that the man who had ruled Russia for eighteen years was dead. In bus queues, shops and restaurants life went on as normal, as if no watershed had been reached, no cataclysmic event had taken place. The dominant feeling was of mild shock mingled with mild regret.

It was a very different atmosphere a few days later when the Central Committee emerged from seclusion to anounce that Brezhnev had been succeeded by Andropov. Suddenly the streets of Moscow crackled into life, and from nowhere squads of police and troops appeared, checking documents at random or simply lining up in side streets in riot vehicles. This was partly the knee-jerk Kremlin reaction to any public crisis, and not due to any real fear of public disorder. But the impressive and overwhelming show of force, with KGB troops as well as soldiers and militia out in strength in the crisp air and snow-lined streets, was also Andropov's first policy move. He was announcing to the Russians, and to the world, that the days of drift and stagnation were over: the new watchwords were efficiency and discipline. As we drove from the Kremlin on the Moscow river to the Politburo residence on Kutuzovsky Prospekt we felt as if we were watching a coup in progress. Formally speaking, the Central Committee had simply elected one General Secretary instead of another. But it was not lost on Russians that the former head of the KGB had taken power, with the help of the military under Marshal Ustinov. The fact that Brezhnev's own choice, Konstantin Chernenko, had lost the struggle meant that we would be living in a very different Russia from now on.

Andropov had given a hint of this in his Lenin Birthday Speech, some six months earlier, which in a way amounted to a declaration of future policy. Sounding what was to become the keynote of the Andropov régime, he launched attack after attack on corruption, embezzlement, bribery, red tape, disrespect for official attitudes to citizens and "other anti-social actions which arouse popular indignation". The Russian people, he said, wanted the Party to take steps to "root out these phenomena". Even though many Russians accept the illegal dealing which makes the cumbersome Soviet system function on a day-to-day basis, Andropov had struck a chord by taking a populist line and posing as the people's champion against abuse of power and privilege. The same people who grumbled as they felt the Andropov lash on their backs while he was in power were later to speak with nostalgia of a strong and intelligent ruler who had seen what was necessary in Soviet public life and had had the courage to do something about it.

One of the unwritten rules of Soviet politics is that the General Secretary must previously have been in charge of one of the Central Committee Departments—that is, one of the Secretaries—and the death of Suslov gave Andropov the ideal opportunity to shed his KGB associations and take on the role of Secretary for Ideology. With the benefit of hindsight it is clear that this was the crucial turning point, not the death of Brezhnev in November 1982. Andropov effectively became the heir apparent at the Central Committee Plenum on 25th May. It was not obvious at the time to everybody that Andropov was moving himself into an unassailable position; all the outward signs still pointed to Chernenko, who was much in the limelight as Brezhnev's own choice for leader. The decisive struggle that Chernenko lost took place at the May Plenum, when Chernenko was proposed for Ideology Secretary but was opposed by senior Politburo members who regarded him as lightweight compared to Andropov. According to Party sources, the key role was played by two senior figures who were to dominate the entire transitional period which began with Brezhnev's decline and continued until Chernenko's own decline and death in 1985: Marshal Ustinov, the Defence Minister, and Andrei Gromyko, the wily Foreign Minister. Between them they ensured that Andropov got the job as Ideology Secretary, which in turn ensured that he also got the job of Party Leader, six months later. Andropov, who had astutely said in public speeches that the armed forces had to be given "everything they needed", had the solid backing not only of Ustinov and the military but also of his own KGB, and the combination proved unstoppable, even though Chernenko appeared to be the front-runner.

The jostling between Chernenko and Andropov went on throughout the spring and summer of 1982, with Andropov speaking in place of Brezhnev at a gala meeting marking the 1,500th Anniversary of the city of Kiev in June and receiving Communist delegations from India, Greece and other countries. On the whole it was Chernenko who dominated the Soviet press and television, and it was Chernenko who was at Brezhnev's side during the summer when the ailing leader conferred with other Warsaw Pact leaders in the Crimea.

At the Kremlin gala marking the 65th anniversary of the Bolshevik revolution, held on 5 November, Chernenko and Andropov sat on Brezhnev's right and left respectively. But it was Chernenko who acted the confident heir apparent, conspicuously consulting Brezhnev from time to time and twisting round in his chair to talk to Candidate Politburo members in the row behind. Andropov by contrast looked thin and unwell, not to say emaciated, and hardly moved at all. The fact that he had made almost no public appearances since stepping down from the KGB in May and becoming Party Secretary only underlined Chernenko's prominence. Mikhail Gorbachov, at this stage still thought too young to be a contender, sat straight-backed and impassive in the front row as Viktor Grishin made the keynote speech, recalling Brezhnev's attack on bribery and corruption during his visit to Baku the previous month. Grishin also called for a return to the ideals on which the Bolsheviks had founded the Soviet state at a time when ideological confrontation with the Western world was on the increase. At the end of the meeting it was Chernenko who accompanied Brezhnev out of the hall and who helped him as he stumbled along.

Presumably on Brezhnev's instructions, Chernenko's writings were extravagantly praised in the Soviet press, and most ordinary Russians, unaware of the intrigues behind the high Kremlin wall, clearly had the impression that when Brezhnev's death took place Chernenko would succeed him. In a way they were right, since Chernenko did seize the opportunity the second time around in February 1984. But when on Wednesday 10 November 1982 the rumours of Brezhnev's death began to spread across Moscow, and television programmes began to be rescheduled, Andropov already had the Central Committee vote in the pocket of his morning suit.

The Wednesday night was tense, with telex and telephone lines humming as diplomats and correspondents saw a pop concert unexpectedly replaced on television by an earnest film about the life of Lenin. An ice hockey match (much to dismay and annoyance of sports fans) was cancelled on the other channel. In what was to become a familiar routine as members of the Kremlin Old Guard passed from the scene, Moscow radio switched to mournful music (Tchaikovsky's *Pathétique* was the favourite choice) and the announcers on *Vremya* (Time), the main evening news at nine o'clock, wore dark suits. But still there was no announcement. Clearly somebody in the Kremlin had died. All the signs pointed to Brezhnev, but it could just as easily have been Andrei Kirilenko, once Brezhnev's choice for successor. His portrait was ominously absent from the long line of giant Politburo pictures which had gone up by the side of the road not far from the Kutuzovsky bridge on the Moscow river.

Then a phone call late on Wednesday night from a source with longstanding contacts within the Kremlin: it was Brezhnev himself who was dead. There was just time to file a brief warning despatch to London to alert readers to what Igor Kirillov, the senior Soviet television announcer, officially declared the following morning in solemn and sorrowful tones: Leonid Ilych Brezhnev had died at 8.30 in the morning on Wednesday 10 November of a heart attack following a long illness.

The indecision of Wednesday night was partly due to the fact that it always takes the Kremlin 24 hours to consolidate arrangements behind the scenes. The Politburo does not like to make a crisis announcement until it is absolutely sure that everything is under control behind the Kremlin wall. Yet Brezhnev had died early in the morning of Wednesday 10th, and it had been clear for several days before that that he was on the verge of death. The temporary Kremlin paralysis was also due to the fact that Russia, which over the next three years was to become so used to Red Square funerals, had not lost a national leader for nearly two decades. Popular reaction was subdued, with Russians in the shops and on the streets expressing respect and sympathy but little obvious grief. On the other hand they had lived with Leonid Brezhnev for eighteen years of their lives, and a generation had grown up knowing nothing but Brezhnev's Russia. Russia was, in a sense, in a state of shock, and it was this, rather than total indifference, which explained the fact that even after Kirillov made his announcement on the Thursday morning, and black-bordered portraits of Brezhnev appeared on television screens, life continued as normal. Reactions to Brezhnev's passing were decidedly understated. Only when Andropov was named as head of the funeral commission in charge of arrangements for the burial on Red Square did people begin to realize that a man very different from Brezhnev, with a KGB background which inspired fear in the hearts of all Russians, already had his hand on the levers of power.

Despite the delays, it did not take long for the Soviet leadership to recover and to put into motion the succession mechanism, which had become rusty for decades but which was to become well oiled over the next few years. A medical bulletin signed by Dr Yevgeny Chazov, Russia's leading cardiologist and the chief Politburo surgeon (his official title is head of the Fourth Department at the Ministry of Health) said Brezhnev had died of a heart attack caused by hardening of the arteries. It confirmed that what Western correspondents had written but Soviet officials had denied was perfectly true, namely that Brezhnev had suffered a number of heart attacks before.

An appeal to the nation, issued by the Party and government, emphasized continuity, saying that Soviet domestic and foreign policy as formulated under Brezhnev's leadership would continue to be pursued "consistently and purposefully" and would ensure détente and disarmament. The statement took up a theme from Brezhnev's final speeches, including his remarks on the anniversary of the Revolution a few days beforehand: military adventurists (meaning President Reagan above all) would never catch the Soviet Union unawares, and potential aggressors should know that a "crushing retaliatory strike" would await them. The statement also attacked unnamed imperialists for trying to undermine peaceful coexistence between East and West by "pushing the peoples on to the path of enmity and military confrontation". It was not exactly a friendly message to the West at a crucial point of Kremlin transition. Even though President Reagan sent his condolences, offering the new leadership co-operation and improved relations, the uneasy state of Soviet-American relations was to dominate the post-Brezhnev era and to dog the steps of both Andropov and Chernenko before the final transition to Gorbachov in 1985. Reagan, who had been woken early in the morning on Thursday to be told of Brezhnev's death, remarked that he looked forward to conducting relations with the new Kremlin leadership "with the aim of expanding the areas where our two nations can co-operate to mutual advantage".

"I have said for many years there are fundamental differences between the Soviet system and our system in the United States," Reagan said. "But I believe our peoples, with all our differences, share a desire and a dedication to peace." For diplomats in Moscow on the other hand, the Soviet attitude remained that summed up by Brezhnev's remarkable address to a gathering of military and political leaders in the Kremlin on 27 October, which in retrospect was his valedictory address. The embittered remarks of a dying man were intended to set the tone for his successor. The speech outlined a programme of high defence spending, powerful commitment to Soviet armed might, and determination to resist pressures on Russia from the outside world. It was meant to warn the West not to try to exploit what was clearly going to be a period of political upheaval inside the Kremlin, but it also augured badly for the revival of the kind of détente Brezhnev had done so much to establish in the 1970s.

For the time being, doubts about the future were submerged in the sheer practicalities of burying the leader and installing a new General

Secretary. Brezhnev's body lay in state at the Hall of Columns, more properly known as the House of Unions, an ornate eighteenth-century, classical, green and white mansion dwarfed by the Stalinist bulk of the Moskva Hotel opposite and the State Planning Committee (GOSPLAN) next door.

For three days factory and office workers were brought in to the sealed-off centre of Moscow in a long line of ramshackle buses and made to shuffle slowly down the street to the Hall of Columns, up the elegant staircase beneath huge chandeliers covered in black crepe, past a military guard of honour and a full symphony orchestra playing funeral music, to what had once been the ballroom of the Moscow Nobleman's Club. There, amid tall white columns and dimly glowing black and red decorations, Brezhnev's body lay on a bier covered in flowers, his numerous self-awarded medals set out on a red satin board at his feet. It was an eerie experience filing through the ballroom with the shuffling line of silent and dutiful specifically selected workers, an experience made all the stranger by the fact that the Hall of Columns is for some reason kept heated at high temperatures. With a hot-house atmosphere and the overpowering odour of funeral flowers, it appeared to acquire the very smell and essence of death and mourning. Outside, in the fresh cold air of slushy Moscow streets, citizens were reading posted-up newspapers announcing that primary and secondary schools were to be closed and that state enterprises would stop work for five minutes during the Red Square burial, with artillery guns firing salutes, and factories and ships sounding their sirens and hooters. President Brezhnev, the newspapers said, had been an ardent champion of peace and Communism, and would live for ever "in the hearts of the Soviet people and the entire progressive mankind".

"Forever" is a relative concept in politics, however, and Yuri Andropov was already planning not only the burial of Leonid Brezhnev but also the burial of much that he stood for. He was devising a political programme which would remove many of Brezhnev's personal cronies from power and launch Russia on a new course of discipline and reform. When Andropov's KGB troops and Ustinov's soldiers suddenly appeared in force on the streets of Moscow, the Russian people snapped out of their state of shock and began to wonder—some hopefully, some fearfully—what the new master in the Kremlin had up his sleeve.

The answer came with Andropov's first speech as leader, which was uncompromisingly tough on both home and foreign issues. The man who had defied the conventional wisdom that a KGB chief could not become Party leader took a no-nonsense approach, stressing discipline and order. He praised his predecessor, saying that he would devote all his "energy, knowledge and experience of life" to carrying out the programme laid down by Brezhnev at the Twenty-Sixth Party Congress of February 1981. But this was clearly only a token nod in the direction of political continuity. Andropov's remarks on relations with the West, for example, went even further than the anti-Americanism of Brezhnev's final days. "We know full well that it is useless to beg for peace with the imperialists," Andropov declared. "Peace can only be upheld if we rely on the invincible might of the Soviet armed forces". Andropov noted that Brezhnev had been not only Party leader and President but also Chairman of the Supreme Defence Council, a crucial post which goes with that of Party leader, even though there is no provision for this either in the Constitution or in Party statutes. The nation's leader is also in charge of the country's defences, and Brezhnev had constantly seen to it that Soviet defence capacity met present day requirements, Andropov said, indicating that he would do the same.

It was particularly bitter for Chernenko to see Andropov present himself as Brezhnev's natural successor. At the extraordinary Central Committee Plenum on the morning of Friday November 12, Chernenko was obliged not only to nominate his rival, after Tikhonov's bid to nominate Chernenko had failed, but also to describe Andropov as "the closest associate of Leonid Ilych", an epithet which was palpably inaccurate and which could have been more properly applied to Chernenko himself. He praised Andropov as a "selfless Communist with multi-faceted experience" in domestic and foreign policy as well as ideology, a prominent Party functionary and diplomat whose concern was for the "interests of the Soviet people", a man "of personal modesty" who was determined to "stand up to the machinations of anti-Soviet aggressors." The pointed reference to modesty was significant, as was Chernenko's assertion that Andropov had assimilated Brezhnev's style of leadership. "It is now twice, three times more important to conduct Party affairs collectively," Chernenko remarked, a clear warning to Andropov that although he may have become General Secretary he was not a dictator and would still have to reckon with other Politburo members, not least Chernenko himself.

To some extent Chernenko's reputation as a political lightweight, and his dismal failure to capitalize on Brezhnev's support by gaining the leadership, masked the fact that he represented thousands of Party officials in both high and low places. He also represented their fears of change. It was not enough, Chernenko said in his nomination speech, to "voice correct ideas without efficient organizational work". In other words, he would speak for the humdrum officials who actually carried out the work of the Party and government apparatus, and who felt they deserved recognition and reward even if they were not as brilliant as Yuri Andropov or the technocrats he was about to try and move into place. The stage was set for a continuation of Andropov's struggle against the Brezhnevites, the crucial difference being that he now had the power to sweep them out of the system, as he began doing within a few days of taking office.

Andrei Kirilenko was allowed to attend Brezhnev's lying-in-state, and even the funeral on Red Square, although not as a Politburo member. But he was clearly in political disgrace. The Brezhnev family was also under a shadow, and even though Galina and others retained some privileges, fear of "Yuri the Long Arm" as Muscovites referred to him (after Moscow's legendary founder) was widespread in the Moscow underworld and the twilight world linking Russia's illegal dealers with corrupt officialdom. As world leaders began to converge on Moscow for the first major state funeral since the death of Stalin thirty years before, Chernenko was already fighting a rearguard action. Yuri Andropov after all was a man of 68, a full decade older than either Brezhnev or Khrushchev had been when they came to power. Would he have the stamina and the endurance to carry out the plans he had nurtured for so long, or had he come to power too late? Was he the Soviet equivalent of a harsh but reforming Tsar, or would he prove merely a caretaker leader who would have to hand over to somebody else, and who might in the end be defeated by the Brezhnevites he had so deftly outwitted in the manoeuvring for power?

CHAPTER ELEVEN

Andropov in the Kremlin

THE ANDROPOV ERA has already been so overlaid with nostalgia and wishful thinking, both in the West and in Russia itself, that there are obstacles to reconstructing it even though it is relatively recent history. Russians who now look back nostalgically on an era of strong leadership and firm measures did not at the time appear so sanguine about the prospect of an iron hand in the Kremlin. Most feared a man who had spent thirteen years on Dzerzhinsky Square and knew the intimate details of Soviet life from a careful study of KGB files. Many resented his swift moves to impose discipline and order in Russia, including the appearance of the People's Control—a kind of inspectorate, with its officers often accompanied by uniformed police—in shops and cinemas, asking Russians why they were not at work, what their business was, and why they were wasting state time and money. At Novgorod, an ancient town not far from Moscow, I saw the People's Control and militiamen pulling over a van marked "Veterinary Surgeon" and establishing that the driver was not on some mercy mission to a stricken animal but using his state-provided van for personal financial gain. In another case the driver of a milk lorry was found to be using his vehicle for "illicit purposes". Although he pleaded that he was having to do so because his family was in dire straits, he was nonetheless punished, in the spirit of the new Andropov anti-corruption drive.

Russians recognized that something needed to be done urgently. The autumn of 1982 witnessed many of the most severe food shortages for a decade. Even before Andropov came to power, it was clear that measures had to be taken to put the economy on the right track. While Brezhnev lay dying, staple products such as meat disappeared altogether from some republics, including the Ukraine and Byelorussia, and remained both scarce and highly priced in Moscow itself. The "food programme" adopted under Brezhnev in May 1982 was clearly not working.

In foreign affairs, too, many of the main features of the Andropov era had already become clear during Brezhnev's final months. As Brezhnev's powers failed, foreign policy decisions came more and more to be taken by a collective leadership with Andrei Gromyko, the veteran

Foreign Minister, beginning what was to be a period of almost personal control of foreign affairs as a series of transitional leaders relied on his skill and experience. The opening to China, begun by the ailing Brezhnev in the spring of 1982, continued with the dispatch of Leonid Ilychov to Peking to begin talks with the Chinese. Afghanistan and Poland remained thorns in the Soviet side, and with Brezhnev in visible decline, the Russians were clearly worried by the challenge from Ronald Reagan, who puzzled and frightened them with his overtly ideological approach. In a magisterial address to the autumn session of the United Nations General Assembly, Gromyko gave an overwhelming impression of consistency and continuity in Soviet policy in Asia, Europe and the Middle East, watching the Western alliance tear itself apart over the controversial question of Western technology supplies for the East–West gas pipeline while the Soviet Union reaped the economic and political benefits.

In his speech to military leaders in the Kremlin in October Brezhnev had observed that the foreign policy principles adopted at the Party Congress in February 1981—which had emphasized the prospects for détente and arms control—were being revised. Moscow was clearly irritated by the American insistence at the Geneva Arms Talks that the Russians in fact had the edge in strategic nuclear weapons, and that there was no possibility of including the British and French weapons' systems in the talks on medium range missiles. Brezhnev accused the Americans of preparing an economic, political and ideological offensive against Moscow "with unprecedented intensity". The theme was taken up by Chernenko in a speech in Tbilisi in which he said Russia refused to be frightened by American sanctions or bellicose posturing. "If Washington proves unable to rise above primitive anti-Communism and persists in its policy of threats and *diktat*, well, we are strong enough, and we can wait," Chernenko remarked.

Andropov's first speech as leader was tough in the same manner, including the almost contemptuous remark that it was "useless to beg peace from the Imperialists". But Western leaders arriving in Moscow for the funeral of Brezhnev were keen to discover whether this was to be the Kremlin's unswerving line under Andropov, or whether there was room for compromise. Chernenko, the most prominent of the Brezhnev men, stressed consumer needs, détente and disarmament in his nomination speech, where Andropov talked of the danger of Western imperialism and the need to maintain Russia's armed might, remarks which won him applause from *Red Star*, the paper of the Soviet armed forces. But would Andropov prove more conciliatory when confronted with

Western representatives, including Vice-President George Bush of the United States, and George Shultz, the Secretary of State?

It was in this atmosphere that we watched the body of Leonid Brezhnev laid to rest on Red Square on 15 November. Only perfunctory attention was paid to Brezhnev and the Brezhnev era, with most eyes focused on the tall, stooping, gangly and bespectacled figure of Yuri Andropov as he walked slowly on to the Lenin mausoleum on Red Square to say farewell to his predecessor, gazing at the ground as he walked. The centre of Moscow was efficiently sealed off by police and troops for an event which had not taken place since 1953, almost thirty years before—the death of a national leader. Specially-selected Muscovites passed through empty and silent streets to the cobble stones of Red Square, the ancient heart of Russia, with the "representatives of the people" holding black-bordered portraits of Brezhnev and falling into line behind phalanxes of police and troops in grey and blue uniforms. The funeral cortège arrived, led by a highly polished gun-carriage, and a military band struck up Chopin's Funeral March. In the Russian tradition, a hangover from the practices of the Orthodox Church, the lid of the coffin was open and Viktoria Brezhnev, the widow, Yuri Brezhnev, his son, and other relatives leaned over to kiss his face. Andropov and the other Politburo members peered down from the top of the mausoleum and delivered suitable eulogies, praising Brezhnev as an outstanding fighter for peace and Communism. "Farewell dear Leonid Ilych," Andropov said. At a quarter to one, with the chimes of the Kremlin clock ringing through relatively mild air, Andropov, Chernenko and other Politburo members carried the coffin on their shoulders to a plot of ground behind the mausoleum reserved for heroes of the state. It was to be the last time the Politburo would enact this tradition, which went back to the funeral of Stalin in 1953, and of Lenin in 1924; for the funerals of Andropov and Chernenko a new practice was adopted whereby troops carried the coffin and the Politburo followed behind, possibly because in 1982 the coffin of Brezhnev was so heavy that it gave the largely geriatric leadership some difficulty. It certainly hit the ground with an audible thud as gravediggers lowered Brezhnev's remains into the earth between the old Bolshevik Yakov Sverdlov, the first President of the Soviet Union who died in 1919, and Felix Dzerzhinsky, founder of the secret police, who died in 1926. Not far away was the grave of Stalin, removed from the mausoleum next to Lenin in 1961, but not of Khrushchev, buried at the Novodevichy cemetery as a private citizen.

There were poignant moments at the Brezhnev funeral: in the

profound silence that followed the firing of artillery salvoes and the sounding of factory and ships' hooters on the river, and before the coffin had been lowered into the ground, a solitary crow swooped down from the Kremlin wall and flapped across the square to the long and ornate façade of G.U.M., the department store, cawing as it went. But then the band struck up a lively march, and the troops, who had been so mournful and solemn only moments before, swiftly removed their black armbands and marched briskly in front of the new leadership across the square and out the other side. The message was plain: the new era had begun. "The General Secretary is dead, long live the General Secretary," murmured one ambassador.

Afterwards, inside the Kremlin, we watched to see how Andropov would receive the foreign leaders who had come to pay homage to him, do business with him, or simply sound him out. Andropov's talks with Vice-President Bush were described as "cordial", but he also gave a conspicuously warm welcome to the Chinese Foreign Minister, Huang Hua. It was an auspicious beginning. Andropov gave the impression of a man in full command of all the details of foreign policy, able to conduct negotiations with a variety of foreign leaders without assistance from aides or prepared props. To some extent, this impression was reinforced by a natural Western desire to give the new Soviet leader the benefit of the doubt and get East–West relations off to a good start after the Brezhnev era. There was, in other words, an element of wishful thinking and exaggeration. It was nonetheless true that Andropov had taken control of Kremlin policy as swiftly and as efficiently as he had taken control of the Central Committee meeting which elected him General Secretary.

In the first days of his rule, details began to trickle out, of the way in which the Andropov election had been stage managed. The proceedings of the Central Committee are strictly secret, and only partial and unconfirmed details emerge of plenary deliberations. The last time Central Committee proceedings were published was under Khrushchev, and even then the debates were not fully revealed. But it became clear that the Chernenko forces, who included the Prime Minister, Nikolai Tikhonov, had put forward Chernenko as the natural successor to Brezhnev. Ustinov intervened to point out, to the dismay of Chernenko, that Andropov had been qualified for the post as a Secretary of the Central Committee since May, and already had sufficient support within the Central Committee to win election. It then fell to Chernenko not only to step down but also to nominate his rival for the leadership, a double humiliation which he was to nurse through the fifteen months of Andropov's rule.

Andropov had come to power after months of manoeuvring, and confronted George Bush, Huang Hua, and other leaders not as a man who had been unexpectedly propelled into the hot seat, but as a leader with carefully thought-out positions. Obviously aware that the eyes of the world were upon him, Andropov proved a master of the political hint while at the same time maintaining the hard anti-Western line taken by Brezhnev in his final months. On Red Square, Andropov said Russia would maintain vigilance and readiness to "give a crushing rebuff to any attempt at aggression", and accused the "forces of imperialism" of pushing the world towards "hostility and military confrontation". Marshal Ustinov spoke of the need for the new leadership to continue Brezhnev's "unflagging attention to ensuring the defence capability of our country". The overtly military nature of the funeral ceremonies was clearly aimed at the Western powers, even though President Reagan had sent his deputy to Red Square as a political gesture of conciliation. Bush and Schultz received no special treatment in the line up in St George's Hall when the foreign visitors paraded before Andropov, and indeed were given only a cursory welcome compared to the Chinese. On the other hand, Bush, ever optimistic in a manner described by Americans as "preppy", was able to emerge from his meeting with Andropov and talk of "frankness, cordiality and hopes for a positive and constructive relationship with the new leadership."

Within days of the Brezhnev funeral a large delegation of American businessmen arrived in Moscow to revive the American–Soviet Trade and Economic Council, and to hear Nikolai Patolichev, the Minister for Foreign Trade, express the hope that the dismal level of superpower trade would prove to be only "a temporary phenomenon". At a Kremlin dinner for 250 American executives, including representatives of Dow Chemicals, Pepsi-Cola, Texaco and Occidental Petroleum, Nikolai Tikhonov called for a restoration of the "normal, and even friendly relations" which Russia had enjoyed with America in the past, and urged the Reagan administration to drop its practice of imposing sanctions and embargoes on Moscow. "Sanctions do not exactly inspire kindly feelings in us," Tikhonov remarked. "And they undermine our confidence in the American market."

There were also hints on Afghanistan, possibly the most sensitive issue Andropov had inherited. In December, barely a month after Andropov had taken over, the former Deputy Head of the Afghan secret police, Lieutenant-General Ghulin Siddiq Miraki, told the BBC in Pakistan that Andropov had opposed the intervention in Afghanistan in 1979 when he was head of the KGB. Whether true or not—and nobody in Moscow was able to confirm it—Andropov certainly made a point of giving General Zia of Pakistan a much warmer welcome at the Brezhnev funeral than he gave to Babrak Karmal, the Soviet-appointed leader of the Afghan government in Kabul. Andropov's cold shoulder treatment of Karmal gave rise to reports that Zia was willing to stop giving assistance to the Afghan rebels in return for a timetable of Soviet withdrawal over a period of up to two years, and that the Chinese were exerting subtle pressure on Moscow in order to remove Afghanistan as an obstacle to "normalization" of Sino–Soviet relations. These were expectations which were to be disappointed, and Afghanistan continued to sour Russia's relations both with the West and with the Islamic world through the Andropov and Chernenko eras and on into the present Gorbachov era.

But the way in which signs of subtle shifts in Kremlin policy were plucked from the air and magnified in the world media testified to Andropov's mastery of public relations. Even the personal image Andropov wished to project was plastered all over the Western press, conveying the impression of a sophisticated and liberal-minded man with a liking for modern art, Johnny Walker whisky and modern jazz, who had strong links with the Moscow intelligentsia through his daughter, and his son-in-law, an actor at the Mayakovsky Theatre.

These details of the private life of a Soviet leader were a sign of the times. The West had known about Brezhnev's penchant for fast cars, and his device for limiting his cigarette consumption. But these intimate details only emerged because of his exposure to the Western media in Washington and Bonn. Glimpses into Stalin's private life, such as the all-night drunken parties at the Blizhnaya dacha near Moscow, or the late-night film shows in the Kremlin, only emerged through Khrushchev's frank memoirs. But by the time Andropov came to power, many people in the West took it for granted that the leader of a superpower in the 1980s was bound to allow something of his private self to come under public scrutiny. Partly because of his long KGB background (the security chief necessarily keeps a low profile) there could hardly have been a more intensely private man than Andropov. The KGB were able to satisfy the Western appetitite for details of the new leader's private life by creating a persona which partly corresponded to the real Andropov. That he lived relatively simply (relatively, that is, in terms of Soviet privilege) was certain, as was the fact that he allowed himself some Western luxuries, including a video system on which to watch Western films. It was also true that he liked modern art, and, like many other Russian intellectuals, collected icons.

Above all, it was no myth that Andropov, probably to a greater extent than any previous Soviet leader, was interested in and aware of Russia's intellectual, political and diplomatic history, and had a firm grasp of the real history of Marxist ideas and the practice of Soviet Communism. When foreign visitors arrived for the Brezhnev funeral they found, as one senior West German official put it, that Andropov was in full command of the smallest detail of policy and had "taken charge from the word go". As former head of the KGB, Andropov knew better than most how to disseminate both information and disinformation. As the world watched to see how the first weeks of his administration would develop, the message he deftly put across was—in the words of *Pravda*—that the Russia he was about to create would be "vigorous and optimistic".

There were still influential Brezhnevites in the leadership, not least in the Politburo itself. But Andropov had the backing of Andrei Gromyko, who had served under every General Secretary since Khrushchev and had begun his career under Stalin, as Soviet Ambassador in Washington. At the time of Andropov's succession, at the end of 1982, Gromyko was a tough, shrewd, cynical politician with a penetrating knowledge of the world which few other foreign ministers could match. Gromyko was the great survivor of Soviet politics, yet had no power base of his own in the Politburo, and therefore presented no threat to the new leader. Although sometimes witty and urbane, Gromyko took an unswervingly hard line when it came to the defence of Soviet interests, and had done so since the first Cold War years when he personified the dour and implacable face of Soviet diplomacy at the United Nations from 1946–48. He was a symbol of continuity, together with other members of the Old Guard who remained in place after Andropov's rise to power, such as Boris Ponomaryov, head of the Central Committee International Department.

There was a daunting array of foreign policy issues on the new General Secretary's desk at the end of 1982, and none appeared easy to resolve, however firm his grasp on foreign policy might be. In the Middle East there was growing Soviet alarm at what appeared to be the possibility of an agreement between the Reagan administration and moderate Arab states on moves toward a peace settlement. Through TASS, the Kremlin praised radical pro-Soviet Arab states like Libya for trying to "foil the sinister designs of imperialism and Zionism" and criticized Arab leaders such as King Hussein of Jordan (indirectly) for "regrettably expressing their readiness to help Washington to implement the imperialist designs of the Camp David framework". Shortly afterwards King Hussein arrived in Moscow and Andropov swiftly put pressure on him not to take up the Reagan proposal for a Jordanian–Palestinian federation. There were Soviet anxieties too over Southern Africa, particularly when Angola, a Soviet ally, held secret talks with South Africa at Cape Verde on the question of the independence of Namibia. Anatoly Gromyko, son of the Foreign Minister, said that there could be no solution in Namibia unless the "racist government of South Africa, backed by the United States" acknowledged Moscow's demands that the South West Africa People's Organization (SWAPO) had the right to hold power.

For most Russians, on the other hand, the question of Moscow's relations with America, China, the Arab world or the African states took second place to the fundamental question of the moment: how long would Andropov remain in power, and what would he be able to do during his period in office? It did not escape the man on the street that Andropov was 68 whereas Khrushchev and Brezhnev had come to power in their fifties. Most of Andropov's colleagues in the Politburo were seventy or over. This highlighted the key problem of generational change in the Soviet political hierarchy, with Andropov representing the generation which had been in the upper echelons of the Party and Government for thirty or forty years, and had filled the shoes of men removed either by Stalin's Terror or the ravages of the war against Hitler. A series of deaths in the Kremlin—Alexei Kosygin in 1980, Mikhail Suslov in January 1982, and now Brezhnev—had driven home the fact that the generation formed by Stalinism and the Second World War was passing away, while the generation of men in their fifties had been held back. Under Brezhnev the "cadres policy" adopted by Khrushchev, which meant a high turnover of personnel in both Party and government, was abandoned. Rigidity set into the system, as Brezhnev and his colleagues sought to ensure that officials to whom they owed their power enjoyed tenure for life. This static personnel policy had an additional advantage: it reduced the risk of an ambitious and rising Party official manoeuvring himself into a position where he could do to Brezhnev and Kosygin what they had done to Khrushchev in 1964. Although Andropov was a man of quite different background and cast of mind to Brezhnev, in terms of political generation he was from much the same mould. The men in their fifties, many still languishing at provincial committee (OBKOM) level, had no way in which to vent their frustration as the economic and social system continued to stagnate. The leader of the new generation, and their only representative in the Politburo itself, was Mikhail Gorbachov, who at the death of Brezhnev was still only 52.

How long would it be before the Gorbachov generation pushed the generation of Andropov and Chernenko on one side in order to put new ideas and policies into practice? The death of Brezhnev and the succession of Andropov had shown that the succession mechanism, although secretive and undemocratic, could function smoothly, without bloodshed or upheaval. But it had still left the ambitious young generation waiting in the wings.

CHAPTER TWELVE

Andropov's Programme: The Turning Point?

IN NOVEMBER 1982, when the Supreme Soviet met for its first session since Andropov's rise to power, the signals about his authority in the Kremlin were mixed. On the one hand the 1,500 member Supreme Soviet—a rubber stamp parliament which only meets twice a year—failed to elect Andropov President (formally speaking Chairman of the Praesidium of the Supreme Soviet), the post which Brezhnev had combined with Party leader in order to give him the authority to deal with foreign leaders and sign state documents. To the surprise of most, the two-day Supreme Soviet ended on 24 November with no election to the post of Head of State, leaving Vasily Kuznetsov, the Vice-President, to continue performing the functions of acting Head of State at the distinctly advanced age of 81. On the other hand Konstantin Chernenko, Andropov's defeated rival for the Party leadership, did not become President either, as some Moscow rumours suggested he might. On the contrary, Chernenko appeared to have sunk without trace since the extraordinary Central Committee Plenum which elected Andropov as Brezhnev's successor. Chernenko had not made a single public appearance for several weeks. He had not even been allowed to speak at the funeral of Brezhnev, a slight which cut him to the quick, since he above all had been Brezhnev's closest associate for many years. The only noteworthy development at the Supreme Soviet came when the head of GOSPLAN, Nikolai Baibakov, noted in his review of the current five year plan that industrial production had increased by only 2.8 per cent, the lowest annual growth in Russia for over thirty years. Clearly Andropov had his work cut out.

The clearest sign that he intended to do something about this parlous state of affairs, and was swiftly gaining a firmer grip on power, came at the Central Committee Plenum which met on the eve of the Supreme Soviet and which promoted Geidar Aliyev into the Politburo in place of the disgraced Andrei Kirilenko, a close Brezhnev aide. Aliyev, an Azerbaijani, was a smooth talker who had shamelessly flattered whoever happened to be General Secretary, lavishing almost grotesquely sycophantic praise on Brezhnev when he visited Baku shortly before his death. On the other hand a group of Western ambassadors who visited

Aliyev in Baku shortly before his elevation into the Politburo and move to Moscow under Andropov, were greatly impressed by his acumen and ability, qualities which Andropov had also obviously spotted. A man of energy and charm, Aliyev had become deputy head of the KGB in Baku in 1965 and head of the security forces in Azerbaijan two years later. In 1969 he was made First Secretary of the Communist Party in the Republic, and became a Candidate Member of the Politburo in 1976. There were marks against Aliyev: to begin with he came from the Muslim South, in itself automatically suspect to Great Russians, even though Aliyev's political loyalty to Moscow was beyond dispute. Aliyev told the Western Ambassadors that Soviet Azerbaijan had become fully developed thanks to Soviet power, whereas Azeris in neighbouring Iran had remained backward, and it was his personal hope that "all Azerbaijanis would be reunited in the future", a rather incautious remark about a politically sensitive border region. Brezhnev's attack on the lack of "socialist morality" in Azerbaijan during his visit to Baku was ambiguous, since Brezhnev appeared to include Aliyev in his list of leaders who were failing to tackle corruption energetically enough. On the other hand Azerbaijan has always been a traditional area for wheeler-dealing and corrupt practices, and as a former KGB man Aliyev had been more successful than most in cleaning up the republic. At the Supreme Soviet Aliyev was further promoted to the post of First Deputy Prime Minister, a bold move by Andropov since it put a man of Southern ethnic origin within striking distance of the premiership.

Andropov's team was thus already beginning to take shape. At the Supreme Soviet Tikhonov, the Prime Minister, Gromyko, the Foreign Minister and Dmitri Ustinov, the Defence Minister, sat in deep conversation in the front row of the Politburo seats on the platform in the Great Hall of the Kremlin, studiously ignoring the isolated figure of Chernenko. Although Andropov did not become Head of State he did become a member of the Praesidium of the Supreme Soviet, thus enabling him to make a bid for the Presidency at a later date. Party officials assured us that the main reason for Andropov's failure to acquire the Presidency was not that he lacked the power to do so, but rather that he felt it would be politically unwise to seek a post which it had taken Brezhnev thirteen years to acquire.

As the grey November light filtered in through the tall windows of the Great Hall, a long narrow room with white pillars and a statue of Lenin set in a niche behind the podium, there was no doubt at all about who was in charge of Russia's destiny. At the deputies' desks, looking rather like school desks, the delegates—sober-suited Party officials mingling with the colourful costumes of Caucasian and Central Asian members—sat talking with unusual animation. As we looked down from the Press Gallery at the normally lifeless legislature, we could see both ordinary deputies and more senior ones, such as Georgy Arbatov of the USA and Canada Institute, reading Andropov's Central Committee speech in *Pravda* with more than usual interest. It was the first time for many years that Russians had read a leader's speech in the certain knowledge that he intended to change their lives, and they were looking for the clues to the immediate and long-term future.

It was Andropov's first major speech since becoming leader a week and a half previously, and he used it to call for a fresh start in arms control and (more importantly for Russians) in tackling the economic ills he had inherited from the Brezhnev administration. Soviet leaders do not directly disparage their predecessors, but it was clear from every word of Andropov's speech to the closed Central Committee plenary session that he was in a hurry to put right the problems that had mounted up during Brezhnev's final years, adding that when Brezhnev was alive Moscow was credited with "all kinds of sinister intentions". "It now turns out they are worried in case this policy could be changed," he remarked. There was no point, he said, in holding talks for the sake of talks with the Western powers, "as happens all too frequently", and the West should not expect the Soviet Union to disarm unilaterally. "We are not naive people," Andropov said, a remark which was used to prove that the Russians regard unilateralism as a naive approach to arms control. Conscious that the Western world was looking for signs of Kremlin intentions, Andropov noted that what he called "the aggressive designs of imperialism" has compelled Russia and her allies to maintain defence capabilities at a proper level. But the tone of his speech was on the whole conciliatory. Détente had not been a chance episode in the history of mankind, "as certain imperialist leaders nowadays assert", it was a policy for the future as well as the past. Difficulties and tensions in Soviet-American relations could be overcome, provided Washington did not demand that Moscow should make preliminary concessions. "We shall not agree, and in any case properly speaking we have nothing to go back on. We did not introduce sanctions, we did not denounce treaties and agreements which had already been signed, we did not interrupt talks which had already begun." It was an astute and well turned speech, with the clear stamp of Andropov's personal style. There was a gesture for China, with Andropov asserting that Moscow wanted an improvement in relations with "all socialist countries" (thus bracketing China with the Soviet Union's allies), and wanted to eliminate the "lack of trust and mutual understanding" between Moscow and Peking.

On the home front, Andropov leaned unmistakeably towards reform by attacking "inertia and incompetence" and calling for decentralization in the economy and the "harnessing of initiative and enterprise", phrases which were to become familiar as the hallmarks of the Andropov régime, and which were to be inherited by his protégé Mikhail Gorbachov. In a characteristic double-pronged approach these moves towards reform were accompanied by a campaign in the press for strict and even dogmatic ideological control, with articles in *Pravda* praising Suslov, who had died in January.

In the Suslov tradition, Andropov stressed the dangers of anti-socialist literature smuggled into Russia by Western intelligence agents "posing as tourists". General Vitaly Fedorchuk, who had taken over from Andropov as head of the KGB in May 1982 but was then named Interior Minister, made a rare public appearance at the Supreme Soviet to speak on the need for vigilance against "imperialist espionage and subversion", introducing a new bill tightening up border controls. The new bill brought the controls up to date by specifically banning video materials as well as the written word. Clearly there was going to be no loosening up intellectually under Andropov, and certainly no importation of dangerous Western ideas. Nonetheless the thrust towards reform was unmistakeable, and at the Central Committee Plenum Andropov pulled no punches in criticizing the drawbacks of the food programme adopted under Brezhnev and calling for local decision-making in farms and factories. He repeated his promise to give the armed forces "everything they needed" but also stressed the need to provide the Russian people with better and more varied consumer goods. "Of course," he added disarmingly, "I do not have ready-made answers, Comrades." But the Central Committee members were not fooled: the message to the bureaucracy was loud and clear. The incompetent and corrupt could expect to be weeded out in a no-nonsense purge, and those with drive, ability and initiative would be brought in in their place. Within a week of Andropov's speech the Soviet Minister for Railways had been removed, a direct result of Andropov's complaint that the transport system was "failing to ensure the needs of the economy" and had shown an increasingly poor performance from one year to the next.

On 12 December, a month after Andropov had taken power, *Pravda* carried a Central Committee statement on its front page launching a comprehensive attack on the inadequacies of Soviet agriculture. Taking a farm in Kazakhstan as the example, the statement said resources had been used unwisely as a result of poor management, there were inadequate storage facilities, low grain figures, inefficient crop rotation, dairy and cattle production, and persistent livestock diseases. Officials recalled Andropov's remark to the Central Committee Plenum: "I have to tell you bluntly, the implementation of the food programme cannot be delayed." They also recalled that Andropov had taken to task managers who "simply do not know how to do their jobs". *Pravda* carried an intriguing article criticizing Russian "gigantomania" and suggesting that the way to economic efficiency lay through smaller decentralized production units based on the experience of large Western companies. On 14 December, following a meeting of transport executives addressed by Geidar Aliyev in his usual plainspeaking manner, *Pravda* published a long Party and government decree calling for stricter labour discipline and announcing that the transport system would no longer receive state funds automatically but would have to earn them by high productivity.

On 21 December the Supreme Soviet gathered again, this time not to discuss legislation or to approve Central Committee decisions, or even to make appointments, but to mark the sixtieth anniversary of the formation of the Soviet Union in 1922. The occasion enabled Andropov to survey sixty years of Soviet achievement but also to take a critical look at the drawbacks he had inherited. As the delegates gathered once again in the Kremlin, General Fedorchuk was moved to the Interior Ministry, placing the police and judiciary under his stern command, and Colonel-General Viktor Chebrikov (later to be made General) became the new head of the KGB after years as Andropov's assistant. Almost immediately the chief of police and the prosecutor at Krasnodar in the northern Caucasus—Andropov's home region—were sacked for embezzlement and abuse of power. *Izvestiya* announced new regulations to come into force on 1 January 1983, strengthening the penalties for corruption and bribery. On Andropov's instructions, the press began to print exposures of corrupt officials and badly managed enterprises, and said the stricter penalties for misdemeanours were the result of "countless requests from workers intolerant of anti-social behaviour".

There were obvious dangers in this change of tack, among them being the hard fact that bribery and illegal dealing are built into the Soviet system. The Soviet economy would grind to a halt altogether if such underground practices did not spring up to fill the gaps left by a hopelessly inefficient system of centralized production and distribution. But Andropov's aim was to clean up the system and make it more efficient, not to revolutionize it altogether. A more serious drawback, one of which his aides were very much aware, was that in shaking up the system Andropov risked the wrath and resentment of thousands of humdrum Party and government officials who kept the wheels of Soviet bureaucracy turning in an unimaginative, often corrupt but on the whole, workable manner, and who did not in the least relish having to roll their sleeves up in order to prove they were in tune with the new era of discipline and initiative. Their champion remained the man who had apparently been so decisively defeated in November, but who was still an influential member of the Politburo and in many ways continued to embody the average Soviet *apparatchik*: Konstantin Chernenko. How long would it be before these simmering resentments were channelled through Chernenko into the political process at the top? Or to put the question another way: would Andropov have the time to push through his reforms before the inevitable bureaucratic backlash?

As 1983 opened, Andropov pursued his anti-corruption campaign with a vengeance. There was trouble brewing on the international scene: Russia began to hint that it might walk out of the Geneva arms talks, and bitterly attacked the American "zero option" on medium range missiles, under which NATO would have forgone the deployment of Pershing and cruise missiles in Western Europe provided the Soviet Union undertook to dismantle the missiles it had targeted on Western Europe, including the infamous SS-20s. The NATO missiles and the Soviet rockets were in no way comparable, *Pravda* asserted, "as any schoolchild can see", since Russia was faced with rockets which could reach the Soviet heartland, whereas Soviet missiles could hit Europe but not the United States. The zero option amounted to Moscow making concessions while Washington gave up not a single missile or aircraft, *Pravda* said. Andropov made it clear what the Soviet position was going to be in a speech just before Christmas, when he offered to balance SS-20s against the British and French nuclear deterrent, despite NATO's argument that the British and French systems were not part of the NATO arsenal but sovereign national defences.

Tackling illegal dealing and streamlining the economy seemed much simpler than the intricacies of arms control. At the end of January the Kremlin warned that profiteering at peasant markets in Moscow and other cities would be thoroughly investigated. At the beginning of February, Andropov launched his personal style by visiting the Ordzhonikidze engineering plant in Moscow and making a speech demanding that workers and managers put their backs into his programme for economic efficiency. There was one minor slip, when Andropov asked an elderly worker how much he earned. The worker gave a figure high above the regular norm, confessing that he was not only drawing a state pension but also drawing wages at the plant, an illegal but not uncommon practice. Not surprisingly, this exchange between the leader and a rank-and-file member of the working class was censored from *Pravda* the next day when Andropov's shop-floor dialogue was re-printed. (Perhaps for this reason, when Chernenko made his obligatory factory visit, about a year later, very few snatches of dialogue were published, and when Gorbachov visited a plant in 1985 no shop-floor exchanges were published at all, despite Gorbachov's outgoing and informal style.)

Very few Russians noted that Andropov's factory remarks had been censored. In any case the main message was plain, and was reiterated again and again by the official media, echoing the new leader: "There are no miracles", Andropov told the Ordzhonikidze factory hands bluntly. If they wanted increased wages and better conditions, this could only come from increased production, hard work, and a crackdown on "shirkers, bad work and idlers." "Without discipline we cannot advance quickly," Andropov said, keeping up the momentum of the campaign which already had members of the public worried because of persistent police and People's Control raids on shops, cinemas and public bars to catch numerous Russians playing truant from work or using office or factory time to stand in queues for scarce goods.

As the Andropov era forged ahead, Chernenko and other followers of Brezhnev were reduced to ensuring that they kept a toehold on power, and ensuring also that the memory of the late leader was not entirely obliterated. Andropov, ever conscious of Soviet political history, seemed in any case reluctant to continue the tradition whereby former leaders were cast into oblivion, perhaps having in mind his own future fate. In February 1983, three months after Brezhnev's death, *Pravda* published a long and laudatory review of the final and posthumously issued sections of Brezhnev's memoirs, entitled *Moldavian Spring*, *Space October* and *A Word about Communists*. These sections, which followed Brezhnev's widely publicized and extravagantly praised first memoirs on the War and Postwar reconstruction, were published in the journal *Novy Mir* (New World), Moscow's leading literary magazine. *Pravda* described them as "works of historical and educational signifi-cance which successfully blend the manifold experience of a leader with a Marxist-Leninist analysis of reality". Yet this was essentially an echo of the fulsome tributes to Brezhnev in November, at the time of Brezhnev's death, rather than a pointer to the future. Although Brezhnev's memory was to be preserved, and a plaque was unveiled to him on Number 26 Kutuzovsky Prospekt, the Politburo VIP block, the personality cult Brezhnev had so painstakingly constructed during his lifetime was being swiftly and quietly dismantled. Brezhnev's name was only rarely heard on Andropov's lips, or indeed on anybody's lips, and his quotations, which once dominated Moscow's billboards and newspapers, had disappeared altogether. The impression given in public speeches in Andropov's first months was that the Brezhnev era was one in which the economy had stagnated lamentably and the Andropovite virtues of hard work and discipline had been neglected. Chernenko was powerless to prevent this subtle denigration of the Brezhnev inheritance. A film of Brezhnev's life was shown on Moscow television, but the career which had once been endlessly publicized, celebrated in films and books and taught in schools across the Soviet Union, was now condensed into a telebiography of a mere twenty minutes.

Russians and foreigners in Moscow alike found Andropov's style intriguing. On the one hand his question and answer session with the Ordzhonikidze workers about living standards was more reminiscent of the Khrushchev era than the grey style of Brezhnev's managerial politics. On the other hand Andropov, unlike Khrushchev, was distant and aloof, inspiring a respect which verged on fear. The shop floor exchanges were not shown on television, but were read out by an announcer, and Andropov generally kept himself firmly in the background. In contrast to the Brezhnev era, Andropov's portrait did not stare down from every wall. His speeches tended to be sprinkled with dry personal asides, and yet he preferred to speak in the name of the Party and government, as though his rule were somehow anonymous. The fact remained that nobody had any doubt that he was in charge, and that he was moving fast to purge the apparatus of those "who are too set in their ways", which often meant those too closely linked with the former régime. On foreign affairs, too, Andropov kept the West on the hop, skilfully exploiting anti-war sentiment in Europe and posing as the true champion of disarmament, while maintaining high Soviet military spending, developing chemical and space weaponry, and turning down Reagan's proposal for a summit meeting on arms control.

CHAPTER THIRTEEN

Tensions in the Kremlin

BY THE END of his first one hundred days, Andropov had the makings of his own team already in place, among them General Fedorchuk, who in December moved from the KGB to the Interior Ministry, and General Viktor Chebrikov, who succeeded Fedorchuk at the KGB. Together with Marshal Ustinov and the armed forces, this gave Andropov a formidable powerbase which no potential challenger could hope to match. Senior casualties of his purge included Nikolai Shcholokov, Brezhnev's 72-year-old Interior Minister, and Andrei Kirilenko, the 75-year-old former Politburo member, who made way for Aliyev. Out too went Alexander Struyev, 76, who had been Trade Minister for seventeen years, making way for Grigory Vashchenko, the 63-year-old head of the Budget Commission. In came a new chief of propaganda, Boris Stukalin, aged only 49, former head of the Komsomol. Even the Sports Committee was not overlooked, with Sergei Pavlov being eased out after fifteen years at the head of the Soviet Olympic and sports bureaucracies. And there were shake-ups in a number of key industries at senior and middle management levels, including the textile industry, where widespread theft and waste were exposed in the Soviet press.

But what of Andropov's role as an intellectual with a mastery of Marxist ideas? From this point of view one of the most worrying developments was the emergence of a group of young unorthodox socialists—officially only a discussion group—with members drawn from sons of the Party and government élite. The group had very modest aims, and was not a particularly significant force; but Andropov of all people was aware of the way in which, in Russia, small groups of intellectuals can in the long run have an impact on policy and power. The young left-wingers, who studied Marxist and left-wing writings outside the framework of Party teaching, had come to the conclusion (hardly startlingly original in the West, but heresy in Russia) that Communism had never been established in Russia at all, and that the system developed since the 1917 Revolution had merely created a new ruling class. These were not the kind of "new ideas" Andropov had in mind when he called for fresh air in the Party and government structure. In a move intended to nip this dangerous heretical development in the bud,

Andropov had nearly all the members of the group arrested, and put pressure on their embarrassed parents to ensure that Marxist orthodoxy was rigorously reimposed.

There was talk of a trial, and Roy Medvedev, the distinguished dissident Marxist historian, who was much admired by the young socialists, was called to the Moscow prosecutor's office for the first time in twenty years and told that the authorities' patience was at an end. Medvedev's voluminous writings on Russian history and socialism were "slanderous", the prosecutor said. Possibly because of the concern these developments aroused among left-wing opinion in the West, especially in Western Europe, the trial of the young socialists was postponed three times following their arrest in April 1982, and in the end the six "ringleaders" were quietly released following promises of good behaviour. Their discussion journal *Socialism and the Future* was suppressed.

The emergence of a "Russian New Left" right at the beginning of the Andropov era was no coincidence. Intellectuals expected something more from Andropov than the usual meaningless ritual Party terminology. Perhaps to meet these expectations, Andropov published a long and detailed theoretical article in the February issue of *Kommunist*, the Party's main theoretical journal, which although for the most part dense, wordy and platitudinous, did contain occasional flashes of incisive intellect. The article, devoted to the centenary of the death of Karl Marx, made no concessions at all however to the liberal wing of the Party. Andropov agreed that Soviet Marxists had much to learn from other Socialist countries, a reference above all to the Hungarian experience, but he was swift to add that this did not mean that Soviet Marxism needed an injection of Western leftist ideas, or that Russia could in any way tolerate "those who oppose their own egotistical interests to those of society as a whole". He even added that such dissident intellectuals needed to be "re-educated", a chillingly ominous reference to the practices introduced by the KGB under his chairmanship, such as the incarceration of dissidents in psychiatric institutes. This was not a "flouting of human rights", Andropov wrote, "but rather the reverse".

The Marx centenary article was defensive in tone, answering unnamed critics who argued that Russian socialism was not taking the course envisaged by Marx. But there was no such thing as an abstract, neat and ideal socialism, Andropov said. On the other hand the article stressed the need for change, for local initiative, and for material incentives in the economy, and in the context of the unimaginative ideology of the

Brezhnev years posed some awkward and challenging questions. "What is holding us up?" Andropov asked. "Why do we not get the right return from massive capital investment? Why are scientific and technological achievements not being applied fast enough? The answer," he said, was that "the perfection and reshaping of the economic mechanism and the forms and methods of management has lagged behind". What were needed were "measures which give broad freedom of action to the colossal creative forces latent in our economy", provided they were "carefully prepared and realistic". The Soviet economy and administration could not merely be run by Communist decrees, Andropov said.

Both Andropov's personnel changes and his careful elaboration of the intellectual foundations of reform were beginning to alarm hidebound and time-serving members of the apparatus who regarded Chernenko as their champion. Unsettling rumours that all was not well at the top began to circulate in Moscow. At the end of February Tass issued an obituary for a leading Soviet mathematician, saying that it had been signed by Andropov and other leaders. Shortly afterwards the same obituary was read out on television, but the announcer failed to mention Andropov's name, and immediately journalists and diplomats were on the alert. Was this perhaps a significant slip? The incident coincided with the swift and sudden return from Budapest of Marshal Ustinov after a visit to Hungary barely lasting one day, and the presence of an unusually large number of police on the streets of Moscow. The following day, *Pravda* carried Andropov's name along with that of other leaders when the mathematician's obituary was published, and Soviet officials hastened to explain that it was not at all unusual for Defence Ministers to pay one day visits to allied countries. Nevertheless observers in Moscow remained aware that the signs surrounding the death of Brezhnev three months before had been so small that they could easily have been overlooked, and in some cases were. Rumours of a crisis in the Kremlin in February 1983 proved unfounded in the short term; but when Andropov died a year later in February 1984 and details of his medical history were released by the authorities, it became clear that he had indeed begun to fall seriously ill only a few months after taking power, and had begun to suffer the kidney ailment which together with other diseases was to kill him after only fifteen months in power. The February rumours were symptomatic of the kind of nervous atmosphere which was to prevail in Moscow almost continuously from the death of Brezhnev until the accession of Gorbachov. The entire three year period appears in retrospect as one of almost constant transition.

Kremlin policy under Andropov, which had got off to such an

energetic and efficient start at the end of the 1982, began to falter in the spring of 1983. The general impression was that the leadership was already beginning to lose direction. Not the least of these signs was the complete misjudgement by the Soviet leadership of the elections in West Germany. Right up to the victory of Helmut Kohl and the Christian Democrats, the Russians continued to support Hans-Jochen Vogel, the leader of the Social Democrats, and even in private firmly believed that the Social Democrats would form the next government in Bonn. The Kremlin even took the risk of sending Andrei Gromyko to West Germany in order to try and boost Vogel's chances, although—as should have been obvious at the time—the move had precisely the opposite effect. The overwhelming election of Helmut Kohl as Chancellor of Germany in March 1983 came as a shock to the Kremlin, despite all the warning signs, and Moscow angrily reacted by advising Kohl not to agree to the deployment of new NATO missiles in Germany despite his victory at the polls.

A second policy failure, or at least loss of momentum, in the spring of 1983 came over the continuing problem of Afghanistan. Under Andropov the Afghan war, which had previously been in the shadows rather than highlighted, received an unusual amount of publicity as the Soviet press began to give detailed accounts of incidents in which young Soviet soldiers had died fighting the Afghan rebels, described as *basmatchi* or *dushmani*, the terms used for mountain fighters in Central Asia and the Caucasus during the 1920s and 1930s. In one article in *Red Star*, the newspaper of the armed forces, a description was given of the killing of three young Soviet recruits in a mountain ambush while they were trying to isolate a burning lorry filled with dynamite. In another case a young army lieutenant was depicted as the hero of an ambush in which he fell while taking on a dozen rebels at once while waiting for reinforcements to arrive. This press campaign was a remarkable admission that the Afghan operation, begun in December 1979, was very far from being the clean-cut, swift and efficient operation initially envisaged, and that Russia had become in effect bogged down in difficult fighting in inhospitable mountainous terrain. On the other hand the press campaign was partly designed to placate the armed forces, who felt that their role in subduing the Afghan rebels had not been sufficiently recognized publicly, almost as if there was something to be ashamed of. It was also intended to impress the Soviet public with the heroism and courage of young Soviet soldiers on the Afghan front. In the Muslim republics of the South, examples of selfless courage were held up before the population, partly to counteract an undercurrent of feeling that

Soviet soldiers of Muslim origin should not be dying in a struggle against fellow Muslims who shared the cultural and religious traditions of Uzbekistan, Tajikistan, Turkmenistan and other Southern Republics. One Party official in Tajikistan even produced the bloodstained Komsomol card of a young Tajik recruit who had died in Afghanistan, citing his death as an example to other Soviet soldiers.

More open descriptions of the fighting in Afghanistan did not however suggest that a political solution was in sight—quite the contrary. Bringing the fighting out of the shadows suggested that the Kremlin envisaged a long-term struggle on similar lines to the Soviet campaign against the *basmatchi* of Central Asia and the Caucasus some fifty years before, and had therefore decided to make the best of it. The official line remained that the Soviet Union had in 1979 gone to the help of a legitimate government threatened by foreign-backed mercenaries, and that Soviet forces were only there because an "undeclared war" was being conducted in Afghanistan by the United States, China and other foreign powers. There were expectations of a possible agreement on Soviet withdrawal when Perez de Cuellar, the United Nations Secretary General, visited Moscow at the end of March for talks with Andropov to seek a formula for a political settlement acceptable not only to Moscow and its puppet régime in Kabul but also to the regional powers involved, such as Iran and Pakistan. In the event de Cuellar emerged from the Kremlin empty handed, and although at the end of his visit he put a brave face on things by hinting at some movement or concession by Andropov, he was unable to explain what such a concession might be. In subsequent weeks it became clear that Andropov's position had not changed one iota. Afghanistan, like the vexed question of Soviet-American arms talks, was to remain a thorny and unresolved problem for his successors, Konstantin Chernenko and Mikhail Gorbachov.

The fortunes of Chernenko meanwhile appeared to be in flux. While Andropov grappled with the problem of power in his first few months, with the added disadvantage of physical disability, Chernenko fought a rearguard action, occasionally disappearing from view but occasionally also returning to the limelight.

In March 1983 Chernenko chaired a two-day meeting of Warsaw Pact ideological secretaries. He lost his influential post of head of the General Department of the Central Committee—formerly his bureaucratic power-base—but retained influence as Secretary for Ideology, the position Andropov had used the previous year as a launching pad for his bid to succeed the ailing Brezhnev. It had become Kremlin tradition that the Secretary for Ideology ranked as Number Two in the hierarchy, and had the best chance of succeeding in the event of the incumbent's death or retirement. The content of the ideological conference was not in itself noteworthy (there was a call for vigilance against Western psychological warfare and reinforcement of Warsaw Pact unity) but the meeting demonstrated that Chernenko was not yet finished as a political figure.

To add to the increasingly nervous political atmosphere—quite remarkable considering that Andropov had only just taken over—Tass suddenly announced at the end of March that Andrei Gromyko, who had been Foreign Minister since 1957, was to become Deputy Prime Minister while retaining his post as Foreign Minister. There were already two First Deputy Prime Ministers: 75-year-old Ivan Arkhipov, and Geidar Aliyev, at that time 59. Aliyev had only become a Politburo member the previous November, and some Party sources suggested that Gromyko had been moved up in the Council of Ministers hierarchy with the rank of Deputy Premier to put a brake on the Azerbaijani's ambition.

The move certainly had an impact on the manoeuvring in the hierarchy which was taking place against a background of uncertainty at the top. Andropov failed to appear at several meetings with foreign visitors, and spent a brief spell in hospital for kidney treatment. Even Nikolai Tikhonov, the Prime Minister, was caught up in the speculation when he was obliged by ill health to postpone a visit to Yugoslavia and was under doctor's orders to rest. This period of feverish speculation in the spring of 1983 contained some downright bizarre elements, including rumours that an unnamed woman had tried to assassinate Andropov in his private office. Some of the rumours suggested the woman was Mrs Shcholokov, wife of the former Interior Minister and Brezhnev associate whom Andropov had so summarily dismissed and disgraced a few months before. The rumour was strengthened later in the year when *Izvestiya* published an article on the assassination attempt on Lenin by a woman Socialist Revolutionary terrorist, in 1918. The rumours were symptomatic of the political atmosphere at the time, and as in the case of many Moscow rumours had some basis in fact—in this case, that Andropov was physically incapacitated just at the time when he should have been consolidating his hold on power.

Although Kremlin officials claim that they pay no attention to the impact of such rumours on foreign opinion, it was striking that at the end of March and the beginning of April the leadership moved swiftly to impose political calm and to give the impression that all was well. Andropov made a public appearance to meet Daniel Ortega, the leader of the Nicaraguan Sandinista government, and Tikhonov made his delayed visit to Belgrade. Officials hinted that the Central Committee would meet shortly to approve further policy and personnel changes by Andropov, although in the event the Central Committee did not convene until June, three months later. Intellectuals who supported Andropov's reform ideas began to publish articles in the press arguing that Russia's economic problems needed tackling urgently, and that Russia could profitably learn from the experience of East European countries, above all the new economic mechanism in Hungary.

In *Pravda* Academician Oleg Bogomolov praised the Hungarian model of decentralized decision-making and profit and loss accounting, and said there was also room for the expansion of private farming plots, adding—to reassure the hardliners—that such proposals would not harm the socialist structure or lead to a return of capitalism in the Soviet Union. At the same time Andropov's campaign to root out corrupt officials continued apace, even claiming as one of its victims the woman director of restaurants in a Black Sea resort, a woman known by the colourful nickname of Iron Bella.

Iron Bella, who operated in the resort of Gelendzhik, had been involved in a web of embezzlement and corruption which included the local chief of police. While such activities were tolerated under Brezhnev in his latter years, Andropov and his stern Interior Minister, Vitaly Fedorchuk, decided to make an example of Iron Bella by sentencing her to death. The case caused considerable shock, partly because the accused was a woman, and partly because corruption in the Black Sea area had previously been regarded as endemic and inevitable. Suddenly the Soviet press was full of cases of corruption and embezzlement, with officials being sacked and punished all over the country for corrupt activities. There were further death sentences, including one in Kirghizia, where the public prosecutor was sentenced to death for bribery, described by the court as a particularly dangerous crime for society.

In March and April Andropov firmly took hold of the reins of foreign policy in order to quash rumours that he was already in decline after only a few months in office. When in March 1983 President Reagan made a speech proposing a more defensive American policy in nuclear deterrence—the germ of what was later to become the highly controversial notion of strategic defence, or SDI, the "Star Wars" system—Andropov was swift to react by saying that this would involve violation of existing Soviet-American arms treaties and was therefore unacceptable. Reagan suggested that a strategy of retaliation for a Soviet nuclear attack could be replaced by the end of the century with a space age protective umbrella based on anti-ballistic missiles (ABM) defences, which he described as "a new hope for our children in the 21st century". The idea was that the United States would destroy incoming Soviet missiles before they reached their targets.

The reaction of Moscow however was that the United States could only redeploy its ABMs within the area surrounding the existing ICBM base at Grand Forks, and that to conduct research and development on space systems was a violation of the ABM Treaty of 1982. In what was to become a familiar theme of Soviet propaganda, TASS said the Reagan plan was part of an overall American strategy aimed at destroying the rough parity between the superpowers and achieving nuclear superiority over the Soviet Union. In an interview with *Pravda* (a device Andropov and Chernenko both used to show the world that they were firmly in charge of policy) Andropov dismissed the Reagan plans for defensive nuclear strategy as unrealistic and extremely dangerous. They might seem attractive to the layman, but they did not appear so "to those who are conversant with such matters". The Reagan concept, Andropov said tersely, would open the flood gates to a runaway arms race involving all kinds of strategic weapons, both offensive and defensive. He warned Washington that Russia would never be caught defenceless, and added: "It is time the Americans stopped devising one option after another in the hope of finding the best way of launching a nuclear war and winning it. This is not just irresponsible, it is insane."

CHAPTER FOURTEEN

Chernenko Fights Back

As Moscow sweltered in an unseasonal heatwave in the spring of 1983 with temperatures in the city soaring to above 20 degrees Centigrade and traffic police hastily donning summer-issue uniforms, the temperature of international politics rose steeply to match the weather. With tensions over arms control dominating the world scene, the Soviet military came increasingly to the fore, a development which was to become even more pronounced later in the Andropov era. Four army generals, including Vladimir Tolubko, Commander of Strategic Rocket Forces, were promoted to the rank of Marshal. After dismissing the Reagan plan for space-based defences Moscow reiterated that it found America's interim proposal on medium range missiles unacceptable and that it was considering ways of hitting back at the United States over the apparently inevitable deployment of new NATO weapons in Western Europe—Cruise and Pershing Two. Having failed to prevent NATO from going ahead with deployment, regarded in the West as a response to the growing numbers of Soviet SS-20s aimed at Western Europe, Kremlin leaders began to talk of striking back by installing new rockets on the territory of Warsaw Pact allies such as East Germany and Czechoslovakia, a move which threatened to raise the stakes considerably rather than taking the heat out of superpower tensions.

In a speech in East Germany Marshal Dmitri Ustinov, the Defence Minister, took the Soviet position even further by making it clear that the Soviet Union would retaliate directly against American territory if it were attacked by Cruise and Pershing missiles based in Western Europe. He did not say how Russia would do this, but conveyed Soviet anger at the latest developments. "If in Washington they think we will only retaliate against targets in Western Europe, they badly delude themselves. Retaliation against the United States itself will be ineluctable." There was growing irritation with the failure of Western peace movements to have a perceptible impact on NATO's determination to counter the SS-20s. A pamphlet called "How to Avert the Threat to Europe", part of the growing Soviet peace offensive, took Western peace campaigners to task, even though the booklet was specifically aimed at them. It was wrong, the booklet said, to blame all governments for the arms race or to suppose that the "battle for peace should always and everywhere have an anti-government thrust". In an atmosphere which also included the expulsion of Soviet diplomats from Britain and France and (in the case of Britain) Soviet retaliation, the Andropov era showed no sign at all of leading to the hoped-for improvement in East-West relations.

There was little doubt in the spring of 1983 that Yuri Andropov did want to improve relations with the United States—Russia's number one priority—despite intense Soviet dislike and mistrust of Ronald Reagan. The prospects for a superpower summit were another matter, however. Much to the surprise of both Russians and foreigners in Moscow, Andropov was not yet President as well as Party leader; at the Supreme Soviet which followed his election as General Secretary, he had merely been made a member of the Praesidium, which entitled him in future to become Chairman of the Praesidium or Head of State. But for the time being he was content, as Brezhnev had been content in his first years in power, to conduct foreign policy as Party leader without at the same time holding the formal position of President, which would enable him to negotiate face to face with his American counterpart. There were some suggestions at the time that Andropov, like Gorbachov later on, had decided there was no need to assume the Presidency since he already wielded real power, and would be content to let some senior figure such as Andrei Gromyko or Marshal Ustinov become Head of State, thus returning to the pre-Brezhnev system in which Russia was ruled by a triumvirate of Prime Minister, General Secretary and President, with the three powers separated. Other reports from within the Party said the truth was not that Andropov had decided he could live without being President, but rather that his position was not as secure as was believed, and there was an internal power struggle going on over who should hold which office. A variant on this was that Andropov wanted Chernenko to become President, not so that Chernenko could enhance his position, but, on the contrary, so that he could be kicked upstairs, the Presidency being a purely ceremonial post unless combined with another power base.

The most valid explanation was that Andropov had decided that there was no need to create unnecessary opposition or resistance, or to alarm entrenched bureaucrats by his fast pace of change, and took the view that since he would become President anyway eventually, there was no need to hurry. But in matters of policy, as opposed to the question of formal titles, Andropov was very much a man in a hurry, both at home and abroad. In March the Soviet press published extensive extracts from letters American citizens had written to Andropov, urging him to improve relations between the superpowers and thanking him for saying in a speech that he wished Americans and their families well. *Pravda* even published photographs of stamps and postmarks to prove that the letters were genuine. At the same time the Kremlin made a gesture towards Western opinion by releasing six Pentecostalist Christians who had spent five long years cooped up in the basement of the American Embassy on the Ring Road in Moscow. The scene of their departure in a minibus, driven through the same gates past which they had rushed to seek refuge in 1978, was flashed on television screens around the world. Shortly afterwards Georgy Vladimov, the dissident writer well known for his novel *Faithful Ruslan*, an allegorical tale about a prison camp guard dog, was given an exit visa to West Germany.

The Russians let it be known that they were reluctant to continue the cycle of tit-for-tat spy expulsions with the West, in particular Britain. When the Western nations met at a summit in Williamsburg, the reconstructed colonial town in the United States, the Kremlin offered a muted version of its usual attacks on Western policies and adopted a tone of sorrow rather than anger. It was a pity, Soviet commentaries said, that the West had used the usual set of phrases, and had shown no sign of a shift in the direction of realism over the impending deployment of new NATO missiles in Europe. It was to be regretted, Tass said, that Williamsburg summit had refused to include the British and French deterrents in the Geneva negotiations.

Against this background there were conflicting signals in the spring and summer of 1983 over the political standing of Chernenko. By now 71, Chernenko was no longer head of the Party's General Department, and Brezhnev, with whom Chernenko was so closely identified, was already a figure of the past and hardly mentioned at all a bare six months after his death. Brezhnev's memoirs were reviewed, and his description of Chernenko as a leader of "great talent and experience" was widely quoted in the press. But the object of this posthumous praise seemed to have disappeared. He was suffering from a lung complaint, emphysema, which was to dog him when he finally gained power after Andropov's death. In April Andropov addressed a Kremlin meeting on agriculture and *Pravda* listed attendance by all members of the Politburo—except for Chernenko. Shortly before this Chernenko had been unexpectedly absent from a conference in East Berlin, and Soviet officials gave ill health as an explanation, even though Chernenko was his usual animated and ruddy-faced self when appearing on the platform next to Andropov and Tikhonov in the Kremlin at a meeting in commemoration of Karl Marx. Chernenko's absence from the agriculture meeting overshadowed the substance of Andropov's remarks, which consisted of a call for new management techniques and praise for the efficiency of Russia's small-scale private farming, a significant reference to the private plots which account for nearly a third of fruit and vegetable output even though they hold only one per cent of agricultural land.

The power struggle took another twist in May, when even as reports of Chernenko's political decline were circulating in Moscow, *Pravda* reviewed a volume by him on Party organizational work in the most laudatory terms. Predictions that Chernenko was on the way out were none the less strengthened when he missed not only the anniversary of Lenin's birthday in April, but also the May Day parade on Red Square, a high-profile public occasion when all members of the Politburo are expected to wave dutifully to the crowd from the top of the mausoleum, and be shown on television. Chernenko's office at the Central Committee on Staraya Ploshchad (Old Square) was obliged to issue an unusual statement saying that Chernenko had been suffering from a "slight cold" (the Kremlin euphemism for something much more serious) but had now returned to work. The *Pravda* review of the book, which appeared on 22 May, said generously that Chernenko's views on how to mobilize the energy of the masses were "profound and comprehensive". Chernenko remained, in other words, responsible for questions on ideology, which were expected to dominate that next Plenum of the Central Committee in June. If he did not make the main speech at the Plenum, or indeed did not speak at all, the knives would be out in the Kremlin and correspondents would dust off their political obituaries. When Arvid Pelshe died at the end of May, at the age of 84, the Politburo lost its oldest member, and the death forcibly reminded the public at large of the mortality of the gerontocracy. On the other hand at the beginning of June Chernenko triumphantly reappeared for Pelshe's funeral on Red Square, looking rather unsteadier than when he had mysteriously disappeared, but still walking on to the top of the Red Square mausoleum not far behind Andropov.

The other question was whether Andropov was strong enough to make further changes in the Politburo. The death of Pelshe had come at just the right time, reducing the Politburo to eleven and leaving vacant the post of head of the Party Control Commission, an important disciplinary body which enforces orthodoxy in Party ranks. Pelshe, a man of skeletal appearance best known for his imposition of rule from Moscow in his native Latvia after the Second World War, was one of the few remaining members of the leadership who had witnessed the

Revolution in 1917 and had known Lenin personally. His death was another reminder that the generation of the Revolution and the War was passing away. Yet the only new appointment to the Politburo since Brezhnev's death had been that of Geidar Aliyev the previous November, and Andropov was widely expected to follow up a steady trickle of lower level and administerial changes with a reshuffle at the top. How far would he go—or to put it another way, how far *could* he go to oust the numerous Brezhnevites who stood in his way?

The Brezhnevites were spreading a rumour that Brezhnev had left a "last will and testament" naming Chernenko as his successor, which Andropov had arrogantly ignored. Ranged against the Brezhnevites were Andropov's bright young men, above all Nikolai Ryzhkov, appointed to supervise the new economic programme and the fight against bureaucracy as Central Committee Secretary the previous November, and Gorbachov, still only 52, and fast emerging as Andropov's favourite son. Gorbachov made a much publicized and highly successful trip to Canada, where despite one or two upsets over the questions of Afghanistan and Human Rights, he came across as urbane, articulate, and a smooth talker. Above all, he was a man cast in a different mould from the series of ailing and ageing leaders the world had become resigned to seeing hold sway in the Kremlin. When Gorbachov returned to Moscow from Canada he was met at the airport by Geidar Aliyev, who was deferential in a way which went beyond Aliyev's usual sycophantic manner.

As the manoeuvring for the Plenum intensified, the world watched for glimpses of the man who had taken power only six months before but who was already faltering. When the veteran American diplomat Averell Harriman and his wife Pamela (the former Mrs Randolph Churchill) came to Moscow, they were quick to suggest that Andropov was really in remarkably good health. Mrs Harriman, looking disconcertingly like Margaret Thatcher in a sky blue dress and pearls, told me that Ambassador Harriman, who had been American envoy to Moscow during the Second World War, had met Andropov for an hour and twenty minutes and found him vigorous, sunburnt, and "taller than I expected, with a good sense of humour." But this was a sad (though not untypical) case of foreign visitors being grateful for and overawed by their reception by one of the world's most powerful men, and putting discretion before unpleasant truths. Similarly, when Neil Kinnock visited Moscow in November 1984 he observed to reporters that Chernenko was in an advanced stage of emphysema, although when Kinnock emerged from the Kremlin after his meeting with the Soviet leader he declined to speculate about Chernenko's illness. A more realistic picture of Andropov's condition emerged on 6 June, when President Mauno Koivisto of Finland visited Moscow for talks in the Kremlin. A Finnish photographer caught the Soviet leader in a pose which dramatically conveyed his physical disability: a frail and wooden figure, puffy faced, with hands hanging at his side, his face hidden by dark glasses and a pork pie hat. Two bulky aides physically manhandled him down the steps as Andrei Gromyko, and Leonid Zamyatin, head of the Party's international information department, looked on anxiously. Finland and the Soviet Union duly renewed their 35-year-old treaty of friendship, and signed a new agreement on co-operation in agriculture and foodstuffs. But it was the insight into the truth about Yuri Andropov which dominated the visit, not trade and treaties.

Up to the very eve of the June Plenum, Party sources maintained, apparently in all sincerity, that a number of senior Brezhnevites were in political peril. Both Chernenko and the ageing Prime Minister Nikolai Tikhonov were in disgrace, the sources whispered, and could even be removed from the Politburo altogether when the Plenum convened. Whether some such plan indeed existed, and had to be shelved, or whether the political rumours amounted to wishful thinking on the part of Gorbachov and other Andropovites is not clear. But those were so confidently predicting the end of Chernenko and Tikhonov in May and June of 1983 had clearly both underestimated the strength of the Brezhnevites and over-estimated Andropov's physical and political condition.

CHAPTER FIFTEEN

Andropov's Invisible Presidency

SIR WINSTON CHURCHILL'S best-remembered remark about Russia is that it was "a riddle wrapped in a mystery inside an enigma", and that its actions could not therefore be forecast. But Churchill also memorably observed that the power struggle in the Kremlin was akin to two dogs fighting under a carpet, an image which seemed particularly apt in June 1983 when Chernenko emerged from a tangle of speculation and doubt to make it clear that rumours of his imminent political demise had been greatly exaggerated.

After all the mixed signals in the press, after his mysterious absences from public view—above all his failure to attend the May Day parade—it was Chernenko who delivered the main speech at the two-day Central Committee Plenum on ideological matters, using the occasion to accuse NATO of a runaway arms race, but at the same time espousing the Brezhnev doctrine of détente and peaceful coexistence. Chernenko accused Washington of pushing mankind towards a nuclear war, but added that "this nuclear madness can be stopped", and that the Soviet Union would in the long run win the East-West battle of ideas by peaceful means. Communist ideology would win the hearts and minds of millions, he asserted, despite the attempts of imperialism to "poison the minds of Soviet people". There was more in the same vein. Significantly, Chernenko went out of his way to praise Andropov, remarking that his statements had had a profound influence on world opinion, and that Andropov's arguments and his "calm and confident tone" were in sharp contrast to the White House's irresponsible and aggressive policy. Possibly this generosity towards his rival marked a kind of political truce between the two men. More likely, Chernenko felt able to speak from a position of greater strength and make the usual obligatory obeisance to the leader. In effect, the subterranean struggle which Chernenko and his followers had been waging against Andropov since the death of Brezhnev had come out into the open with Chernenko's remarkable political comeback.

There was at least no fundamental difference of principle between Chernenko and Andropov as far as ideology and dissidents were concerned. Chernenko's remark that while the Soviet constitution guaranteed freedom of conscience, "subversive political activity" would be severely punished even if "it were covered up by religion", fully reflected the views held by Andropov himself. When Andropov rose to speak at the Plenum as General Secretary the danger of ideological heresy was clearly uppermost in his mind, not least in Eastern Europe and above all in Poland. The Polish Pope, John Paul II, formerly Cardinal Wojtyla of Krakow, was about to visit Warsaw, and Andropov went out of his way to warn the East Europeans not to fall for "bourgeois reformism" or the recipes of "self-styled defenders of the workers", a reference to Solidarity. "When the guiding role of the Communist Party weakens, there is always danger of slipping into bourgeois reformist paths of development," Andropov remarked. Russia would enhance its armed might under his leadership, Andropov said, but it might also be possible to reduce the level of military spending in the East and West, which would be "a great boon for all countries and peoples". It seemed a remote expectation.

The personnel changes Andropov made at the Plenum reinforced his position, but he made no changes to the Politburo itself, reinforcing the impression that after an initially dynamic start he was now slowing down. "The old man is no longer in such a hurry", was a remark often made by Soviet friends. The stalemate was in effect a standoff between Chernenko and Andropov, and although the two men had achieved a *modus vivendi*, this inevitably made for a certain amount of stagnation at the top. Andropov had turned 69 during the Plenum, but there were no public celebrations of the event.

Perhaps the most significant personnel move was the transfer of Grigory Romanov, the Party boss in Leningrad for thirteen years, to Moscow to become a Central Committee Secretary while remaining a member of the Politburo. This gave Romanov, at sixty considered a member of the younger generation, similar status to that of Chernenko and Mikhail Gorbachov. Romanov lacked the power-base which Gorbachov had been able to build up in Moscow over several years, a deficiency which was to prove crucial in 1985 when Romanov and Gorbachov fought it out for the succession to Chernenko.

But no less significant, in retrospect, were the Plenum decisions on the sacking of Nikolai Shcholokhov, the once powerful Interior Minister, from the Central Committee, and the appointment of Vitaly Vorotnikov, as candidate member of the Politburo. The expulsion of Shcholokov, and also of Sergei Medunov, the former Party boss at Krasnodar in the Black Sea region, was a further nail in the coffin of the Brezhnev system of nepotism and corruption. The mini-purge was a dramatic reminder to the rest of the Central Committee that those practices would not be tolerated by Andropov despite his failing power. The simultaneous elevation of Vorotnikov to candidate membership of the Politburo carried the same message. Few Party members had forgotten that it was Vorotnikov, once exiled to Havana as Soviet ambassador by Brezhnev, who had been installed as Medunov's successor at Krasnodar in 1982 by Andropov with the specific mission of cleaning up malpractice and abuse of power in the Black Sea area. Vorotnikov had made his career in Kuibyshev, subsequently climbing up the ladder in Voronezh as first secretary and then becoming Deputy Prime Minister of the Russian Federation under Mikhail Solomentsev. It could only be a matter of time before Vorotnikov became Russian Federation Prime Minister. Solomentsev now became chairman of the Party Control Commission in succession to Pelshe, although without rising from candidate to full Politburo member.

It was a cautious but significant Plenum. The appointment of Romanov as a Central Committee secretary in Moscow made him joint heir with Gorbachov for the mantle of Andropov when the time came, provided Romanov could overcome his image as a rather crude politician with an extravagant and self-indulgent life-style, and provided he could build up a power-base in Moscow. There was no comfort in the Plenum speeches and resolutions for Moscow intellectuals.

One writer told me that the best thing for intellectuals to do would be to "keep our heads down for a while", especially since both Chernenko and Andropov had called for an "intensification of ideological warfare" to counteract Reagan's "crusade against Communism". There was alarm in Moscow artistic circles at Chernenko's criticism of what he described as "artistic futility" in books, plays and films, and his ominous remark that film makers seemed to prefer unhappy destinies and whining characters to noble revolutionary ideals and ideological convictions. He also attacked writers who idealized religion and the eternal values of the Russian people rather than Marxism-Leninism.

The general lack of exhilaration as the Andropov régime entered its eighth month was reflected at the Supreme Soviet inside the Kremlin the following day, when Andropov was finally named Chairman of Praesidium of the Supreme Soviet, or President. Andropov walked unsteadily on to the platform from the wings to applause from the 1,500 deputies below, and had to hold on to the backs of chairs as he skirted his way round to the front row. There was a microphone on the desk in front of him, and when he made his acceptance speech he stayed where he was, speaking in a thin and rather distant voice, rather than coming down to the podium in the normal way. Once again, as in the election for the Party leadership the previous November, Andropov was proposed by Chernenko, who was able to speak from the podium. Chernenko declared, without noticeable enthusiasm, that Andropov was an outstanding leader of the Leninist type and had been unanimously nominated for the post by the Supreme Soviet Praesidium. Andropov looked neither pleased nor displeased by his appointment but simply sat expressionless, as if this were something of a chore instead of one of the political high-spots of his career.

It was, in retrospect, an important political stage in the career of Chernenko, whose praise for Andropov as a man of "human qualities, wisdom and experience" disguised his own ambition to succeed Andropov in all the important jobs—the Party leadership, the State Presidency, and chairman of the Supreme Defence Council—and take revenge for his defeat in the power struggle eight months before. This, perhaps, was the main point of the Supreme Soviet, which otherwise merely automatically approved the decrees which had piled up in the previous six months. It was remarkable only for speeches by Andrei Gromyko, the Foreign Minister, and Boris Ponomaryov, the candidate Politburo member and powerful member of the Central Committee Secretariat. Gromyko, obviously having in mind the Pope's visit to his Polish homeland, picked up Andropov's East European theme and reminded the Poles that they were an inalienable part of the Soviet bloc despite "ideological subversion" by the West. Ponomaryov, for his part, suggested a five-power nuclear arms freeze involving Britain, the United States, China, France and Russia, and called on the other nuclear states to show responsibility and political will by agreeing to it. Geidar Aliyev also figured in the proceedings, introducing a new law on "workers' collectives" in agriculture and industry, a move intended to reinforce democratic procedures in factories and farms, although in practice the new structure was to prove as empty as before.

The consensus among foreign observers as the deputies departed for their farms and factories, and in some cases institutes and ministries, was that Russia was being ruled by a triumvirate consisting of Andropov, Gromyko and Marshal Ustinov, with Chernenko making a remarkable come-back and acting as a kind of counter weight to the Andropov troika. Andropov had been able to make Vorotnikov a candidate Politburo member; but the Politburo remained static at eleven members, and there was now the distinct possibility that Chernenko would be able to slow down Andropov's anti-corruption campaign by protecting former Brezhnevites who had fallen foul of Andropov's stern demands for higher standards of public behaviour. Andropov announced that a new Party programme would be worked out to replace the outdated and disgraced Khrushchev Party programme, and that this would be done at the next Party Congress, due to take place in 1986. But would Andropov, now a physically sick man, be able to carry through the new programme, and would he indeed be present at the next Party Congress?

There had been no talk at the Plenum or the Supreme Soviet of the dynamic economic and administrative reforms Andropov had hinted at the previous November, and there had been practically no movement at the top. He had berated the West in the kind of ideological platitudes the Plenum itself had criticized as stale and lifeless. This was no longer a man in a hurry, it was a man rapidly running out of steam. "The Soviet political system needs continuity and firm leadership to avoid disintegration", *The Times* noted editorially. "There is still no constitutional means of selecting the top man in the Soviet Union, and Politburo wheeling and dealing takes time."

While the manoeuvring went on, the world watched for further signs of Andropov's decline as he received Helmut Kohl, the West German Chancellor. The mood in Moscow of suspicion of the outside world and defensive aggression—characteristic of periods of intrigue in the Kremlin—became stronger, with Marshal Ustinov echoing the themes of the Plenum and the Supreme Soviet by telling a closed Party meeting at the Ministry of Defence that the world was witnessing a "tense and sharp clash" between the two ideologies of East and West, and that Russia was threatened by a growing military alliance between the NATO powers and Japan. There was a flurry of alarm when Chancellor Kohl's first meeting with Andropov had to be cancelled because of illness. Although he subsequently did hold talks with the West German leader, the general impression of intrigue and decay was only intensified by the Kohl visit.

On June 28 the Warsaw Pact leaders held a one-day summit in Moscow, accompanied by a *Pravda* editorial stressing the need for cohesion within the Socialist community and a closing of ranks not only against the West but also against ideological heresy in the socialist system, which *Pravda* said tended to lead to "serious miscalculations". There was even an attack on that favourite bogeyman of Soviet propagandists, Ian Fleming's James Bond, described by *Pravda* as a "super spy and daredevil from Her Majesty's Secret Service". It was significant, *Pravda* said, not altogether in jest, that the fictional Commander Bond had an ardent admirer in the real President Reagan, who liked the intrepid agent not for his indulgence in strong drink, or his way with women, but for his stature as "an outstanding personality" who could bear comparison with the great soldiers, law givers and heroes of the past. Perhaps, *Pravda* noted acerbically, Mr Reagan also dreamed of having a licence to kill, and hero worshipped Bond because he had fellow feeling for a man who "shoots first and uses his brain afterward". The words were to have an ironic ring only just over a month later, when the Soviet Union shot first and asked questions afterwards, killing 269 people on board a Korean Airliner (ironically numbered Flight 007) over the Kamchatka Peninsula.

International attention continued to focus in the summer of 1983 on whether or not Andropov was firmly in charge of the Kremlin. Soviet Foreign Ministry officials were aware that despite their dislike of President Reagan, he was already preparing for the presidential elections in the United States in 1984 and might very well win a second term. When an eleven-year-old American girl called Samantha Smith came to Moscow at Andropov's personal invitation (she was one of many children who had written to the leaders of the superpowers about the future of the world), many expected that Andropov would scotch the rumours about his health by receiving her in the Kremlin before the world's press and television cameras, and by having his photograph taken with this somewhat precocious self-possessed young envoy from the United States. But although Samantha and her parents enjoyed sight-seeing trips and a four-day stay at a youth camp in the Crimea, Artek, and were able to pronounce Russia "a beautiful country which does not want to harm anyone", the Soviet leader did not appear, excusing himself on the grounds that he was too busy.

He was preoccupied with his domestic reform package, knowing that his time was limited. In July the Kremlin announced "limited industrial experiments". They disappointed those who had expected something with a broader sweep, but the experiments nonetheless laid the ground work for the invigoration of Soviet industry through decentralization and material incentives. The new measures were confined to factories responsible to the Ministries of Heavy Industry, Electro-Technical Industry and to collective plants in the Ukraine, Byelorussia and Lithuania. Under the scheme, which came into force on 1 January 1984, wages and bonuses were more closely linked to production, marketing and sales, and factory managers were given some control over the allocation of resources, production decisions and the distribution of profits. The reaction of many Russians was not interest and expectation but rather puzzlement and resentment that Andropov was continuing with his government programme during the summer months. Andropov showed no sign of following Brezhnev's example by taking an extended break on the Black Sea coast for most of July and August.

At the end of July the Politburo passed yet another resolution, this time "on the establishment of political organs in the Ministry of the Interior", a euphemism for stricter political control over the police and judiciary. The resolution followed widespread criticism in the press of the traffic police, known by its Russian initials as the GAI, and the revelation by General Fedorchuk that senior police officers in Odessa and Georgia had been dismissed and disciplined for embezzlement and negligence. To many, especially Chernenko and fellow Brezhnevites, it clearly seemed only a matter of time until the previous Interior Minister, Nikolai Shcholokov, was put on public trial.

At the other end of the spectrum, on the liberal wing of the Party, there was disgruntlement of a different kind: dissatisfication with the rather timid and vague nature of the recently announced industrial experiments. At the beginning of August a confidential report written by Dr Tamara Zaslavskaya, a sociologist at the influential Academy of Sciences branch at Novosibirsk was leaked to the Western press—in itself an almost unprecedented step—after the report had been discussed and rejected by a high level policy-making group within the Kremlin. The report stated bleakly that many of Russia's problems were due to the fact that the system had not been fundamentally altered since the days of Stalin, when managers and workers alike were regarded as cogs in a machine driven by state terror. "People behaved accordingly, as if they were machines and materials, passive and obedient", the report said. The system had failed to respond to social and political changes by adapting new economic mechanisms more suited to the means and abilities of a sophisticated work-force with rising expectations, and anachronistic planning and management methods were being perpetuated by a rigid and self-serving bureaucracy. The document underlined the fear felt by many Russian liberals that Andropov was failing to take on the entrenched bureaucrats and adopt the necessary radical methods.

Still Andropov kept at his desk without going on holiday to his favourite resort in Kislovodsk, the spa near his birthplace in the northern Caucasus, preferring instead to operate from a new dacha at Barvikha, on the road to Uspenskoye, in the woods just outside Moscow. He took part in celebrations marking the eightieth anniversary of the Russian Communist Party, and met Le Duan, the Party leader in Viet Nam, and the Portuguese Communist leader Alvaro Cunhal. Still the *Pravda* editorials kept coming, with new warnings on labour discipline making it clear that those who followed Andropov's lead and worked diligently would be rewarded, while slackness, absenteeism and alcoholism would be severely punished. At a time when most Russians were on holiday and trying not to think about work at all, the Soviet papers published new penalties for poor work perfomance and drunkenness, with the new element that slackness and alcoholics would be sacked on the spot and would be rehired only at a lower wage, with half the usual monthly bonus entitlement. General Fedorchuk wrote in *Pravda* on 10 August that the police had been "revitalized", and were under firm instructions to crack down on drunkenness, hooliganism, idleness, speculation and theft of socialist property.

On 15 August, Andropov held what was perhaps one of the most significant meetings in this final and almost desperate phase of activity: a conference of Party veterans at which he sat on the platform flanked by Mikhail Gorbachov on his left, and Grigory Romanov on his right. "We have not been vigorous enough", Andropov remarked. "We not infrequently resort to half measures and have been unable to overcome accumulated inertia. We must now make up for what we have lost." Russia could not otherwise enter the next Five Year Plan in two years "fully armed". "We have reached the stage where we need to turn our entire huge economy into an uninterruptedly functioning well-adjusted mechanism," Andropov declared. Yet only days after this address, members of the Old Guard in the Kremlin felt sufficiently self-confident to drag their feet in public. Nikolai Baibakov, Head of GOSPLAN for nearly twenty years and now 72 years of age, told us that the Andropov industrial experiments would have to be cautiously conducted "in view of the size and scope of our economy", perhaps an ironic reference to Andropov's demand that the "huge economy" should be turned around. Clearly for Baibakov the half measures Andropov was so bitterly criticizing were quite enough, if not already too radical. It was a sign that Andropov's grip on the Kremlin might be loosening. His presentation of Gorbachov and Romanov as joint heirs apparent only served to underline this impression.

There were meetings too on the international front—Andropov's final appearances on the world stage, although few guessed it at the time. He met the remarkably named William Winpisinger, vice-president of the AFLCIO, the American trade union organization, and told him that Moscow was ready to meet Washington half way "on many points". Ill or not, Andropov was clearly looking ahead, possibly to disguise the fact that the Soviet Union would pursue a constructive and flexible line at the Geneva talks until December, when NATO reviewed the deployment of new missiles in Western Europe. If America extended the hand of friendship to him, he said, it would always be given "a sincere handshake by the Soviet people".

Shortly afterwards Andropov received his final foreign visitors, a delegation of Democratic Senators. He launched a new Soviet arms proposal, vowing that Russia would not be the first to put an anti-satellite weapon into space, and imposing a moratorium on such weapons providing the United States did the same. He described this as an "exceptionally important decision". There was Western scepticism, since Russia had already tested killer satellites and laser weapons in space. In any case anti-satellite weapons were not the central issue of the moment between East and West, and had nothing to do with either the medium range missile talks or the strategic arms reduction talks at Geneva. Andropov was ominously pessimistic about the talks, noting that the United States would "feel the difference between the situation which existed before the deployment [of NATO missiles] and that which will take shape afterwards". It was, it turned out later, an indication that the Soviet Union was considering walking out of the Geneva talks altogether.

Andropov had a further proposal up his sleeve: an offer, made in an interview with *Pravda*, to "liquidate a considerable number of SS-20 missiles" as part of an overall agreement on medium range rockets, with the vital qualification that this reduction in the number of Soviet missiles would depend on a deal under which Soviet weapons were balanced against the independent deterrents of Britain and France. It was in effect a refinement of the proposal Andropov had made the previous December. Although it had some effect on Western opinion, as it was intended to, it did not materially affect the growing gloom at Geneva.

There was one more American visitor to Moscow that summer: John Block, the American Secretary for Agriculture, who signed a new agreement for the export of American grain to Russia over a period of five years. But Andropov did not receive Block, who instead held "business like" talks with Geidar Aliyev. Andropov, having made his final offers to the West on arms control and his last attempt to persuade Russians to raise production and stamp out corruption, finally left for the northern Caucasus and Red Rocks, high above the soothing waters of the spa of Kislovodsk. Within a few days of his arrival in the Caucasus, Andropov's rest was to be rudely shattered by a crisis which finally put paid to an improvement in East-West relations for some time, and almost certainly took a final fatal toll on his state of health.

CHAPTER SIXTEEN

Andropov's Final Days

IN THE SMALL hours on the night of 30 August–1 September 1983, Western correspondents in Moscow were wakened by telephone calls from London, New York and Australia. A jumbo jet belonging to Korean Airlines, with 269 people on board, had disappeared near the Soviet Far East coast over Sakhalin Island. Most of the passengers on the missing plane were Japanese and Korean, but there were also a number of American citizens, including Lawrence McDonald, the head of the House of Representatives Armed Services Committee. Gradually, in the course of the day, details began to emerge: flight KAL 007 from New York to Seoul via Anchorage had plunged from a height of 10,000 metres, and in the space of twelve minutes had disappeared from radar screens in the Far East after straying over 700 kilometres off course into Soviet airspace over Sakhalin and the Kamchatka Peninsula. But most of the details of the disaster were coming from Japan and the West, with almost complete silence about the fate of the Korean airliner in Moscow itself. In the outside world, evidence began swiftly to emerge that the plane had been deliberately shot down by Soviet fighter aircraft. Yet the Soviet media and Kremlin officials had almost nothing to say about why the unarmed jumbo jet had been attacked and 269 innocent people had been killed. It was as if the Kremlin was hoping this terrible tragedy would somehow go away and the crisis which was about to engulf Soviet-American relations, barely a year into the Andropov leadership, could be somehow averted. The KAL disaster was not only an appalling human catastrophe, it also exposed the nerve ends of the superpower relationship in the 1980s—and provided both Moscow and Washington with a crucial test of leadership.

With Andropov recuperating on holiday, desperately trying to regain his health, there was a potential power vacuum in the Kremlin at this critical juncture. Whatever other role it may have played in East-West relations, the Korean airliner crisis dealt a deadly blow to the declining Andropov leadership, complicating Andropov's relationship with his fellow Politburo members, and placing a profound strain on the always complicated and delicate relationship between the Soviet Communist Party leadership and the Soviet military, who in the first instance were responsible for border defences in general and the destruction of "the Korean intruder" in particular.

It is not my intention to go into the Korean airliner tragedy in detail. Even now the details of exactly what happened remain controversial, and the incident deserves a volume to itself. What interests us here is the impact of KAL 007 on the Kremlin and the armed forces at a time when there was already concealed manoeuvring in the Soviet leadership for the succession to Andropov. Just as Andropov himself had manoeuvred for position in Brezhnev's declining years and months, so now Andropov's rivals and supporters were engaged in a lethal battle for influence in the Kremlin corridors of power. The transition struggle, indeed, had in a sense never ceased. Andropov had taken over as General Secretary and then as President at a relatively advanced age and in an already poor state of health, so that his leadership was increasingly seen as interim even before KAL plunged into the Sea of Japan.

With Andropov on holiday at the end of August, the running of the country had been left in the hands of two men who were to play a crucial role in subsequent events: Marshal Dmitri Ustinov, the veteran Defence Minister, and Konstantin Chernenko. It was never finally established at what level the decision to open fire over Sakhalin Island had been taken, but the decision had been referred to the regional command in the Far East at Chita and had not immediately gone to Moscow, even though the Korean airliner had first strayed into Soviet airspace over Kamchatka two hours before it was destroyed. Nonetheless Ustinov and Chernenko were ultimately responsible for the decision, even though it had been taken at a local military level under standing orders of military engagement governing the defence of Soviet frontiers. Above all they—and when he came back from holiday, Andropov—were certainly responsible for the paralysis which appeared to seize the Kremlin in the face of an embarrassing and damaging storm of protest from abroad. Having at first said nothing at all, the Soviet authorities gradually began to admit that an airliner had indeed disappeared off the Soviet far eastern coast. But they maintained, to universal disbelief and ridicule, that they did not know what the fate of the aircraft had been. The most Tass would say was that the plane did not have navigation lights and failed to respond to Soviet queries, and that fighters of the Soviet anti-aircraft defence forces had tried to direct the plane to the nearest airfield. KAL 007 had failed to react to Soviet signals and warnings, and had then "continued its flight in the direction of the Sea of Japan".

Unfortunately for Moscow, the United States and Japan had kept close track of the aircraft's movements and had monitored its communications with ground control (so much so, indeed, that the Russians were later able to argue that the intrusion was a deliberate provocation by a spy plane under close Western and Japanese control). As a result George Shultz, the Secretary of State, was able to give details of the shooting down of the plane at precisely the time when the Russians were denying they knew what had happened to it. On 2 September Tass acknowledged that there had been loss of human life, and said the 269 deaths were due to "criminal disregard" on the part of those who had used the passenger jet as a spy plane. The Tass statement, issued just as the United Nations Security Council was going into emergency session, admitted for the first time that Soviet fighters (they later turned out to be Sukhoi 15s rather than the MiGs originally mentioned) had fired warning shots with tracer shells along the route of the plane. But still the Kremlin was refusing to admit that the fighters had actually shot the aircraft down. All Moscow would admit was that an unidentified plane had violated Soviet airspace, had flown 310 miles over Soviet territory and had spent more than two hours above the Kamchatka peninsula, the Sea of Okhotsk and Sakhalin. The Politburo was in almost continuous extraordinary session to deal with the crisis, yet the only tactic it had come up with was to try and turn the tables on the United States by saying as loudly and as often as possible that the tragedy was the fault of the United States rather than the Soviet Union, and that Washington was trying to smear Moscow and "sow hostility towards the Soviet Union". But international pressure for an explanation was building up, and by Sunday 4 September fingers were being pointed at senior Soviet military officers, above all General Vladimir Govorov, the Commander of Soviet forces in the Far East, and Marshal Alexander Koldunov, Commander in Chief of the Air Defence Forces. Suggestions began to be made that the shooting down of the plane was a deliberate attempt by the military to sabotage the arms control process at Geneva and disarmament measures favoured by Andropov.

At this point, according to Soviet sources, an angry and embarrassed Andropov decided that the Soviet military, including the Head of the Air Force, Marshal Pavel Kutakhov, and of the Chief of Staff, Marshal Nikolai Ogarkov, should bear the brunt of the crisis and explain to the world what had happened. But still the military could not bring itself to admit in public that it had made an error of judgement. On the contrary, the instinct of Russia's senior officers was to maintain that they had fulfilled their duty in defence of the motherland.

Colonel-General Simeon Romanov, Chief of Staff of the Air Defence Forces, was put forward to justify what had happened, but even five days after the disaster he could still not bring himself to tell the truth. (In May

1984, nine months after KAL, Red Star reported that General Romanov had died suddenly "while carrying out his official duties", seen by some as an act of poetic justice or even divine intervention.) The most he would admit was that Soviet radar and intercepters had mistaken the outline of the Korean jumbo for an American RC 135 reconnaissance plane, adding that American spy planes had been in the region at about the same time and that therefore mistaken identity was not only understandable but also reflected America's sinister intentions. Even ordinary Russians—hitherto baffled by the fuss because of lack of information and oblique references in the Soviet press—began to realize that the aircraft involved was carrying Americans and that loss of life had been heavy, and that Russia had perhaps committed an appalling crime.

Although the Kremlin does not have to deal with public opinion as understood in the West, this was a difficult moment. Fortunately for the Kremlin, most Russians seemed so appalled by the possibility of confrontation with the United States that they took refuge in the traditional Russian desire to believe that the authorities were ultimately competent and omniscient and would provide an explanation for the inexplicable. On the whole it was foreigners and diplomats who agreed with a visiting American Congressman that the Soviet explanation was unsatisfactory, and that Soviet radar ought surely to have been able to distinguish between a civilian jumbo jet and an American reconnaissance plane in a period of over two hours.

It was not until Tuesday 6 September that Moscow finally admitted that the Korean plane had been shot down—and even then the tone was defiant, suggesting that those in the leadership who took an aggressive line over the incident had prevailed over those whose instinct was to acknowledge a measure of culpability. A Soviet statement said that Soviet fighters had fulfilled ground control orders to "stop the flight" when the Korean jumbo jet failed to respond to signals and warnings, and that the Kremlin regretted the death of innocent people and shared the sorrow of the bereaved. But the statement added: "the entire responsibility for this tragedy rests wholly and fully with the leaders of the United States", and the Soviet action was "fully in keeping with the law on the state borders of the Soviet Union". It fell not only to Andrei Gromyko to maintain this line, at a Foreign Ministers' meeting in Madrid, but also to Marshal Ogarkov, at a unique press conference in Moscow in which the Chief of Staff defended the Soviet actions with reference to a large map showing the extent to which KAL 007 had mysteriously strayed from its flight path. This was Marshal Ogarkov's finest hour—although in retrospect his performance at the unprecedented press conference may also have been a prime cause of his subsequent downfall a year later, when he was sacked abruptly as Chief of Staff. At the time, in the face of international fury and furore, Marshal Ogarkov won a reputation for icy calm, intellectual arrogance and mastery of detail under intense pressure. He showed not a trace of regret—something which may have persuaded the Kremlin that his performance was not altogether beneficial to the Soviet image—and referred in Orwellian language to the "termination" of the flight, giving a detailed account of the interception.

On the face of it the Ogarkov press conference was a brilliant tour de force. But it did leave world opinion with a number of unanswered questions, including why the Russians had taken so long to admit that they had shot the plane down. Ogarkov's claim that Soviet reports had talked of "stopping the flight from the very beginning" was transparently absurd. President Reagan's popularity meanwhile leapt in the opinion polls and the United States kept up relentless pressure on Moscow, accusing the Russians of perpetrating a crime against humanity and then trying to cover up the massacre. Subsequent suggestions that the Korean airliner might have indeed had an espionage role and might not have strayed altogether accidentally from its flight path tended to be lost in the barrage of anti-Soviet criticism.

The Russians continued to use the once rare medium of press conferences to advance their case, but the tone continued to be defensive. When George Kornienko and Marshal Akhromeyev, the Deputy Chiefs of Staff, spoke in mid-September about the impending round of Geneva arms talks, they were at pains to stress that Moscow would not make arms control concessions simply because it was considered to be in the wrong over the Korean airliner disaster. Andropov himself sought to give an impression of normality by resuming his holiday in the Caucasus and assessing the damage to East-West relations while taking a rest cure. Soviet sources subsequently maintained that he had been "personally appalled" and had considered punishing those responsible, demanding scapegoats among the military. However when the Politburo met in emergency session following the disaster it decided that attack was the best form of defence, and that the best tactic was to blame the tragedy wholly on the United States. By the time Andropov resumed his interrupted rest cure, the tactic appeared if not wholly successful, then at least partially so. The decision not to send Andrei Gromyko to the United Nations General Assembly—the first time he had been absent during 27 years as Foreign Minister—was a further attempt to avoid international opprobium and limit damage to the Soviet image. Gromyko's decision not to go to New York was ostensibly because the Americans refused to allow his Aeroflot aircraft to land at a commercial airport, but there is little doubt that his unprecedented absence was a tactical Kremlin decision as well as a reflection of his personal anger and pique at the American attitude. The Soviet counter attack continued in late September with the claim, advanced by military officials in *Pravda* and *Red Star*, that the ill-fated Korean jumbo had co-ordinated its flight with the overhead path of a Ferret American reconnaissance satellite. When Andropov emerged from seclusion to make his first public statement since the disaster, he avoided all mention of the KAL tragedy, as if it had not taken place, referring instead in a reply to an appeal from West German Social Democrats to Moscow's concern at the lack of progress at Geneva and offering a "qualitative and quantitative freeze" of nuclear arms, a repetition of the proposal he had advanced at the Supreme Soviet in June.

There were nonetheless unmistakeable signs, both in public and behind the scenes, that the Korean airliner disaster had shaken the Kremlin and was sowing confusion in the Andropov leadership in its waning months. A pilot on leave in Moscow from the Sakhalin fighter base broke down and cried in the bar of the Central Committee hotel, to the dismay of officials. In Britain an official from the Party's information department, attending a conference in Edinburgh, admitted to the BBC that it had been a mistake to shoot down the Korean jumbo, and said the "trigger happy" Soviet pilot had mistaken the airliner for an American military spy plane. The official, Viktor Linnyk, subsequently disavowed his own statement and reiterated what he revealingly described as the "official Russian line", namely that KAL 007 had been on a spy mission and had to be stopped. The gaffe highlighted one of the main contradictions in successive Soviet versions of the incident, with some military officers maintaining that the jumbo had been mistaken for an American spy plane, and other Soviet accounts insisting that the 747 had itself been a spy plane. The two versions existed side by side, and were never satisfactorily resolved. It became increasingly apparent that the local air defence forces in the Soviet Far East had taken a hasty decision in confused circumstances, and that the political leadership had had to deal with the disastrous consequences. There was also the vexed question of whether the Russians had realized that there were civilians aboard the plane, with Marshal Ogarkov saying vaguely that the military "might have assessed things differently" had they known, but with one of the fighter pilots involved observing in *Red Star* that it had "never entered his head" that the plane was carrying civilian passengers. With the Kremlin in disarray, Soviet leaders both military and political resorted to hardline Cold War rhetoric to cover up the confusion, and *Izvestiya* carried a further statement by Ogarkov lashing out at the United States for its "lies and slander" and accusing America of planning a first nuclear strike against the Soviet Union despite the Geneva arms talks.

Andropov was making even fewer public appearances than usual, and his photograph had not appeared in *Pravda* for over a month. He had made his statement on the Geneva talks—rather oddly, a response to a two-month-old West German appeal—but the words "Korean" and "airliner" had not passed his lips. "Mr Andropov is no liberal civilian trapped by the military", I wrote in *The Times*. "In Russia communism, nationalism and militarism are all entwined in a system of coercion and privilege sustained by the police and the armed forces. What is remarkable is that the generals and marshals have been making politically charged statements on East-West issues." . . . "It is too early to say whether Mr Andropov has bungled the crisis by comparison with Khrushchev's U2 crisis or Brezhnev's Czechoslovak crisis, but he has allowed Russia to appear inconsistent, foolish, callous and deceitful, reinforcing widely held views of Russian behaviour, while in turn Russians have had their prejudices about America reinforced by men in uniform."

Andropov's reaction to the crisis was to push the military to the forefront, a position they were not used to occupying in Soviet political affairs, and the result was not altogether a happy one. There were confusing indications over whether Russia might take the ultimate step of withdrawing from the Geneva arms talks if NATO persisted with its dual track policy and stationed Pershing Two and Cruise missiles in West Germany to counter Soviet SS20s. Andropov referred nostalgically to the détente of the 1970s, laying the groundwork for a last minute compromise at Geneva, yet began to suggest in public statements—all released in his absence, since he was still out of the public eye—that any hope of "evolution for the better" in Reagan administration policies had been finally dispelled. The Reagan proposals at Geneva, he said, were "selfish, shortsighted and suicidal". Further indications of how far Andropov was prepared to go to ensure that the new NATO missiles were not installed was expected to come from his trip to Sofia in the second half of October.

The trip never took place. It was the first serious public sign that Andropov might be dying. There were further indications of a health crisis in the Kremlin as 1983, on the whole a dismal year for East-West relations, drifted towards its end. Andropov had still not been seen since August, and in a curious slip, reminiscent of Brezhnev's final days the previous year, a television announcer reading out Andropov's harsh response to American arms control proposals inexplicably inserted a passage on Warsaw Pact manoeuvres which bore no relation to the rest of the Andropov statement and did not appear in the public version in the press the following day. The broadcasting authorities were reprimanded for the slip-up, but the lingering impression was that all was not well in the Kremlin. Andropov was reported to have met President Ali Nasser Mohammad of South Yemen at the same time that he made his anti-Reagan statement, but there was no proof, and no indication of where the meeting had taken place. A visit by Andropov to Tbilisi was cancelled, and so was an impending visit to Moscow by General Jaruzelski of Poland.

For a while, at least, world attention was deflected from the Kremlin's problems in late October by the American invasion of Grenada, and the subsequent Caribbean crisis. There were in any case contradictory indications of what was going on behind the Kremlin wall, with Dr Yevgeny Chazov, the Politburo surgeon, conspicuously attending an international seminar in Moscow and making as clear as possible that his services were not urgently required. With the United States under fire for its "imperialist" behaviour in the Caribbean, Andropov chose the end of October to make a further statement to *Pravda* and Moscow television, issuing a final ultimatum to the West over the Geneva arms talks on medium range missiles, and confirming that the talks would be broken off if NATO went ahead with the deployment of Cruise and Pershing Two in December. This would make "continuation of the present talks impossible", Andropov said. Behind the scenes Soviet officials rubbed their hands over the Grenada crisis, obviously hoping that the Andropov *Pravda* statement and anti-American feeling in Western Europe would somehow sway public opinion against the NATO missile deployment.

This brief respite coincided however with the disclosure on the front page of *Pravda* that Andropov was suffering from "a cold", a phrase which quickly became a byword for the much more serious kidney and heart diseases from which he was in fact suffering. The admission that Andropov was unwell—a remarkable concession in the Communist system—came in a message to the Moscow conference of World Physicians for the Prevention of Nuclear War, co-chaired by Dr Chazov, in which Andropov regretted that a cold "has prevented me from meeting you personally in Moscow". "President Andropov, himself a product of the established system, has not yet shown the ability to overcome its fundamental inertia", *The Times* wrote in an editorial. "If he is to succeed in extricating the Soviet Union from its growing difficulties at home and abroad, he needs time and energy, but now seems to be running short of both." He was indeed, and, after the "cold" incident, Moscow was abuzz with speculation over whether Andropov would be fit enough to attend the annual Kremlin meeting marking the anniversary of the Revolution on 5 November and the Red Square parade two days later. If Andropov did fail to appear, would Chernenko or some member of the younger generation come to the fore to fill the vacuum? A year after the death of Brezhnev, Chernenko's mentor, both Brezhnev and Brezhnevism were hardly mentioned, and the somewhat absurd personality cult with which Brezhnev had surrounded himself when in power had been swiftly dismantled, with scarcely a trace remaining. Kremlin officials, who once had quoted Brezhnev, now referred anonymously to "decisions of the Twenty-Sixth Party Congress". The laxity and drift of the final Brezhnev years were still being contrasted with the Andropov period of austerity and hard work.

This did not mean that the Brezhnevites were defeated—far from it. They were beginning to gather their forces for the impending struggle for the succession. That struggle came out into the open when Andropov did indeed fail to appear at the Kremlin anniversary meeting of 5 November, and Chernenko walked into the hall to occupy his place as acting leader. As if to underline the fact that the younger generation was also very much in the running to succeed, the main speech at the anniversary meeting was made by Grigory Romanov, who punctuated his speech with references to Andropov which only served to underline the ailing leader's absence. Romanov warned the West that Moscow would take steps in response to the deployment of Cruise and Pershing by stationing its own missiles in Eastern Europe, adding, "we will not sit by with our arms folded". Up above him on the podium, Chernenko, looking fit, confident and ruddy faced, chatted amiably to Viktor Grishin, the veteran Moscow Party boss, and a key Chernenko ally, while further along the row Marshal Ustinov, who had helped Andropov to power and was playing a key role in the current power brokering, sat in uniform gazing at the neat and dapper figure of Romanov below.

The shockwaves which greeted Andropov's absence from the Kremlin meeting were reinforced when he failed to appear two days later on top of the Lenin mausoleum for the 7 November parade, normally an occasion for affirming national unity and military power and faith in the Communist future. Giant portraits of Andropov carried on floats, and blown-up quotations from his speeches, had much the same effect as Romanov's frequent references to the absent leader shortly beforehand. Some Soviet newspapers (though not *Pravda* or *Izvestiya*) deliberately omitted photographs of the parade the following day, an apparent reflection of the Kremlin's awareness that parading likenesses of Andropov only served to underline the growing crisis behind the scenes. But as if to stress that the succession was by no means cut and dried, the press failed to emphasize that Chernenko was acting leader in Andropov's place. Instead it gave equal prominence to Chernenko and the three younger contenders for power: Grigory Romanov, Geidar Aliyev—and Mikhail Gorbachov.

CHAPTER SEVENTEEN

The Death of Andropov

IN A BIZARRE incident which had about it an ominous symbolism, a protester set fire to himself on the steps of the Lenin mausoleum shortly after Red Square had emptied at the end of the 7 November Parade in 1983. The man became engulfed in flames while a fellow protester shouted something incomprehensible to passers by. What lay behind the incident was never clear, because both men were swiftly bundled into the ever-ready police vans and never seen again. But it was an unsettling sign of the times.

The traditional winter session of the Central Committee and the Supreme Soviet had still not taken place, and were clearly being delayed because of Andropov's deterioration. The overall impression was of an increasingly immobile and embittered old man who, after initial hopes and drive, had become obsessed with the issues of medium range missiles. Pershing rather than Cruise aroused most alarm in Russians—not surprisingly, since Pershing could in theory reach the Soviet Union within eight minutes, and the Kremlin was only too aware of the way in which its air defences had bungled the response to the Korean airliner with a whole two hours in which to make a considered decision. There were also repeated demands that British and French missiles had to be taken into account if the Geneva talks were to have any chance of success. At the end of November Andropov made yet another statement through the press and television, stating categorically that the Geneva talks had broken down, and indicating that Russia would not return unless the United States withdrew its missiles from Europe. He added that Moscow would hit back at Washington by deploying new Soviet missiles which could threaten American territory "from the oceans and the seas", an apparent reference to submarine launched missiles. The West Germans, Tass said shortly afterwards, had crossed the Rubicon by accepting Pershing missiles. "The Russians seem to have forgotten that when Caesar crossed the Rubicon in 49BC he was heading for victory", was the comment of one Western diplomat in Moscow.

And still the Central Committee Plenum did not convene. A report in a London paper that Yuri Brezhnev, son of the former president and

Deputy Minister for Foreign Trade, had shot and wounded Andropov— in itself absurd—reflected not only the genuine grievances of the Brezhnev family, but also the increasingly febrile atmosphere in which Soviet politics were taking place. Soviet sources were beginning to refer to "extraordinary tensions" in the leadership, with a number of factions emerging as the contenders for leadership taking stock of their positions. A curiously timed article in *Izvestiya* on 15 November, on the attempt on Lenin's life by Fanny Kaplan in 1918, stressed that even when incapacitated Lenin had continued to rule and to hold all the levers of power in his hand because of his "strong constitution", and there had been "no confusion in the ranks of the people". This was "highly topical even today", *Izvestiya* said. But the rumours that Andropov was losing control and had undergone a kidney transplant rather than "a cure for a cold" gathered strength as the factions crystallized. A key figure in the manoeuvring was General Vitaly Fedorchuk, the tough Interior Minister and a key Andropov ally. Fedorchuk was not in the Politburo, but he did wield enormous power and influence through his control of the police and the judiciary, while retaining his links with the KGB. As the factions formed, the Politburo approved new measures strengthening the ties between Fedorchuk's Interior Ministry and the Party structure. Although he was considered an Andropov man, Fedorchuk was now supporting the candidacy of Chernenko, who after all was unquestionably the beneficiary, and probably the initiator, of a campaign to restore the memory of Brezhnev which began with a fulsome tribute to the former leader in *Pravda* three days after Andropov failed to appear in Red Square.

The younger generation faction appeared to be headed both by Romanov and by Gorbachov, aged 60 and 52 respectively. Gorbachov, apparently conceding that he had little chance of becoming General Secretary this time round, formed a temporary tactical alliance with his powerful rival. Gorbachov had accompanied Romanov in June when Romanov toured Leningrad to say farewell to the city he had ruled for thirteen years, before moving down to Moscow to become a Central Committee Secretary. On 22 November *Pravda* marked the anniversary of Andropov's first speech as Party leader the previous year, but only mentioned his name once in a front page editorial. The press ignored altogether the anniversary of Andropov's election as General Secretary, while commemorating Brezhnev in terms which included criticism of the slackness and inefficiency of the Brezhnev years but also included praise for the former leader as "an outstanding figure" who had laid the basis for Soviet policy. The *Pravda* editorial on 22 November recalled

Andropov's promise at the November 1982 Plenum to improve Soviet living standards, and praised the subsequent drive for efficiency, labour discipline and economic growth, without referring specifically to Andropov himself.

On 24 November Andropov made another of his policy statements through the press, this time stating categorically in *Pravda* that the Geneva talks on medium range nuclear missiles had broken down, and that Russia would not return until and unless the United States withdrew all its missiles from Europe. Because Washington had torpedoed the chances of agreement, Moscow had decided that "further participation in these talks is impossible", and the Geneva negotiations could only resume if America and NATO showed "a readiness to return to the situation which existed before the deployment of new NATO missiles". But still Andropov himself did not appear. Only at the last minute did the government observe the one month ritual by announcing at the beginning of December that the Supreme Soviet would convene by the 28th. At a press conference on the future of Soviet-American arms talks on 5 December, Leonid Zamyatin, who claimed that Andropov had a cold, asserted that Andropov was "recovering from an illness" and carrying out a full range of Party and state functions. Was Zamyatin seriously suggesting that the Soviet leader had been absent for 110 days merely because he had a cold? Zamyatin, an irascible man at the best of times, grew red in the face and said angrily that reports of a serious operation were "insinuations which do not correspond to reality". But he added enigmatically: "I have already said all that it is possible to state officially", a remark taken to mean that Andropov's illness was more serious than had been officially admitted. (Zamyatin lost credibility over this, and was flatly challenged when he later claimed Dr Sakhorov was in good health).

Andropov was in fact at this crucial period in the Politburo hospital at Kuntsevo, on the outskirts of Moscow, receiving a stream of Politburo colleagues and other high level officials in his sickroom, and working on papers in his dressing gown. His mind was still active, although his body was fast deteriorating. To this extent Zamyatin was right in saying that Andropov was "carrying out state and Party functions". To the world at large, on the other hand, the general impression was that an announcement of Andropov's death could be expected at any moment, and there was talk in Moscow of the need for him to resign before he became fully incapacitated. When the two cosmonauts who had spent 249 days on the space station Salyut 7, and returned at the end of November, were awarded medals in the usual way, the awards were announced in the press, and there was no presentation ceremony at the Kremlin, as might normally have been expected. Pierre Trudeau, the Canadian Prime Minister, sought a meeting with Andropov for late December, but was told that Andropov would be "unable to receive him".

It was less than surprising when on 26 December the Central Committee finally convened in plenary session, and Andropov was not there. The announcement nonetheless came as a tremendous political shock. Andropov sent a message expressing his deep regret that he had been prevented from appearing in person by "temporary causes", instructing the Party from his sickbed "not to lose the tempo and the general positive intent to get things going". The speech he would have made at the Plenum was circulated to Central Committee members instead. "I have attentively studied all the materials which underlie the Plan for the coming year," Andropov wrote. "I have thought a great deal about them, and was preparing to speak and outline some of my ideas." This was obviously supposed to give the impression that Andropov had recently recovered and had then suffered a temporary relapse. The speech did have an impact, although not quite the impact it would have had if he had been able to deliver it in person. Strict implementation of the Plan, Andropov said, was a patriotic duty at a time when aggressive imperialism was aggravating the international situation. He called for harder work and extra labour discipline, sounding the familiar themes of the Andropov era in an almost desperate attempt to ensure that they survived despite his decline. There had been changes for the better, the absent leader said, adding that "this is only the beginning". The 1984 Plan to be adopted by the Supreme Soviet would raise consumer goods production while also maintaining the country's defences at a proper level. "I have to say bluntly that proper concern for reducing labour costs is not being shown in some sectors," he declared sternly, lashing out at incompetent managers who paid workers undeserved bonuses, at factories which failed to reduce costs by using their resources wisely, at absurd planning agency jargon, and at consumer goods shortages. "Inefficiency and ignorance of real market conditions mean that products are either scarce or pile up unwanted, and this gives rise to popular discontent," Andropov warned.

Perhaps the most convincing sign that Andropov was not finished yet was his ability to make several key changes in the Politburo at the December Plenum, including the promotion of Vitaly Vorotnikov and Mikhail Solomentsev to full Politburo membership. General Chebrikov, head of the KGB, became a candidate Politburo member. Solomentsev, at 70 something of a survivor from the old régime and a veteran *apparatchik*, was not a man particularly identified with Andropov. But Vorotnikov—candidate Politburo member since the previous June Plenum—clearly was one of Andropov's right-hand men and a potential holder of high office in government. Equally, General Chebrikov was unquestionably a close Andropov associate, having served as his deputy in the KGB for thirteen years. Chebrikov had begun his career in the Ukraine, where he was linked with Brezhnev, but his KGB links with Andropov were even stronger. Vorotnikov was 57, Chebrikov 60. In another significant move Yegor Ligachov, who was to play a crucial role in both the Andropov and Gorbachov eras and later to become second in command to Gorbachov in the Party hierarchy, was moved from the relative obscurity of Tomsk in Siberia, where he had been a local official, to become a Central Committee Secretary in charge of Party cadres, thereby gaining a crucial role in the Andropov purge of Brezhnev era officials.

The Supreme Soviet session which met on 28 December was a curiously lame occasion. It was dominated, like the Central Committee Plenum the previous day, by a man who clearly still had the power and the strength of character to shape the Russia of the future and whose spirit hung over the hall like an invisible presence as the snow drifted past the high windows of the Great Kremlin Palace. All the members of the Andropov generation were there—Nikolai Tikhonov, Andrei Gromyko, Marshal Ustinov and, of course, Chernenko. Down in the hall a ghost from the past appeared in the form of Andrei Kirilenko, once Brezhnev's chosen successor but removed from the Politburo by Andropov the previous year. Kirilenko walked among the 1,500 deputies, occasionally glancing up at the platform at those who now held power. Also down in the hall was Marshal Ogarkov, in uniform, gripping the elbows of fellow deputies, and sitting as he always did, at a desk completely uncluttered by unnecessary papers, his hands gripping the sides of the desk as he listened in obvious boredom to Nikolai Baibakov, the head of GOSPLAN, making his ritual incantation of industrial statistics for the following year. Speaker after speaker in the formal debates which followed referred repeatedly to Andropov and his policies, with economic officials outlining a programme designed to yield an annual growth rate of four per cent, twice the rate of the previous year and (if fulfilled) a considerable improvement on the final Brezhnev years. The Supreme Soviet foreign policy statement was read out by Boris Ponomaryov, head of the International Department, and a candidate Politburo member, which again served only to underline Andropov's absence. The statement condemned the Reagan administration's "reckless and bellicose" policies, but expressed the hope that the Stockholm Disarmament Conference and other East-West forums would lead to a change for the better in the international situation.

It was clearly a provisional statement, made by a provisional administration. The invisible Andropov sent the Supreme Soviet deputies his best wishes for the new year, but many in the hall, not to mention many Russians outside it, doubted whether he would live to see it. This feeling was reinforced when, on 1 January 1984, *Pravda* carried the text of a message congratulating Fidel Castro, the Cuban leader, on the 25th anniversary of his rule, and the telegram was signed by the leadership collectively rather than by Andropov personally. Similarly a telegram to the Sultan of Brunei was sent in the name of the Praesidium of the Supreme Soviet rather than Andropov as head of state. It was announced that Andrei Gromyko would meet George Shultz in Stockholm on 18 January for the first East–West encounter since the Korean airliner crisis the previous September.

The Andropov "limited industrial experiment" came into force at the beginning of January, confined to five industrial ministries and designed to show results over five years. It was a pale echo of the 1965 Kosygin economic decentralization measures, and Soviet officials made it clear that although managers had the power to sack surplus manpower under the Andropov scheme, the sacked workers would be reabsorbed into understaffed industries rather than becoming unemployed. Otherwise the measures boiled down to a limited delegation of powers to factory managers over resource allocation, production decisions, investment and the use of profits, with the central planning mechanism retained if not reinforced.

Two weeks later the editor of *Pravda*, Viktor Afanasyev, claimed that Andropov had been suffering from a kidney complaint complicated by influenza but "would reappear shortly". Rumours of the first COMECON summit to be held for twelve years waxed and waned. Clearly no summit, whether of COMECON or the Warsaw Pact, could possibly be held in the circumstances of Andropov's continuing absence.

The machinery of government rolled on regardless. Andropov was even named as a candidate for the Supreme Soviet elections in the Proletarski district of Moscow on 4 March. Whether he bothered to prepare his election address is not known; at all events he did not live to deliver it. Potential foreign visitors to Moscow began to wonder who would receive them in the Kremlin. "Mrs Thatcher could visit Moscow later this year," I wrote in the *Sunday Times*, "but last night it was not clear whether she would be going for a summit with President Andropov or to attend his funeral." The immediate cause of alarm was the cancellation by Marshal Ustinov of a longstanding visit to India, allegedly because of Marshal Ustinov's "domestic concerns". This evidently referred, not to problems in the Ustinov household, but to the crisis in the Kremlin as Andropov's illness reached a critical stage at the beginning of February. The streets of Moscow remained eerily calm, with no unusual activity, no lights burning in the Central Committee, and no extra troops or soldiers on the street.

But behind the scenes there was political turmoil. Younger Soviet officials began putting it about that Andropov's chosen successor, whether in a formal political testament or simply by understanding, was Mikhail Gorbachov, despite his relative youth. By now, sources pointed out, Gorbachov was not only the Politburo expert on agriculture but also had responsibility for cadres and some industrial matters. Moreover he had master-minded the internal Party elections in the autumn, together with Yegor Ligachov, and the Party purge had ended with the replacement of over 20 per cent of Party secretaries at the OBKOM level. Most of the new men in the OBKOMs were in their forties or fifties, and many could eventually expect to serve on the 300-man Central Committee. Surely the man who commanded the loyalty of the new generation of officials, who represented the future of Russia, and who moreover was Andropov's own choice for leader, was destined to succeed to the office of General Secretary? But as the funeral music began to be played on Moscow Radio on 9 February, and Soviet television altered its programmes in the time honoured indication of a death in the Kremlin, Chernenko and the Old Guard *apparatchiks* had quite different ideas.

CHAPTER EIGHTEEN

Chernenko in Charge

ANDROPOV HAD BEEN seriously ill for about half of his fifteen months in power. In February 1983, when he had been in the Kremlin for only a few months, Andropov had to use a kidney dialysis machine as his condition deteriorated, and by autumn, as we have seen, he was confined to a Kremlin hospital on the outskirts of Moscow. By October Andropov had had the kidney operation which Kremlin officials so strenuously and pointlessly denied at the time, and was more or less permanently attached to the dialysis equipment. The constant stream of messages and statements in his name in the Soviet press helped to give the illusion that he remained politically active, and the events of the autumn and winter of 1983–4 did indeed bear his stamp. It was a remarkable reflection of the awe in which he was held that he continued to direct policy from his sick-bed, summoning Politburo members—and above all Mikhail Gorbachov, his young protégé—for consultations at the Kuntsevo Hospital. But the end came at the beginning of February, when he entered a coma from which he never recovered, and when Andropov's death was announced on 11 February many Russians who had had their hopes raised by his programme of action were fearful of a return to the old days of stagnation and corruption.

As a man who knew the true situation in Russia from his time at the KGB, and who was not afraid to draw attention to the gap between the self-comforting fantasies of Soviet propaganda and the dismal reality of Soviet life, Andropov had aroused hope and expectation both in Russian intellectuals and in ordinary working class people. He had begun the vital process of generational change, promoting the men who were later to form the kernel of the Gorbachov team: Yegor Ligachov, Nikolai Ryzhkov, Vitaly Vorotnikov, and others. He was impatient, knowing— as he told a leading Moscow intellectual—that his action programme needed at least ten years to be properly carried out, whereas his time was in fact distinctly limited. Kremlin doctors told him he might have only five years to live when he took power in 1982. As it turned out, he had even less time at his disposal. He impressed Russians by living modestly, both at his VIP apartment on Kutuzovsky Prospekt and at his dacha outside Moscow at Barvikha, and by concentrating on what needed to be done to pull Russia into the 21st century rather than on his own personality as previous leaders had done.

Chernenko, by contrast, was a man who made most Russians' hearts sink. His first appearance before the nation, at Andropov's funeral, was a pathetic performance. The doddery Chernenko was unable to raise his hand in salute as the clock on the Spassky Tower chimed in the chilly February air and the guns of ships on the river boomed in honour of the dead leader. It was Andrei Gromyko, the veteran Foreign Minister, who appeared fit, alert and in command, and Gromyko's eulogy for Andropov was clearly intended to contrast the intellectual and political quality of the late leader with the mediocrity and unsuitability of the man who now stood in his place on Red Square.

Chernenko won power, as Stalin had done so many years before, by mastering the administrative machine and exploiting the loyalty of second rank and second rate Party bureaucrats who owed him their careers and their allegiance. He had manipulated the levers of the Soviet political system brilliantly, but was not himself a brilliant, innovative or forceful man. He was mediocrity raised to the highest office in the land, and although the system was arguably designed to have precisely this result, the effect was extremely depressing for those who had been encouraged by the Andropov phenomenon, which now began to look like an aberration from the normal pattern of Soviet politics. Party *apparatchiks* throughout the country, on the other hand, were secretly delighted that their futures were no longer in jeopardy and that demands of imagination and innovation beyond their powers were no longer being made of them.

Chernenko had no programme of action, indeed very little programme at all. To some extent the Andropov policies continued as before, with Soviet industry going through the motions of following the economic experiments laid down by Andropov. Anti-corruption cases which were already in the judicial pipeline were carried to their logical conclusion. These included the case of Yuri Sokolov, the manager of Gastronom No. 1, Moscow's main grocery store, who despite Chernenko's protection was finally executed for embezzlement, and Nikolai Shcholokov, the disgraced Interior Minister, who committed suicide during Chernenko's time in office and was buried without the usual honours. But the country was again drifting, as it had during the final Brezhnev years. Andropov's plans for drastic reductions in the cumbersome and overmanned bureaucracy were quietly shelved, with a return to the previous Soviet practice whereby officials were guaranteed sinecures for life.

And yet, paradoxically, it was under Chernenko that foreign policy took on a new lease of life, not the least in the sphere of Soviet-American relations, which had suffered such damage under Andropov despite the high hopes of the immediate post-Brezhnev period. As Chernenko moved into the General Secretary's office in February 1984, many observers in Moscow noted that the Andropov era had seen both the collapse of the Geneva talks on medium range and strategic missiles, and the icy superpower atmosphere which followed the Korean airliner crisis of September 1983. Chernenko, on the other hand, was closely associated with the policy of détente pursued by his lifelong mentor, Leonid Brezhnev, and appeared to have a sentimental as well as political attachment to the concept of peaceful coexistence with the West, particularly the United States.

The first public indication that Chernenko was in an advantageous position in the power struggle came when he was named as chairman of the commission in charge of Andropov's funeral, usually a reliable pointer to the succession process. Andropov had headed the funeral commission after the death of Brezhnev. The thirteen man Politburo, with Marshal Ustinov once again playing the role of kingmaker, had decided that the younger generation headed by Mikhail Gorbachov and Grigory Romanov should for the time being be passed over in favour of a fellow member of the Old Guard who was likely, after all, to prove an interim leader. His uncertain gait and shortness of breath in the days following Andropov's death suggested that Chernenko, like Andropov himself, was not in the best of health.

A medical bulletin signed by Dr Chazov and published in the Soviet press underlined the frailty of the generation which still held power in Moscow. It said that Andropov had suffered from fluctuations of blood pressure and diabetes complicated by chronic kidney insufficiency, and that he had died from heart and respiratory failure. The bulletin confirmed that Andropov had needed dialysis treatment from February 1983 onwards, and while the treatment had initially been effective, his condition had worsened towards the end of January 1984 with "degenerative changes in internal organs and progressive hypotonia". The announcement, read out on Moscow radio and television, informed the Soviet people "with great sorrow" that Andropov, described as "an outstanding leader of the Soviet Communist Party and the state" had died at 4.50 p.m. on the afternoon of Thursday 9 February after a long illness. "The name of Yuri Vladimirovich Andropov, a staunch fighter for the ideas of Communism and peace, would always remain in the hearts of the Soviet people and all progressive humanity," the announcement said. In an address to the Soviet people the Kremlin called for national unity "in these dark days", and pledged commitment to a policy of "peace, restraint and vigilance designed to thwart the designs of imperalism and consolidate the country's defensive might." As in previous succession crises, the Kremlin statement described the leadership as collective and said that Moscow remained committed to a policy of détente, adding: "we want to live in peace with all countries and co-operate with governments prepared to work honestly and constructively in the name of peace". It noted that Andropov had secured a "confident advance" in economic and social policies during his brief period in office and referred to his management reforms and his discipline campaigns, describing him as "a principled and modest leader" who had been close to the working people.

The leadership was not as panic-stricken this time as it had been at the death of Brezhnev, which after all had followed a period of thirty years during which no Soviet leader died in office. Announcements of Andropov's death were followed on television by a return to coverage of the Winter Olympics at Sarajevo in Yugoslavia and other normal scheduled programmes. Mourning in Moscow was distinctly low key and shops and theatres on the whole remained open, except in the centre near Red Square, which was sealed off by troops, police and civilian auxiliaries (*Druzhiniki*) with red armbands on. As we passed through numerous police cordons for the second time in two years to attend the lying-in-state at the Hall of Columns, a young policeman checking my pass in an otherwise deserted street near the Kremlin remarked: "We have been through this all before", when I commented on the relative political calm. At the Hall of Columns itself a middle aged woman in a sheepskin coat said, with a bit of prompting, that this was "the end of an era". "He was part of our lives for a long time," she said thoughtfully. "Now I feel simply sad. Andropov was a good and strong man, but he did not have enough time." Even the black-edged flags hanging from Moscow's gargantuan public buildings seemed to have an understated air, fluttering in the icy breeze but not dominating the scene. At the Hall of Columns itself an apparently endless stream of factory workers and soldiers shuffled forwards through the crystal clear winter air towards the ornate doorway, almost as a matter of routine.

Inside the hall, the chandeliers covered in black crepe cast a faint glow on the white and waxen face of Andropov, whose body lay on a flower-covered bier, though without the vast number of medals which had lain at the feet of Brezhnev. The mourners included Igor Andropov, the late leader's son, a member of the diplomatic service who had been Soviet delegate to the Stockholm disarmament conference. Igor Andropov had left Sweden for Moscow the previous Tuesday, two days before Andropov breathed his last, one of the first signs that the final crisis was at hand. At the Hall of Columns Igor, later to be named Soviet Ambassador to Greece, sat with his hands in his lap staring through his spectacles at the flower-covered bier. Not far away Konstantin Chernenko stood without a trace of a smile on his high cheekboned face as he gazed at the coffin of his former rival, displaying nothing of the emotion he must have felt at the Politburo decision to hand him supreme power only fifteen months after he had been written off as a political has-been. Also in the room was Andropov's widow Tatiana, the first official public confirmation that Andropov had a wife at all—a remarkable insight into the traditional secrecy which surrounds the private lives of all Soviet leaders. It was some time, indeed, before it became officially known that Chernenko, too, had a wife, the grandmotherly Anna Dmitrievna, who at this stage remained as shadowy a figure as Andropov's wife before her.

"The Brezhnev age has resumed", one Western diplomatic observer commented when the news of Chernenko's selection came. Others openly hoped that Chernenko would prove to be "the Malenkov of our time", a reference to the fact that Georgy Malenkov had only briefly held power in the Kremlin after the death of Stalin before being eased out by Khrushchev. "He is only formally Number Two", liberal intellectual friends assured us, and themselves; "he is the obvious choice for acting leader". In the sixties and seventies Chernenko had risen as Brezhnev rose, and fallen with him when Brezhnev suffered setbacks. Only in 1982, after the death of Mikhail Suslov, had Chernenko become a figure in his own right, taking over from Kirilenko to become the second most senior Central Committee Secretary. But there were fears that Chernenko, unlike Malenkov, might prove to be more than an interim leader and would prove effective against those, such as Gorbachov, who were fighting to preserve Andropov's somewhat tenuously-rooted reform programme and anti-corruption drive.

Chernenko's biography showed that no political figure reaches the very top in the Kremlin without both political skill and ruthlessness. Chernenko's career demonstrated the danger of underestimating a man of resourcefulness and singleminded ambition, who made his way to the top by choosing the right patron. Chernenko was born on 24 September 1911 in distant Siberia, in the village of Bolshaya Tyes, in the region of Krasnoyarsk. His was a lonely upbringing in the depths of the Russian empire; Chernenko's mother died when he was only a small boy. By the time of the Revolution in far away Petrograd in 1917, Chernenko was only six years old. He left school at the age of twelve and joined the newly formed Komsomol because—so he later claimed—he "felt the fresh winds of the Soviet order and envisaged the country's radiant future". He served in the border guards in Kazakhstan on the Chinese border in the 1930s, an episode of which the Soviet press was later to make much in order to compensate for Chernenko's lack of a war record. He then became regional Party Secretary in Krasnoyarsk, professing to find the world of Party officialdom "engrossing", and stayed in Siberia during the war to supervise evacuees—and labour camps.

In 1948 Chernenko went to Moldavia, formerly Bessarabia, on the borders of Romania, and it was here that his long association with Brezhnev began. Two years later, in 1950, Brezhnev, who was party chief in Moldavia at the time, made Chernenko head of propaganda. Brezhnev's protégé, conscious of the fact he was not an educated man, took a correspondence course at Kishinev Pedagogical Institute (although in the eyes of Party intellectuals this never quite counted as a higher education). In 1956, when Brezhnev went to Moscow, he took Chernenko with him to work in the Central Committee propaganda section, and from then on the fortunes of the two men were inextricably entwined. It was always Chernenko who was at Brezhnev's elbow, running his private office when Brezhnev was President of the Soviet Union, and later when Brezhnev had achieved the post of General Secretary. It was always Chernenko who was leaning to speak in his master's ear, shuffling his papers, carrying his briefcase, ensuring that his cigarette-dispensing machine was in order, filling his glass of water. Because of this role as the leader's *chef de cabinet*, Chernenko was not taken seriously by many ambitious Party leaders, not even when he was brought into the Politburo by Brezhnev.

This man, once dismissed as an administrator *par excellence*, now held the reins of power and commanded the destiny of Russia at a time of tense East-West relations. The Central Committee and the Politburo took five full days after Andropov's death to come up with the name of Chernenko, and Party sources confirmed that his nomination had not been uncontested within the inner councils of the Party. There was an important faction which felt that Andropov's work should be continued by someone like Gorbachov. But with the traditional instincts of a Kremlin leadership faced with the death of a forceful leader, the Old Guard plumped for continuity and caution, knowing full well that Chernenko's stewardship might not last for all that long. In his acceptance speech to the Central Committee, Chernenko deliberately spoke of continuity, but also of caution, too much so for those like Gorbachov who hoped to take up where Andropov had left off. "It is necessary to evaluate realistically what has been achieved," Chernenko said, "without exaggerating and also without belittling it. Only this approach prevents mistakes in politics, the temptation to indulge in wishful thinking." This seemed a clear hint that excessive hopes had been placed in Andropov's tentative reform measures. Significantly, Chernenko referred to dissatisfaction among the cadres—meaning middle and lower level Party and government personnel—over Andropov's tactics of bringing in technocrats and specialists to key economic and administrative posts over the heads of run-of-the-mill *apparatchiks*. This practice of replacing personnel "harbours the danger of weakening the role of Party committees as bodies of political guidance," Chernenko said. He praised Andropov's measures to intensify economic development and accelerate the introduction of new science and technology into production, and agreed that the whole system of economic machinery needed "serious restructuring". "Work in this direction has only been started," the new leader said. But he added pointedly: "we would be well advised to observe in this field the old wives' saying, look before you leap." This made Chernenko's praise of his predecessor for achieving a great amount of work in a "short, painfully short time", and his vow to build on the "new and fruitful things Andropov has introduced", somewhat insincere.

On foreign affairs, Chernenko told Western leaders what they wanted to hear: that détente could and would be revived. Chernenko attacked the "reckless, adventurist actions of imperialism", and vowed "to see to it that our country's defence capacity is strengthened". But the thrust of his remarks was in favour of the détente policy identified with Brezhnev. He made no reference at all to the deterioration of Soviet-American relations under Andropov, or to the collapse of the Geneva arms talks, preferring instead to stress that Moscow was "open to peaceful mutually beneficial co-operation with all states" and "serious equal and construc- tive talks". Russia would restrain "hot-headed imperialists", but would "co-operate in full measure with those states prepared to reduce tensions through practical deeds". His election as General Secretary, Chernenko told the Central Committee, was a great honour and an enormous responsibility, and there was "important and exceptionally difficult work" to be done. The Politburo and the Central Committee had to act "in concord and unity", an appeal to the younger generation to work with him rather than undermine his period in office.

As world attention focused on the Andropov funeral and Chernenko's meetings with world leaders, it emerged that a bargain had been struck during the five-day gap between the death of Andropov and the succession of Chernenko, with Gorbachov, Romanov and other members of the younger generation agreeing to wait their turn, on the clear understanding that Chernenko's period in office would be finite. Chernenko was nominated for the post of Party leader by Nikolai Tikhonov, the Prime Minister, now 78. There was historical irony here; when Brezhnev died, it was Tikhonov who put forward Chernenko, only to have his proposal overturned by Ustinov, who revealed that Andropov had already gathered the necessary support. There had been repeated rumours during Andropov's stewardship that Tikhonov would be replaced by a younger man, but here he was, still Prime Minister, and able finally to propel Chernenko into the Number One slot. Chernenko, Tikhonov said in his nomination speech, had known "hard peasant labour" as well as Party work, and was a talented organizer, an ardent propagandist and a Lenin-type leader in the mould of both Brezhnev and Andropov.

None of this was accepted by the majority of Russians, and for that matter it aroused scepticism in the Party itself. The world could see in mid-February 1984 that a wheezing old man of limited abilities had gained power in the Kremlin as a compromise candidate, largely because he had been acting leader under Andropov and had been confirmed in that place by the powerful Old Guard of Gromyko, Tikhonov and Ustinov. From the very beginning Chernenko had an image problem which was only intensified by his meetings with Western leaders after the funeral ceremonies on Red Square. Only George Bush, the American Vice President, was boyishly optimistic, as he had been during the funeral of Brezhnev and the accession of Andropov fifteen months before. After half an hour of talks with Chernenko, Bush said he thought the "good mood and excellent spirits of the meeting" could lead to an improvement in East-West relations. Bush went out of his way to contradict the emerging impression of Chernenko as an interim and somewhat ineffectual leader, an impression which gained ground during the lying-in-state of Andropov at the Hall of Columns. Although younger contenders for power such as Gorbachov, Aliyev and Vorotnikov were placed fairly low down in the pecking order, with the Old Guard dominating the scene, it was Gorbachov and other Andropov protégés who comforted the obviously distressed Andropov family: his son Igor, his daughter Irina and his widow Tatiana Filipovna, a clear signal to television viewers that the younger leaders represented the Andropov legacy and hence the future of Russia. But Chernenko, Bush told reporters, had appeared self-assured, had "run the agenda" during the meeting and had behaved "graciously" responding to Bush's remarks without reference to notes.

Bush's portrait turned out to be rosier than the facts justified. The truth was that Chernenko relied heavily on Gromyko and Gromyko's expertise in foreign affairs, an area in which Chernenko's own experience was distinctly limited. As we stood in the ornate splendour of St George's Hall in the Kremlin, where the Tsars had once received guests, to watch Chernenko, Gromyko and Tikhonov receiving their long line of guests, the word that came to mind was "gerontocracy". The succession struggle was continuing despite the choice of Chernenko. Gorbachov and Romanov would now be seen as rivals not only of Chernenko but also of each other, and rather than settling down after President Andropov's long absence to cope with serious domestic and foreign policy issues, the Soviet leaders continued to devote a disproportionate amount of their time to promoting their own careers.

At St George's Hall, as the world's leaders filed up the carpeted stairs and under the chandeliers, past the great marble plaques with the names of Tsarist and Soviet regiments on them, Chernenko gave little hint of what his foreign policy would be. This was in contrast to the Brezhnev funeral, which Andropov used to send signals to China, America and Afghanistan. At the funeral on Red Square, under a bright and frosty sky in which the clouds had again been dispersed by chemicals seeded at dawn from the aeroplanes of the Soviet meteorological office, Chernenko climbed to the top of the mausoleum and spoke in a thin and hesitant voice as the Spassky Tower clock struck noon. He stumbled now and then as he lost his place in the funeral oration, and, wheezing badly, called for a "realistic and honest dialogue" with the West. Andropov's relatives and fellow Politburo members paid their last respects as Andropov's body made its last journey to the plot reserved for him at the rear of the Lenin mausoleum, by the Kremlin wall. Mrs Margaret Thatcher, the British Prime Minister, repeated her desire for dialogue, since Russia and the West "had to live on the same planet", but noted that progress in East-West relations would be a "long, slow task with setbacks and interruptions". A start had been made, Mrs Thatcher said, and there was "a new confidence" in East-West relations, but results would be seen "over years rather than months". This seemed to augur badly for Chernenko, who looked increasingly as though he might last months rather than years.

This impression was reinforced by the other funeral orations on Red Square, made by Marshal Ustinov and Andrei Gromyko in strong clear voices. Like Chernenko, they called for peace with the West combined with strong Soviet defences. But the most striking speech was by Gromyko, who eulogized Andropov as a man of remarkable intellectual ability and great personal charm, neither of which qualities could be easily discerned in the elderly figure in the shiny blue suit who now stood beside Gromyko as Russia's new ruler. Foreign leaders were polite as they left for home, with Pierre Trudeau of Canada noting that Chernenko had "lowered the megaphones". *Pravda* carried three columns of congratulatory messages on its first and second pages. Some Kremlin officials even openly pinned their hopes and career prospects on Chernenko; Ivan Kapitonov, Secretary for Personnel noted during a speech for the coming Supreme Soviet elections that Chernenko was a man of "rich and versatile experience", and Mikhail Zimyanin, of the Propaganda Department, said Chernenko's acceptance speech to the Central Committee had been "enthusiastically received", which was something of an overstatement. Yet it was not long before rumours began to surface that Chernenko, unlike Brezhnev and Andropov before him, might not become President, or chairman of the Praesidium of the Supreme Soviet, and that the powers of Party leader, Head of State and Prime Minister might again be separated. Elections for the new Supreme Soviet were in full swing, and the Supreme Soviet would convene in March to decide the issue of the Presidency. Partly because of their obvious stature during Andropov funeral, the names of both Gromyko and Ustinov were openly mentioned in both Party and government circles as candidates for the post of head of State.

Only a few days after Andropov's funeral on 14 February, the official pamphlet on the extraordinary Central Committee Plenum which had elected Chernenko, issued by Politizdat, revealed that Tikhonov and Chernenko were not the only speakers to have addressed the Plenum. Gorbachov made closing remarks at the meeting which had not been reported by *Pravda* and the Soviet press at the time. Seven of the twelve man Politburo were 70 or older—in most cases older—and the Old Guard felt that Gorbachov posed a threat. The initial suppression of Gorbachov's remarks, which were in themselves fairly innocuous, was otherwise inexplicable. Gorbachov's speech, which took up only two pages of the official account of the plenum, described the election of a General Secretary as a "responsible moment in the lives of the Party and people". Gorbachov called for unity and unanimity, and stressed continuity, putting the leadership choice in the context of the Twenty-Sixth Congress of the Party, and the Central Committee Plenums of November 1982 and June and December 1983—in other words, the

Brezhnev and Andropov eras. Gorbachov ended with a call to the Central Committee members to "go back to their places of work in a spirit of unity", having unanimously elected Chernenko as Party leader.

Since there was nothing remotely offensive to Chernenko and the Old Guard—if anything quite the reverse—the obvious conclusion was that Gorbachov had either made remarks which did not appear in the printed version, or that the Old Guard was so nervous of his continuing influence in the Party that it had decided to ignore Gorbachov's contribution to the Plenum, but was then obliged to place it on record when the full account was published in pamphlet form. Gorbachov made prominent appearances on television in the days following Chernenko's election. Curiously, the first Politburo meeting to be held under Chernenko's chairmanship, on the first Thursday following the funeral, was not reported by *Pravda* and Soviet television in the way which had become customary under Andropov. Chernenko was a leader who, although described by visiting statesmen as "authoritative", "strong willed", "practical and humorous", not to mention "cordial" and "refreshingly free of polemics", came across to the Russian people as a man who could barely walk or talk, who on Red Square lost his place in his speech several times, and who kept mopping his face with his handkerchief. At the reception at St George's Hall he walked unaided in and out of the room, his hands stuck deep in the pockets of his blue suit; but he was still stiff and short of breath, a symptom of the disease identified by Dr David Owen, the leader of the British Social Democrats and a member of the British delegation, as emphysema, an ailment involving fibrosis of the lungs with heart complications.

Hardly surprisingly, the KGB was less than happy with the rise of a man who done his best to frustrate Andropov's drive against incompetence and corruption. Security, initially lax following Andropov's death, soon became far stricter amid a much tenser atmosphere. The five-day hiatus ended in a transition to a man who did not command the respect of Russia as a whole, or of key institutions like the KGB and the military. He was a man who had no war background or military service to his credit, and who had never actually run a farm or factory, or indeed done anything very much except run departments of the bureaucracy. Chernenko had come to power with the reputation of the consumer's champion, emphasizing the need for defence spending to go hand in hand with economic growth. But the watchwords of his régime were likely to be conservatism and ideological rigidity combined with the turning to the West promised in his initial speeches.

CHAPTER NINETEEN

The Chernenko Cult

IT WAS NOT long before the portraits of Andropov started to disappear from Moscow streets and offices, and roadside hoardings of quotations from his speeches vanished overnight. In their place appeared portraits of Chernenko's high-cheekboned, Siberian peasant features, together with quotations from his speeches embodying the new official wisdom. Chernenko's family began to come to the fore, a phenomenon reminiscent of the Brezhnev era rather than the Andropov era. *Pravda* carried a back-page article by Chernenko's daughter Yelena, a senior researcher at the Institute of Marxism-Leninism. The 13 February Plenum which elected Chernenko was increasingly referred to as the basis of all Soviet policy. On the other hand, the continuing influence of the Andropov protégés made itself felt in a decision to perpetuate Andropov's memory by giving his name to a number of schools, shops and factories, as well as to the thousand-year-old Volga city of Rybinsk, where Andropov had begun his political career in the 1930s. The same honour was accorded to a girls' school in the north Caucasus town where Andropov had worked as an apprentice screen projectionist in his youth, and Pioneer palaces and children's community centres at Petrozavodsk, the capital of Karelia, were renamed. A granite bust was erected at Nagutskoye, the tiny village on the railway where he had been born.

Nikolai Ryzhkov, one of the key Andropov supporters in the Central Committee Secretariat, gave an election address at Sverdlovsk in the Urals which made a passing reference to the "satisfaction" which had greeted Chernenko's election, but concentrated on the economic experiments begun under Andropov, which Ryzhkov said were bound to become "the basis for the entire national economy". Since Ryzhkov had responsibility for the economy in the Secretariat, this pointed to a policy struggle behind the scenes on the future course of Soviet domestic affairs. Similarly General Chebrikov, head of the KGB, had little to say in praise of the leader when he made his electoral address at Sukhumi in Georgia, concentrating instead on the dangers posed to Russia by imperialist intelligence services, and praising the KGB for having unmasked scores of Western agents in recent years.

The main question in the minds of Russian readers and viewers was whether Chernenko himself would be able to cast his own vote in the Supreme Soviet elections in March and make a purposeful speech—a sign that Chernenko was already regarded as a shaky leader only weeks after his triumph at the Plenum. Andropov himself had been put forward as a candidate at the election in order to prove (vainly as it turned out) that he remained politically active—although for the last few months of his rule the leader had only appeared as a two dimensional portrait waved at the end of sticks at televised Supreme Soviet election meetings. As if to demonstrate the nature of Soviet democracy, Andropov's place as candidate in the Proletarski District in Moscow was taken by a worker from a ball-bearings factory. But Chernenko was still due to stand at the Kuibyshev district, a sprawling area which included some of Moscow's most spacious parks but also some of its most dismal working class houses and factories. There was no doubt that Chernenko, and all the other candidates in the election, would win the traditional 99.9 per cent of the vote, since the vast majority were nominated by the Communist Party and the election was a pure formality. The question was whether Chernenko would appear for the traditional election rally in the Kremlin and the poll itself.

On 2 March Chernenko did appear at the Kremlin to make an election speech calling for the United States to follow its conciliatory rhetoric with concrete action in the interests of an improved East-West relationship. But Chernenko delivered the text so poorly that the message was almost lost. The Soviet Union, Chernenko said, wanted a drastic change in the East-West climate, and would respond to any positive moves from the United States. "It is up to Washington to act." Unfortunately the speech was broadcast live on Moscow television so that ordinary viewers could see how poor an orator Chernenko was as he stumbled over his text and mumbled inaudibly, running short of breath in mid-sentence. At one point there was an embarrassing pause of half a minute while he lost his place completely, and the Politburo members ranged behind him on the stage of the Palace of Congresses tried to pretend that everything was normal. When Chernenko finally resumed reading, he missed an entire page of his address, and it was only later, when Tass published the full text of his address, that it emerged that he had omitted a call to Washington to respond to Soviet initiative in freezing nuclear missile deployment. Chernenko accused America of pursuing a policy of blatant militarism, but also remarked, in a phrase which clearly was to be the hallmark of his rule, that "détente had struck deep roots".

On this showing, it was far from certain that Chernenko would be around long enough to ensure that détente was revived in the 1980s. Two days later, on March 4, Chernenko had trouble walking as he arrived at the polling station in Moscow to cast his vote in the Supreme Soviet elections. Accompanied by his wife, Anna Dmitrievna, Chernenko swept up to the Krasnaya Presnaya polling station in his black limousine surrounded by outriders and bodyguards, but had to be helped from his limousine up to the drafty hall where Russian VIPs cast the inevitable vote in favour, and could barely make it to the ballot box to insert his paper. Moscow intellectuals, already steeped in gloom by the dismal showing Chernenko was making as the nation's leader, were further depressed when one of Moscow's leading theatre directors, Yuri Lyubimov, was dismissed from his post at the celebrated avant garde Taganka Theatre while on a prolonged visit to the West, and then expelled from the Party. Lyubimov, an energetic, complex and vivid director, had been protected by Andropov, who was grateful to Lyubimov for having persuaded Andropov's children not to take up theatrical careers (Andropov's daughter Irina was married to a well known actor at the Mayakovsky Theatre).

Chernenko remained active in foreign affairs in March, despite his poor public performance, receiving Hans-Jochen Vogel, leader of the West German Social Democrats, and observing to the West Germans that superpower tensions were "dangerous but not irreversible". Nonetheless the main impression which emerged from the Vogel-Chernenko meeting was yet again that Chernenko had appeared short of breath and had to support himself on a chair back. Similarly, at the end of March, when the Central Committee held a meeting on agriculture addressed by Chernenko, the leader was shown on television leaning forward and supporting himself on the desk in front, once again speaking poorly with obvious shortness of breath. The main speech at the agriculture conference was made by Mikhail Gorbachov and not by Chernenko, and although both men called for "new methods", Gorbachov was clearly referring to the Andropov reforms and deliberately keeping them alive. In terminology which instantly reminded readers and viewers of Andropov, Gorbachov called for dynamism, initiative and discipline, and said officials should be "politically mature, literate and competent organizers with a feeling for the new", a sideswipe at the bureaucrats Andropov had tried to purge but who now felt protected by Chernenko. Gorbachov and like-minded Kremlin officials also stressed that the brigade system of payment by results favoured by the Andropov-Gorbachov team would be expanded, with brigades paid according to productivity and a distribution of profits to the best workers. In order not to be left behind with all this talk of new methods and new spirit, Chernenko himself noted that the 1982 food programme associated with Brezhnev was only the beginning, and that it needed a decisive improvement in management organization. "Frankly speaking, there is little time left," Chernenko said, perhaps mindful of his own lack of time. "It is vital to find urgent and thorough solutions."

The mortality of the older generation was underlined by the absence from the agriculture conference of Nikolai Tikhonov, the Prime Minister, who had overall responsibility for economic affairs, but was also a figure from the past rather than the future. "On nie tot", Russians said as they watched Chernenko's performance, a phrase literally meaning "he is not the one", although "he is not up to it", conveyed the meaning—and the implied comparison was with Andropov and Gorbachov. A photograph in the press of Chernenko posing as a proud grandfather, standing in shirt-sleeves with his grandson and his wife and daughter either side of him, appealed to Russians, as it conveyed an appropriate patriarchal image. But the positive overtones of this attempt to create a personality cult around Chernenko and his family were overshadowed by embarrassment as it became clear that Chernenko's abysmal performance during the funeral of Andropov had not been an aberration. It seemed increasingly likely that Chernenko would after all be made President as well as Party leader at the Supreme Soviet in April. But this was not confirmation of his power so much as a gesture to a man who was not likely to hold office for all that long.

Despite Moscow's insistence that détente had benefited mankind in the 1970s, Chernenko took a harsh and uncompromising line towards the United States in a front page interview with *Pravda* on 9 April. Russia would on no account return to the Geneva talks, he said, unless American missiles were first withdrawn from Western Europe. Despite the "peaceloving rhetoric" coming out of Washington, Chernenko declared, it was impossible to discern any signs that Reagan was ready to back up his words with deeds "however hard one tries". Chernenko denied that he waiting for the outcome of the American presidential election before reaching agreement with the United States. "Those who circulate such ideas either do not know our policy, or more probably deliberately distort it. Ours is a principled policy and is not subject to transient vacillations."

The following day, 10 April, Chernenko addressed the first full Central Committee Plenum to be held since his election, and there were definite signs of a growing personality cult around the new leader—yet Chernenko was unable to bolster his position by making changes in the

Politburo, and there were no policy innovations either. At the Plenum Chernenko promised not to relax his efforts in "improving the system of economic management and looking for new forms and structures". But he was being obliged to promise continuation of Andropov reforms somewhat reluctantly under pressure from Gorbachov, Vorotnikov and other members of the younger generation. Chernenko hinted at possible government changes when he said that the Supreme Soviet would approve the composition of the Council of Ministers, that officials had to show "personal creative initiative", and that there should be a "steady influx of fresh forces". But in fact there were no new faces either in the Government or in the Politburo, and in retrospect Chernenko's remark at the Plenum that in some cases the structure should be improved rather than shaken up took on new significance.

The following day, at the Supreme Soviet in the Great Hall of the Kremlin, Chernenko was duly elected Chairman of the Praesidium of the Supreme Soviet, or Soviet President, and was nominated for the post by the man who appeared most likely to succeed him: Mikhail Gorbachov. Tikhonov was confirmed as Prime Minister, even though he was 78, and even though Geidar Aliyev, the Deputy Prime Minister, had received growing publicity of a kind which suggested that he might be being groomed to take Tikhonov's place. Aliyev featured prominently with Gromyko at meetings with Colonel Mengistu, and had been highly visible when he accompanied Tikhonov to an international metal working exhibition in Moscow shortly before the Plenum. Yet in the event the Old Guard remained firmly in charge, symbolizing an administration of continuity rather than change.

For most Russians the Plenum and the Supreme Soviet took second place to the absurd attempt by *Red Star*, the armed forces newspaper, to extol Chernenko's role in the border guards in the thirties and thus add extra weight to the growing Chernenko personality cult. The paper published a 1930s group portrait identifying Chernenko as one of the soldiers in the back row. Underneath the photograph was an article recalling the performance of Chernenko's posting to Kazakhstan, on the Chinese border, which claimed that Chernenko had been a fine horseman and a crack shot when courageously fighting anti-Communist bandits on the Central Asian frontier. "He could fire accurately from a rifle or machine pistol, and his hand grenades never failed to hit their mark," *Red Star* said, arousing general hilarity in view of the striking contrast with Chernenko's shuffling gait and faltering delivery. This somewhat pathetic attempt to present Chernenko as a leader of superhuman qualities contrasted unfavourably with Andropov's austere and remote style, which involved keeping his personality and his family as much in the background as possible.

It was in a way a triumph for Chernenko that he should have become Party leader and President against all the odds, having been written off a year and a half after his defeat by Andropov. Gorbachov, speaking in a strong clear voice, said when nominating Chernenko that combining the functions of Party leader and President was of "tremendous significance" for Soviet foreign policy, which was "indivisible from Party policy", suggesting that Chernenko had been made President because Brezhnev and Andropov before him had combined the two posts. To some extent this was true, although Gorbachov's dictum on the desirability of combining the two jobs rebounded on him when he himself became Party leader the following year. Gorbachov chose not to take the title of Head of State, preferring instead to remove Andrei Gromyko from the Foreign Ministry and give him the title of President as political compensation.

Gorbachov praised Chernenko in his nomination speech as a "staunch fighter for Communism and peace" who had "outstanding political and organizational abilities and immense experience". This sounded more like an obituary than a nomination speech. Gorbachov recalled that Chernenko had been chairman of the foreign affairs committee of the Soviet of the Union, one of the Supreme Soviet's two chambers, a post to which Gorbachov himself now succeeded. This was more than purely symbolic; it made Gorbachov the official Number Two in the hierarchy, and confirmed that he now held the ideology portfolio in the Central Committee Secretariat.

That post had traditionally been associated with the foreign affairs committee chairmanship since the time of Mikhail Suslov. In his reply Chernenko said he was aware of his great responsibilities and of the need for "major, carefully considered decisions" to improve the economy, scarcely a reassuring form of words for the more ardent Andropov-style reformers. On foreign affairs Chernenko observed that Moscow was "firm and consistent" in its search for sensible agreements. Only a few days before, further signs of stormy waters in Soviet-American relations had arisen over the future of the 1984 Summer Olympics in Los Angeles, with the Soviet Union demanding an emergency session of the international Olympic Committee to discuss alleged violations of the Olympic Charter by the United States, which Moscow said had unleashed "an anti-Soviet campaign by reactionary forces" to the point where the security of participants in the Los Angeles games could not be guaranteed. It was the first firm hint that Moscow was about to cause an international sensation by boycotting the 1984 Games.

Unlike Andropov the previous year, Chernenko looked very pleased indeed to be President. He beamed, smiled, and waved delightedly to the deputies, holding his hands above his head in a kind of victory salute. Even his appearance was transformed, and although he still had to support himself on the backs of chairs as he walked stiffly down from the platform to the podium to make his acceptance speech and say what a high honour it was to be Head of State, he looked sun-tanned and even relatively fit. He had reached the pinnacle of power despite having been written off by those who thought of Brezhnev's office assistant and protégé as a figure of the past. Chernenko went to the podium again to nominate Nikolai Tikhonov as Prime Minister, or Chairman of the Council of Ministers, and although his voice was breathless and faint as usual, he did not lose his place in his text for once. Outside the Kremlin, on the streets of Moscow, giant red posters went up with quotations from Chernenko's speeches, the white text on a red background glistening in the spring sun after a burst of April rain.

The editor of *Izvestiya*, Lev Tolkunov, was eased out by Chernenko to be made chairman of the Soviet of the Union, one of the two chambers, a largely ceremonial post. Tolkunov, a former director of Tass, had been an Andropov appointee.

With the next Party Congress in 1986 in mind, Chernenko presided over the Party Commission formulating a new programme. In an address to ideologists working on the project, he noted that the capitalist system would eventually and inevitably succumb to Communism, but pointedly avoided giving a Khrushchev-style definite date either for a world Communist victory or for the achievement of the abundant society in Russia. It would be wiser, Chernenko said, to abandon the "superficial concept" of laying down a timetable for the transition for the supreme phase of Communism, something which had been mistakenly attempted during "a certain period of Soviet history". Chernenko went even further and told the meeting that although capitalism was of course unquestionably doomed, it was far from beaten yet and it possessed "quite substantial and far from exhausted reserves". There was a need to remove the "discrepancies" between Khrushchev's 1961 programme and the "real course of social development", and the authors of the new programme should aim at a bold and expressive picture of the future "without attempting to envision the details". At 72, Chernenko was no more likely than Khrushchev or Brezhnev to witness the advent of full Communism, defined in 1961 as a system in which the Soviet Union enjoyed higher wages, better housing and fuller shops than the West.

Chernenko was also, as it turned out, unable to preside over the Twenty-Seventh Party Congress in 1986, a task he was to hand on to his youthful successor, together with the modest draft programme.

As if to compensate for these intimations of mortality, the Chernenko personality cult, which had begun with *Red Star*'s extravagant praise of Chernenko's role in the border guards in the 1930s, took off with a vengeance in May 1984, beginning with Chernenko's visit to the giant Hammer and Sickle Foundry in Moscow on the eve of May Day. Andropov had made a much publicized visit to the Ordzhonikidze Engineering Works the previous year, and it was becoming almost obligatory for the Soviet leader to be seen talking to workers on the factory floor, a practice allegedly reminiscent of Lenin's personal style. Chernenko was not shown emerging from his black limousine at the Hammer and Sickle factory, largely because he had to be helped from the car by burly aides. His conversation with workers in hard hats inside the plant was painfully stiff and artificial, with none of the personal rapport with the working class which the Kremlin image-makers must have hoped would come across.

Apart from discussing wages and production methods with the workers in a staged conversation, Chernenko offered them a lecture on international affairs, declaring that confrontation in East-West relations could be turned into détente, but that the Soviet Union would "keep its gunpowder dry" in case the forces of Western imperialism proved stronger than Communism. He thanked thousands of Soviet patriots for offering to work longer hours and to set up a national defence fund. Russia's economic and defence capabilities were adequate, Chernenko said, although he admitted "far from everything has been done" to supply the population with food and consumer goods. That at least was something that the workers at the Hammer and Sickle factory could agree with, not that they were allowed to say so.

"You can't have a personality cult without a personality", was a widespread comment in Moscow, but to Chernenko this was obviously no obstacle. As he waved shakily from the top of the mausoleum on May Day, looking down over a sea of rippling red flags, and thousands of well-drilled workers marching under a sunny spring sky, the scene was dominated by giant portraits of himself and giant blown-up photographs of the *Pravda* report of his meeting with the steel workers at the factory. It was in striking contrast with the previous year's May Day parade, when Chernenko's absence had sparked off intense speculation about his political future. But when in mid-May King Juan Carlos became the first Spanish Head of State to visit Russia, the most striking fact to emerge from the Spanish royal visit was that Chernenko had suffered a relapse and was once again in poor physical condition, having to be helped out of his car and supported under each elbow. Chernenko's condition was strongly reminiscent of Andropov's disability during the visit to Moscow by President Koivisto of Finland, when photographs showed Andropov being helped down the stairs. This time the Kremlin were careful to ensure that there were no photographs, but the impression was similar. By the time Chernenko had completed his first 100 days, the most common observation in Moscow was not that he achieved so much in his first three months, or indeed that he had achieved anything at all, but rather that he had managed to make it this far.

CHAPTER TWENTY

Gorbachov on the Verge of Power

IN THE MIDDLE of June 1984, the shade of Yuri Andropov returned to haunt Chernenko, just as rumours were circulating in Moscow that Chernenko had fallen ill at the long delayed COMECON summit. The rumours were false, but the tribute to Andropov which appeared in the pages of *Pravda* was real enough. The article, entitled "A Life devoted to the people", marked what would have been Andropov's seventieth birthday, and was in marked contrast to the relative silence in the media over the legacy of Brezhnev. By now very few articles were extolling the praises of the Brezhnev years or Brezhnev's style of leadership; yet here was *Pravda* charting Andropov's rise to the top by way of his career at the KGB, and describing him as an experienced and wise leader who had understood the Soviet masses. Whereas Brezhnev had hardly been mentioned after his death in November 1982, and the anniversary of his death in November 1983 had passed with very little comment, Andropov's protégés, chief among them Mikhail Gorbachov, were clearly doing their utmost to ensure that Andropov's memory and achievements were kept alive under Chernenko. Even as Chernenko was opening the COMECON summit, a plaque bearing a portrait of Andropov was unveiled at No. 26 Kutuzovsky Prospekt, the block of flats where he and other Soviet VIPs kept their town residences. A similar plaque at the other end of the block commemorated the fact that Brezhnev had lived there, but it was striking that Andropov's memorial was surrounded by mounds of freshly cut red flowers days after the unveiling, whereas Brezhnev's commemorative plaque went virtually unnoticed.

Perhaps to counter the impression this made, the Soviet media gave massive coverage to Chernenko's talks with President Mitterrand of France, who visited Moscow towards the end of June. At the same time *Pravda* published a long and laudatory review of a collection of Chernenko's speeches, in glowing terms, under the title "Towards the perfection of developed socialism". The *Pravda* review described Chernenko's analysis of world events and Soviet domestic affairs as "comprehensive and profound", and said that his speeches and writings would greatly contribute to the elaboration of a new Party programme.

Curiously, Gorbachov did not occupy his by now familiar position as Kremlin Number Two in the Chernenko-Mitterrand talks; instead Geidar Aliyev was shown on television and in *Pravda* standing at Chernenko's right elbow, as if to emphasize that Gorbachov was not the only contender for the succession. Chernenko also made the point indirectly that the anti-corruption drive was not the monopoly of the Andropovites, and over a hundred top officials in Latvia were expelled from the Party for embezzlement and abuse of power. The Soviet press also reported widespread corruption in Uzbekistan and other Soviet republics.

Both officials in the Mitterrand party and Soviet officials were at pains to correct any lingering impression in the Western mind that Chernenko was a stiff figure lacking in authority. The Kremlin image-makers sought to convey the idea that during their private tête-à-têtes Mitterrand and Chernenko had discussed a thorough range of world issues without reference to advisors or prepared texts, and that Chernenko had been in complete command of Kremlin policy throughout rather than relying on senior aides such as Gromyko. Where has this idea come from, Soviet officials asked reporters testily, that Chernenko is a man of insular or parochial views? After all, he had served for many years at Brezhnev's side, they said, and was fully conversant with the major problems of East and West. The youthful Andropovites struck back at this attempt at image-making with an article in *Kommunist*, the Party's theoretical journal, which once again portrayed Andropov as the very model of a Soviet leader and an outstanding statesman who had managed during his brief period in office to "implant in our social life much that is novel and useful". If anything the eulogy in *Kommunist* was couched in even more glowing terms than the unusual tribute in *Pravda* marking Andropov's seventieth birthday.

Kommunist pointed to Andropov's efforts to speed up economic growth, strengthen discipline and enhance the responsibility of workers, key Andropovian themes which Chernenko had played down. The list of Andropov's sterling qualities seemed endless: his energy, his use of the creative initiative of the masses, his campaign against corruption, bribe-taking, embezzlement and excessive bureaucracy. The short-lived Andropov era had already led to policy shifts in the Soviet economy, the journal suggested, and had promoted the prestige of the Soviet system around the globe. Andropov had been "a Party man to the marrow of his bones, dedicated to the principle of collective leadership", *Kommunist* pointedly recalled, adding that when he took over in February Chernenko himself had acknowledged his predecessor's qualities both as a politician and as a man, saying that Andropov's merits had been "vividly demonstrated" in his activities as both Party leader and President.

Gorbachov remained away from the political limelight, relegated to the sidelines while Aliyev continued to hold centre stage, both during the Mitterrand visit and during subsequent visits by foreign statesmen. While the Chernenko-Mitterrand exchanges were the focus of world attention, Gorbachov was addressing the Supreme Soviet foreign affairs commission on the training of third world students in the Soviet Union, a subject which, as one Western diplomat remarked at the time, was "not exactly in the mainstream of Kremlin preoccupations". Chernenko and Gromyko dominated talks between the Soviet leadership and Sir Geoffrey Howe, the British Foreign Secretary, who arrived in Moscow at the beginning of July. Howe found the two men implacably negative on the question of a possible Soviet return to the Geneva arms talks and disappointingly suspicious about the United States' positive response to a proposal by Moscow for discussions on space weapons to begin in September. The West tried in vain to persuade Chernenko and Gromyko to back down from what Howe called "the politics of the empty chair" at Geneva. The Soviet leaders took the hardline view that Washington was laying down preconditions for the space weapons talks by linking them firmly with the abandoned talks on medium range and strategic missiles. The Russians had become increasingly preoccupied with the issue of space weapons, not only with anti-satellite systems but also with President Reagan's Strategic Defence Initiative (SDI), popularly known as the Star Wars concept, which he had put forward in a major speech in March.

The Soviet press ran a spate of articles warning Russians of the dangers of talking to foreign visitors to Moscow, on the grounds that many of them were spies. President Reagan unwittingly underlined the Kremlin's xenophobic message by making an ill-judged joke during a microphone test before a radio broadcast, remarking facetiously that he had signed legislation banning Russia forever and that the bombing would begin in five minutes. The Kremlin issued a grave statement deploring this invective, and accusing Reagan of blurting out what he really thought. "These blasphemous words, once uttered, have gone down in history and cannot be erased like the infamous Watergate tapes", was *Izvestiya*'s comment.

The sensation over Reagan's unfortunate joke was soon overtaken by fresh speculation about the health of the man in charge of the Kremlin's response to the Reagan administration. Chernenko went on holiday in

August to the Black Sea resort of Oreanda, shortly after the Mitterrand and Howe visits to Moscow, but had not been shown on television taking his ease in the summer sun. No sooner had he disappeared from Moscow than strong rumours about his ill health began to circulate. Rather as in the case of Andropov the previous year, this was the beginning of a series of rumours and reassurances, ending ultimately in the leader's decline and death, even though Kremlin officials were still trying to pretend that everything was normal within the leadership. As I found when I visited the Yalta area in August, the complex of white Politburo villas at Oreanda, high above the sparkling waters of the Black Sea, is hidden by high fences and lush foliage and well guarded by the security forces. What could not be hidden was that Chernenko, taxed by his series of visits by foreign statesmen, was using the services of top class clinics in the area which specialize in both cardio-vascular and lung complaints. Those few officials who admitted that Chernenko was receiving treatment insisted that he was merely undergoing "routine tests", but local residents at Yalta had heard reports from the Oreanda complex of a more serious setback. Back in Moscow the Kremlin resorted to the by now familiar device of publishing a series of messages in Chernenko's name in the Soviet press in an attempt to calm the rumours. *Pravda* published a front page message from Chernenko to an international conference on nuclear free zones in Manchester, clearly a desperate measure. Much in the same category was a message from the absent Chernenko to the Japanese publishers of his collected speeches. On 12 August, at the time he was taken ill, the Soviet press issued a reply from Chernenko to Sean McBride, the Irish president of the International Peace Bureau, maintaining that Russia was ready for good relations with the United States provided there was good will and concrete deeds on both sides.

In fact, during the August hiatus, power in the Kremlin was in the hands of Marshal Ustinov and Mikhail Gorbachov, who appeared to have regained his place as the acknowledged Number Two and to have elbowed Aliyev to one side. At the end of August Ustinov departed for Prague, a move which went some way towards dampening speculation about Chernenko's disappearance, which at this stage had lasted a month and a half. Kremlin sources revealed that Gorbachov was now chairing Politburo meetings. It was Gorbachov who saw Ustinov off to Czechoslovakia and who welcomed him on return a few days later. The pointers to a growing crisis in the Kremlin were clear: official accounts of the Politburo sessions began with a wholly artificial invocation of Chernenko's name, even though he had not been present, in one case noting that the Politburo session had "discussed and approved Konstantin Chernenko's proposals on the construction industry".

Speculation became feverish when Chernenko, who had received no visitors since Perez de Cuellar on 12 July, failed to appear for the opening of the grand style Friendship '84 Games, Russia's propaganda answer to the boycotted summer Olympic Games in Los Angeles. Even a front page "interview" with Chernenko in *Pravda* on 2 September on the crucial issue of Star Wars failed to dispel the mystery. Suspicions were aroused by the fact that Chernenko's return to Moscow had still not been announced two months after his departure for the Crimea. Chernenko had been hospitalized, officials confided, first in the Crimea and subsequently in the capital.

Chernenko's *Pravda* message was that the Soviet idea of resumed talks was to confine them to space weapons, whereas the United States wanted to replace the very subject of negotiation by including the disrupted Geneva missile talks as well. "The American approach is directly opposed to ours," he remarked. "So what would be the point of holding talks?" The only optimistic note, which held the key to the future, although little noticed at the time, was Chernenko's remark that if America and Russia did manage to reach agreement on Star Wars questions, this would facilitate a solution of limiting and reducing other armaments. "I would particularly like to emphasize that," Chernenko said, in what appeared to be an attempt to inject a personal note into the interview.

Vladimir Lomeiko, who had taken over from Leonid Zamyatin as the chief Kremlin spokesman, did his best to calm the speculation about Chernenko's health, but like Zamyatin only succeeded in arousing suspicion. When pressed on the question, Lomeiko maintained that Chernenko was "carrying out his duties". He used this phrase however without confirming that Chernenko was back at his desk in the Kremlin. Was the *Pravda* interview on Star Wars a sign that Chernenko was back and firmly in charge? Lomeiko hesitated, and then said the *Pravda* answers "showed that Konstantin Ustinovich is carrying out his duties as General Secretary of the Central Committee and chairman of the Praesidium of the Supreme Soviet". On 4 September *Pravda* published a front page editorial on preparations for the next Party Congress, but managed to avoid mentioning Chernenko at all, even though it was the President and Party leader who was presiding over the commission for the new Party programme which the Congress was to adopt.

Sovietskaya Rossiya carried a front page article on the death of Lenin's mother at the age of 73, almost Chernenko's own age. "At that age any ailment can take you by surprise", *Sovietskaya Rossiya* said, noting that Lenin had learned about the illness of his mother by "reading between the lines" of a telegram. Chernenko himself was not quite 73—his birthday was at the end of September—but the implication was clear. Even more significantly, the *Sovietskaya Rossiya* article was part of an occasional series called "Reading Lenin Anew", and the previous article in the series had appeared during Andropov's decline and had been used to point cryptically to Andropov's impending demise.

It was not until 6 September, after a mysterious seven-week absence, that Chernenko reappeared in public to pin medals on three cosmonauts at a Kremlin ceremony: Svetlana Savitskaya, Colonel Vladimir Dzhanibekov, the handsome mission commander, and Igor Volk, the flight engineer, the crew of Soyuz T-12 which had docked with the space station Salyut 7 in July. It was supposed to be a triumphant return to public life, but in fact the impression was painful: Chernenko seemed even shorter of breath than usual, walking stiffly into the room and barely smiling despite his description of the occasion as "joyous". Television film of the ceremony was edited to show him in the best light, but Chernenko was still easily outshone both by Dzhanibekov and by Miss Savitskaya, who made a fluent speech of thanks in reply, apparently speaking confidently without notes. Chernenko used the occasion once again to appeal to the United States over the Star Wars' talks, calling on Washington to show political foresight, and recalling that the Soviet space programme, beginning with Yuri Gagarin's legendary space flight 23 years before, was a blend of daring scientific thinking and the courage of individual cosmonauts.

Most Russians had their eyes on earthly problems rather than the mysteries of the cosmos. The death in East Germany of Leonid Kostandov, a deputy prime minister, at the age of 69 had once again focused attention on the mortality of the Kremlin gerontocracy. Kostandov, who specialized in economic affairs, was given a full ceremonial funeral in Red Square. Kostandov's death was soon to be vastly overshadowed however by a far more traumatic event within the Kremlin leadership, and a sign that all was far from well in the crucial relationship between the military and the political hierarchies: the sacking of Marshal Nikolai Ogarkov, 67, as chief of staff and Deputy Minister of Defence.

CHAPTER TWENTY-ONE

Chernenko Makes a Comeback

THE OGARKOV AFFAIR remains an enigma. On the one hand it shows that Chernenko still wielded power in his declining months, since it was Chernenko as General Secretary, Head of State and Chairman of the Supreme Defence Council who sanctioned Ogarkov's dismissal. On the other hand this public breach between the Kremlin and the military— the first since the KAL disaster in Andropov's final days—underlined the atmosphere of chaos and intrigue at the top.

The fall of Ogarkov was one of the most extraordinary political events between the death of Brezhnev and the accession of Gorbachov. He was—and is—a brilliant and aloof man, a military man with powerful intellectual qualities and political ambitions. He had dominated events almost exactly a year before, at the press conference on the downing of the Korean airliner. We had often watched him from the press gallery of the Supreme Soviet, where he sat at his desk as an ordinary deputy, gripping the sides of his desk with an air of bemused tolerance at the banalities of the speeches from the platform, his desk entirely clear of unnecessary papers, a smile of rather haughty superiority playing around his lips. Occasionally he would glance up at the press gallery, obviously conscious of the fact that he was a luminous figure in an otherwise rather dull firmament of political and military leadership.

Marshal Ogarkov had previously fallen out with other senior military leaders, above all Marshal Ustinov, the Minister of Defence, over military strategy. In particular this meant the question of whether the Soviet army should re-fight the Second World War with tanks and heavy missiles, as the majority of generals seemed to believe, or whether, as Marshal Ogarkov recommended, Russia should instead concentrate on high technology armaments and high precision weapons of the new era. He was on record as having differed with Marshal Ustinov over the winnability of a nuclear war. Ogarkov declared in 1981 that a nuclear war could be won by the Soviet Union, but subsequently backtracked under pressure and toed the official Kremlin line, which was that a nuclear war with the other superpower would be futile and suicidal for the globe as a whole. But there was little doubt as to the real reason for Ogarkov's disgrace: he was a man of intellectual brilliance who was regarded as dangerous by the political hierarchy of the Communist Party, and who had "Bonapartist ambitions". This was an emotionally charged accusation which harked back to the days of Trotsky. It suggested that Ogarkov had committed the ultimate sin for a senior military officer; that he had realized that since the armed forces were the backbone of the Soviet system, it was the armed forces who ultimately should influence if not dictate many of the decisions at present in the hands of the civilian power. Under Marxism-Leninism the military power is theoretically at all times subordinate to the civilian power.

Red Star, the organ of the Soviet armed forces, made it quite clear that Ogarkov was being neutralized. *Red Star* carried the announcement of a new Chief of Staff, Marshal Sergei Akhromeyev, formerly Ogarkov's deputy, in a prominent position, while merely noting in passing that Ogarkov had been "relieved of his duties" as both Chief of Staff and Deputy Defence Minister and was being "transferred to other duties", without specifying what those duties were. Ogarkov had been Chief of Staff since 1977 and widely tipped to succeed the ailing Ustinov as Defence Minister—yet suddenly his career was apparently in ruins, not least because of upheavals within the Kremlin over the future af arms control talks, a subject Ogarkov knew well, having taken part in the Salt I talks. This in turn crucially affected the relationship between the armed forces hierarchy and the Party leadership in the Kremlin.

As it happened, both Mikhail Gorbachov and Grigory Romanov, the rivals for the succession to Chernenko, were out of the country at the time of the Ogarkov crisis, Gorbachov visiting Bulgaria and Romanov attending the founding conference of a new Communist-style party in Ethiopia. Both Gorbachov and Romanov had received extensive coverage in the Moscow television news bulletins, whereas the fall of Marshal Ogarkov was passed over almost in silence. *Pravda* offered a neutral account of the affair, with equal weight given to both Ogarkov and Akhromeyev. But *Red Star* carried a front page photograph and biography of Akhromeyev and only mentioned the Ogarkov removal in small print, omitting the usual references to his services to the state and the armed forces.

It subsequently emerged that Ogarkov had been given command of Western theatre forces at Minsk in Byelorussia, a post which would become operational only in wartime and was therefore largely theoretical. This appointment was confirmed by Romanov several months later when he visited Helsinki and was asked—as a known Ogarkov ally—about the fate of the former Chief of Staff. As Secretary for Defence Industries within the Secretariat, Romanov was closely linked to senior officers, including Ogarkov, and Ogarkov's downfall was one of the factors which led to a weakening of Romanov's political position at the time of manoeuvring for the succession.

Chernenko was absent from the lying-in-state of Leonid Kostandov, the Deputy Prime Minister who had died suddenly in East Germany, and also failed to attend Kostandov's Red Square funeral. Even the funeral itself was part of the enigma: Kostandov was scarcely a politician of the first rank, and yet received a lying-in-state at the Red Army Hall attended by Politburo members (other than Chernenko) and his ashes were interred in the Kremlin wall.

Had Ogarkov indeed espoused "Bonapartist" ambitions? In the literal sense, probably not. But during the Korean airliner crisis, in which he defended Russia's actions with superb and icy calm, Ogarkov had given the impression that it was the armed forces which were the main force in the Soviet structure, not the Party. His intellectual arrogance and high public profile tended to reinforce the views of those who held that ultimately, once Communist ideology had been seen to be bankrupt, it would be the armed forces who would step into the vacuum of power, with an ideology of discipline and patriotism but without the trappings of Marxism-Leninism. Ogarkov's performance as Chief of Staff had been widely admired, but it had led to charges inside the Party that the Chief of Staff was too clever by half. His enemies had moved adroitly. Only a few days before his removal Ogarkov played a leading role in talks in Moscow with General Jakko Valtaanen, the head of the Finnish armed forces, and *Red Star* carried a front page photograph of Marshal Ogarkov sitting next to Marshal Ustinov. Ogarkov had been born in 1917, the year of the Russian revolution, and had served with engineering troops on the Ukrainian front during the Second World War and in the Soviet Far East in the 1950s, briefly becoming a troop commander in East Germany before taking part in the Salt talks and climbing the ladder as deputy Defence Minister and Chief of Staff. But it was a sign of his unusual status and intellect that he was capable of formulating unorthodox views. The political leadership hoped that Marshal Akhromeyev, a product of the Heavy Armour Military and the Academy of the General Staff, would prove a more manageable and loyal military figure, as indeed he did.

Behind the upheaval to the military in September 1984 lay not only the Kremlin power struggle and the future of arms talks with the United States, but also an issue which had featured prominently in previous succession struggles—the battle for allocation of scarce resources between the defence budget and the consumer sector. At this crucial stage in the succession struggle, Mikhail Gorbachov emerged as the champion of the consumer, noting in his speech in Sofia that although the Soviet state was right to give unflagging attention to strengthening Russia's defensive capacities, this was deflecting a considerable part of Russia's domestic resources. The Warsaw Pact allies could not do otherwise, Gorbachov hastened to add—"We all have to do this"—but Russia had other economic priorities and needed disarmament abroad in order to concentrate on pressing tasks at home, a principle which was to become one of the leitmotifs of the Gorbachov era when he finally succeeded Chernenko in March the following year. Grigory Romanov, on the other hand, was busy in Addis Ababa maintaining his reputation as a hard line ally of the military, launching attack after attack on the United States in cold war language, and accusing Washington of threatening the world with nuclear war and staging barbarous acts of aggression around the globe—a tone of anger, rather than the tone of regret adopted by Gorbachov in Bulgaria.

On the face of it, it was Romanov who was more in tune with the times. Yet within a few weeks Gromyko's visit to Washington for talks with President Reagan produced the result which both Chernenko and Gorbachov strongly favoured: the resumption at last of dialogue on disarmament with the United States. Gorbachov's Sofia speech underpinned the Kremlin's new line, not least Gorbachov's declaration that the Soviet Union favoured realism, common sense and businesslike co-operation. Although the West was trying to weaken the Soviet bloc by differentiating between liberal and illiberal East European states, Gorbachov said, and although Reagan was conducting a crusade against Communism and "relying on brute force", the Socialist countries had enough good will and determination for détente to be resumed. "If the West shows it understands that nowadays one can only speak to the socialist world on equal terms, then of course a change for the better will occur," was the Gorbachov line. There were still vicious attacks on Reagan in the Soviet press: "the ugly face of malignancy" was one of *Pravda*'s cracks, to show that the Kremlin was not about to help the President in his campaign for re-election. The reality, however, was that Reagan and Gromyko were to meet after the United Nations General Assembly at the end of September. NBC Televison was even able to broadcast its morning show from the gigantic Rossiya Hotel not far from Red Square and interview senior Soviet officials about the forthcoming Soviet-American encounter. Eventually even the Soviet people were informed about Gromyko's trip to Washington, although not until Dr Billy Graham, the evangelist preacher, had told the congregation of a

Moscow church about the forthcoming encounter in one of his passionate and eccentric sermons, apparently oblivious to the fact that the Russian people had not yet been informed.

There were other distractions in Moscow that September. For many Muscovites the focus of attention was not the Soviet-American dialogue, or even Chernenko's state of health, but the opening of the chess championship between Anatoly Karpov, the highly strung World Champion, and the mercurial and unorthodox Gary Kasparov from Azerbaijan. There was also Billy Graham's evangelical tour of Russia, and the dramatic return to Moscow of Oleg Bitov, the *Literary Gazette* journalist who had defected to Britain by way of Venice, but who now claimed, at an extraordinary press conference, that he had been drugged and manipulated by the British intelligence services and had not wanted to live in the West at all.

But in the Party press, the leadership of Moldavia was once again under fire, a repetition of indirect attacks during the Andropov era on Chernenko himself, who had been closely associated with Moldavia and was still strongly linked with the republic. Once again attention became focused on Chernenko's absence, and there were reports (only subsequently confirmed) that Chernenko had returned to hospital after the cosmonauts' ceremony on 5 September. When he finally did reappear on Moscow television, on 18 September, his appearance was truly shocking. Far from having a reassuring effect, the heavily-edited film of Chernenko presenting the Greek Communist leader, Harilaos Florakis, with the Order of Lenin was visual proof that Chernenko was declining fast. Shortly afterwards Chernenko made a further television appearance, this time giving a recorded address to Finnish and Soviet viewers on relations between Moscow and Helsinki. But once again the film had been put together from short takes, and the impact on viewers was painful and embarrassing. The subject of the address (the fortieth anniversary of Russia's armistice with Finland) was ignored as people studied the position of Chernenko's hands in the re-edited film to see how many times it had been cut and spliced together. Whereas during the Florakis ceremony Chernenko had stood stiffly reading with great difficulty from a piece of paper, the address to Finnish viewers was made sitting down. Chernenko was now 73, and it was common gossip in Moscow that Chernenko's grip on power as General Secretary was slipping. On the day of Chernenko's birthday *Pravda* carried a front page announcement of the award to the Soviet leader of the Order of Lenin and the gold Hammer and Sickle medal (one of several he possessed), but there was no photograph, and no mention of the birthday as such. The wording of the award appeared to be a summing up of Chernenko's achievements, an obituary as much as an eulogy.

Against the odds, Chernenko was able to make a physical recovery in late September and early October. He suddenly reversed the image of an incapacitated and declining old man with a series of powerful speeches which, although edited for television, did not have quite the same disastrous effect on public opinion. Chernenko's address to the Writers' Union jubilee meeting in the Kremlin at the end of September 1984 was a strong restatement of his orthodox views on ideology. Giving his first sustained address for some months, Chernenko insisted that Soviet writers and artists had to toe the Party line and adopt the Stalinist concept of socialist realism in the ideological struggle against the West. The meeting marked the fiftieth anniversary of the founding congress of the Writers' Union held in Moscow in 1934, and Chernenko duly paid tribute to Maxim Gorky, who had founded the concept of socialist realism, although he avoided mentioning the hundred members of the Writers' Union who had subsequently met their deaths in Stalin's labour camps and prisons after the founding congress.

Focusing instead on the future, Chernenko recalled his own demands for ideological orthodoxy and the Plenum of June 1983 before he became leader, and said that all Soviet writers had to assert "the lofty ideals of socialism". Too many writers, he complained, had abandoned positive heroes, and novels of industrial achievement. Chernenko recalled Lenin's demand for "sincerity in politics", and looked ahead to distant objectives such as the formulation of a new Party programme at the next Party Congress adding, perhaps a little wistfully, "this may seem somewhat abstract", evidently thinking of his own uncertain health and political future. To assist the Party in its ideological struggle, he said, there should be more books on military and patriotic themes and a stern defence of Soviet values against Western psychological warfare. There was a warning too for dissidents. Chernenko remarked that it was "naive to think that people could blacken the moral and political foundations of the Soviet system and simultaneously expect the benefits of recognition from it". There was very little about foreign affairs in the speech, and no response at all to a call from President Reagan for a high level of exchanges to break down barriers between the superpowers, perhaps leading to a summit of the Soviet and American leaders. On the contrary, the Soviet press dismissed Reagan's conciliatory remarks, made at the United Nations, as "a vessel with nothing inside it", pointing up instead Chernenko's accusation at the Writers' Congress that Washington "either does not want or is not ready to understand that there is no sensible alternative to the normalization of relations." This was followed by a meeting between Chernenko and Kalevi Sorsa, the Prime Minister of Finland, during which Chernenko again ignored Reagan's overture and referred instead to "dangerous tensions" between the superpowers.

Once again Chernenko's television performance was carefully staged to disguise his disability. The front page photograph of the Politburo at the Writers' Congress deliberately showed Gorbachov sitting in a prominent position between Marshal Ustinov and Prime Minister Tikhonov. But there was doubt that Chernenko had made a come-back of sorts: apart from the Writers' Union and the meeting with Sorsa, he was also presented with the Order of Lenin by Marshal Ustinov, and pointedly recalled in his speech of thanks that he held all the offices of state formerly held by Brezhnev and Andropov. And with Gromyko meeting President Reagan in the White House, Chernenko began to take a more doveish line, noting that the capitalist countries should know "that they will always have in the Soviet Union an honest and well-intentioned partner."

CHAPTER TWENTY-TWO

Gorbachov Manoeuvres

AN UNUSUAL BUT effective way of gaining perspective on what was going on in the Kremlin in the autumn of 1984 was to visit, not the Kremlin itself, but the former country estate of the mayors of Moscow beyond the city limits where Lenin had died sixty years previously. Walking among the silver birches of Leninsky Gorki, where Lenin had spent his last years, gazing at the bed on which he breathed his last, one saw clearly that what was happening resembled attempts during earlier succession crises to disguise the fact that the leader was incapacitated and a struggle for power was taking place. As we crowded in from the crisp autumnal air to look at Lenin's reading glasses, winter boots and tea service inside the modest mansion, we were struck above all by a blown up photograph in a downstairs room of Lenin walking in the grounds of the estate. The photograph had been taken in the summer of 1922 by a *Pravda* photographer with the specific aim of scotching rumours about the leader's health. The historical ironies and parallels were all too apparent. The only difference was that Lenin, had television existed in the early 1920s, would undoubtedly have been obliged to do as Chernenko had done and make a number of staged appearances.

So far, Chernenko had handed out medals to cosmonauts, and had a medal handed to him by Marshal Ustinov; he had received a Greek Communist leader and the leader of South Yemen, Ali Nasser Moham-med; he had made his long speech to the Writers' Union and had subsequently made an equally demanding speech to the People's Control, the national inspectorate, demanding tough measures against corruption, embezzlement and the abuse of power, a further marathon performance which was evidently taking its toll on Chernenko's physical stamina. But what would happen when the chill autumn air of October gave way to the often sub-zero temperatures of November, and Chernenko was forced to stand on top of the mausoleum on Revolution Day, the 7th of November? It was not enough to argue, as Soviet officials were tending to do, that the leadership was essentially collective, and that at 73 Chernenko was among the youngest of an ageing leadership, with Tikhonov aged 79, and Ustinov and Gromyko both a vigorous 75. Ustinov and Gromyko were still prominent, with Gromyko going almost directly from his talks with Reagan to East Berlin where he attended celebrations marking 35 years of the East German state.

There was growing unease at the immobility at the top in the Kremlin, and a growing nostalgia for the leadership of Andropov. The Andropov era was increasingly idealized by many younger officials who wanted to move Russia out of its isolationist phase and invigorate its domestic policies. There was talk of whether or not Chernenko might use the Central Committee Plenum to take the "Tsedenbal Option", a reference to the leader of Mongolia who had resigned in September, allegedly on the grounds of ill health. Tsedenbal was subsequently spotted in the Lenin Hills in Moscow in apparent perfect health near a VIP dacha as he took the air, shadowed by a large black limousine. There were rumours that Chernenko too might step down "at his own request", as Khrushchev had done twenty years previously, while retaining all his privileges, and handing over to a younger, more vigorous and forward-looking leadership. His decline, like Lenin's decline in 1924, was painful to observe, but unlike Lenin's last years it was all being played out in the grim limelight of international publicity, including television.

At this crucial point, rumours began to proliferate that Gorbachov, still acknowledged as Number Two in the Kremlin, would be relieved of his responsibilities as Secretary for Agriculture at the forthcoming Central Committee Plenum, and his rival Grigory Romanov began to feature prominently on the international scene and in the Soviet media. Romanov used the occasion of a visit to Finland in mid-October to advance his cause. Although Moscow had announced that it was deploying air and sea launched long-range cruise missiles, accusing the United States of "unleashing the nuclear dogs of war" by deploying Cruise and Pershing Two, Romanov was quick to see that détente was in the air and declared that the Soviet Union was after all ready for negotiations with the United States. This was a piece of deliberate image building by Romanov, who was only too well aware that he was held to be a tough and rather rough edged hardliner in the Kremlin succession stakes. It subsequently emerged however that for most of his visit to Helsinki Romanov had been much the worse for wear, on some occasions becoming totally incoherent because of his heavy drinking, which in recent years had become a serious problem. This was used against him by the austere and definitely non-alcoholic Gorbachov. Romanov's drunken performance in the Finnish capital was doubly embarrassing since he had been sent not only to make an address marking the fortieth anniversary of the armistice between Russia and Finland, but also to try and sort out the quarrel in the Finnish

Communist Party between pro-Moscow Stalinists and moderate Euro-Communists, a task in which he signally failed.

Romanov's appearance in Finland as a rising star of the Kremlin coincided with a partial comeback by Marshal Ogarkov, with whom he was closely allied. Ogarkov reappeared in Berlin and held talks with Erich Honecker, the East German leader, accompanied by General Mikhail Zaitsev, Commander of the Soviet forces in East Germany. Oddly, Ogarkov's Berlin talks were reported in *Neues Deutschland*, the East German Communist paper, but not in *Pravda*, and *Neues Deutschland* simply referred to him as Marshal, without giving his functions and responsibilities. Viktor Afanasyev, the chief editor of *Pravda*, chose this moment to add further fuel to the Gorbachov-Romanov rivalry, by deliberately referring, during a meeting with Japanese journalists, to Gorbachov as "our second General Secretary", a remark which in the Byzantine world of Soviet politics could only be interpreted as meaning that the editor of *Pravda* himself thought Russia had two leaders: Chernenko and Gorbachov, and that the time could not be far off when Gorbachov and not Romanov would succeed for the leadership, becoming Russia's first rather than second General Secretary.

However, there were still growing reports in the Party that Gorbachov might lose responsibility for agriculture in the Secretariat, possibly because of dissatisfaction with a series of bad harvests for which Gorbachov could be held primarily responsible. This was the beginning of a series of ups and downs for Gorbachov in the late autumn of 1984 which reflected the bitter power struggle behind the Kremlin wall. The last Politburo meeting before the October Central Committee Plenum produced a curious hint that personnel changes might be in the offing. The Politburo, according to the official account in *Pravda*, discussed Chernenko's "proposals on several questions of current cadres policy", a reference in Soviet political jargon to Party appointments and dismissals.

Speculation about a change in the agriculture portfolio rose when Chernenko made a hard hitting speech attacking inefficiency and corruption in agriculture. Criticism of disorganization and slowness in the use of animal fodder was followed by a purge of collective farm managers. Chernenko further sought to reinforce his political authority by giving an interview in Moscow to the *Washington Post*, providing written answers on arms control and Soviet-American relations, but also speaking for twenty minutes off the cuff, without notes, and generally giving the impression that he was firmly in charge of foreign policy. At the same time, yet another article in praise of Andropov and Andropovite ideas appeared in *Pravda*. Spread over seven columns and headed "Under the banner of Leninism", the *Pravda* piece said that Andropov's writings reflected his "titanic activities" and the way in which Andropov had guided the Party in "enriching our experience in the building and the perfecting of a new society". The *Pravda* article reviewed a new collection of Andropov's speeches entitled *Leninism is the Inexhaustible Source of Revolutionary Energy and Creative Activities of the Masses*. It noted that, like the plaques on various government buildings in Moscow, the new volume was part of a Central Committee resolution on the "perpetuation of Andropov's memory as an outstanding figure of the Party and state".

When the long awaited Plenum finally did convene at the end of October, after weeks of rumour and counter rumour, it confirmed by implication that Gorbachov was no longer in charge of agriculture. But the Plenum otherwise failed to throw much light on the Kremlin power struggle and generally baffled observers by concentrating on the relatively arcane subjects of land reclamation, irrigation and drainage. These were the kind of subjects usually discussed by special Party conferences on agriculture, but Chernenko insisted on using the full Plenum to expound ideas close to his heart about large-scale cultivation of soil, and irrigation techniques. It was a return to the grandiose schemes of the 1950s associated with Khrushchev and subsequently (although he later played this down) with Brezhnev. The speeches on agriculture at the Plenum took up nearly four full pages in *Pravda*, yet significantly Gorbachov did not speak at all, even though he had been responsible for agriculture in the Politburo since 1980. There were no personnel changes, suggesting that Chernenko had been forced to abandon them.

Gorbachov's supporters, of whom there were many in the Party apparatus at this point, argued that Gorbachov was well rid of the burden of farm policy, the traditional Achilles heel of Soviet politics, and pointed out that he had after all acquired responsibility for the economy as a whole, ideology and for personnel, so that to be associated with harvest failures was an unnecessary luxury. The occasion was not used, as it could have been, to lambast Gorbachov and undermine his position by pointing at agricultural shortcomings, especially since one of the worst annual grain harvests, ever, was widely expected. But on the eve of the Plenum, a photograph published on the front page of *Pravda* showed Gorbachov for the first time in a less prominent position than Romanov, with Gorbachov standing some distance away from Chernenko in the Politburo line-up. A similar scene was shown on Soviet television.

Immediately after the Plenum, Romanov continued his climb to the top by meeting the new leader of Mongolia, Zhambyn Batmunkh, at Moscow airport on behalf of the Politburo and subsequently taking part in talks alongside Chernenko in the Number Two position formerly occupied by Gorbachov himself. While Romanov was being featured on the front page of *Pravda*, Gorbachov was meeting a relatively low-level delegation from East Germany. It was beginning to look as if the remarkable *Pravda* photograph of 18 October, in which Gorbachov's position had slipped significantly, might be more than an isolated case.

It was not until the 7 November parade, and accompanying ceremonies, that Gorbachov was able to restore his position. Politburo portraits on Moscow streets proved that he had not lost his place in the Soviet hierarchy despite his absence from view for several weeks, his relegation to low-level Kremlin talks and his failure to address the October Plenum on agriculture. In some Politburo portrait line-ups, particularly on the Gorky Street telegraph office—often a guide to the ups and downs of Politburo fortunes—Gorbachov was placed right next to Chernenko, out of alphabetical order. By then the focus of attention was in any case no longer Gorbachov's absences and his place in the pecking order but the disappearance of a member of the old generation who had played a key role in the power structure in the past, and had often been able to influence the choice of General Secretary: Marshal Dmitri Ustinov, the Minister of Defence, who had not been seen for a month.

Ustinov failed to appear for the Red Square military parade on the anniversary of the revolution. He had not been seen in public since 27 September, when he had presented medals to Chernenko, and subsequently he had failed to receive the visiting Indian Minister of Defence, S. B. Chavan. Kremlin officials insisted that the missing Ustinov had a "cold" and a "sore throat", but by now such reassurances had been completely devalued. Ustinov, by now 76, had never missed the annual military parade before. His place was taken by Marshal Sergei Sokolov, the Deputy Defence Minister, who made a speech from the mausoleum denouncing the United States as the cause of East–West tensions but deliberately avoiding any reference to the re-election of Ronald Reagan as President of the United States. Viktor Grishin, the Politburo member and Moscow city Party boss, said, as he climbed down from the top of the mausoleum, that Marshal Ustinov had a cold and would return to his duties shortly, but very few people believed it. In a ghostly replay of previous deaths in the Kremlin, television announcers appeared dressed in black and some radio stations began to play solemn music and military songs, leading to powerful rumours that Ustinov had already died. At the gala revolutionary anniversary in the Kremlin, Ustinov again failed to appear for the keynote speech on Soviet-American relations by Andrei Gromyko. Gorbachov walked on to the platform in the Palace of Congresses together with the inner circle of Old Guard Politburo members (minus Ustinov): Chernenko, Tikhonov and Gromyko. Gorbachov spent most of the time chatting to Viktor Grishin instead of listening to Gromyko, and his supporters were at pains to let it be known that Gorbachov had chaired the special Plenum on agriculture the previous month, even though he had not spoken. In other words, they maintained smoothly, the apparent black marks against Gorbachov in recent weeks could safely be discounted. Gorbachov, they said, was in any case about to make a visit to Britain on behalf of the Kremlin. It was subsequently announced that Gorbachov would go to London for a week in December, a visit which was to be of major importance for his image both in the Western world and within the Soviet power structure at home.

There are nonetheless lingering mysteries about Gorbachov's position as he manoeuvred for power, not the least of which is the strange case of the Central Committee Plenum which did not take place. The special Plenum on agriculture in October had by no means precluded the normal Central Committee Plenum on the eve of the Winter Supreme Soviet, to discuss the budget for 1985 and general economic policy. On the contrary, the Kremlin said that the Central Committee would convene on the eve of the Supreme Soviet as usual. In the event, however, an enlarged Politburo session, attended not only by full and candidate members of the Politburo but also by provincial and regional secretaries, was held instead. It was addressed by Chernenko, who outlined economic policy and the progress of the Five Year Plan. Gorbachov did not attend the enlarged Politburo session, which amounted to a mini-plenum, and neither did one of his chief lieutenants and allies, Vitaly Vorotnikov, who was said to be on holiday.

The enigma was compounded when Neil Kinnock, leader of the opposition Labour party in Britain, visited Moscow in November and held talks with Chernenko, but not with Gorbachov—a strange omission considering that Gorbachov was about to visit Britain and was bound to meet the Labour leader as part of his programme in London. Was this an attempt by the ailing Chernenko to reassert his authority and ensure that Gorbachov did not usurp the functions of General Secretary of the Party? Already Chernenko had asserted his position by obliging the Central Committee to adopt those very ideas in agriculture which

Gorbachov had specifically criticized in the past as grandiose and unworkable. Gorbachov preferred to concentrate on better use of existing resources, not on large scale land reclamation. To add insult to injury, *Pravda* announced that the land reclamation scheme would begin in Stavropol, the region in which Gorbachov had begun his climb to the top. *Pravda* also published a full list of all those who had attended the enlarged session in November, a most unusual move which appeared to be designed to draw attention to the fact that Gorbachov and Vorotnikov had been absent.

There were internal Politburo strains over military as well as economic policy. Some elements of the leadership, and some members of the military structure too, were anxious over the dramatic decision by the Kremlin to resume arms negotiations with the United States in the form of a framework discussion, on the arms control agenda, between Andrei Gromyko and George Shultz in Geneva in January 1985. This was the culmination of a process which had begun with Gromyko's visit to the White House in September, and had advanced behind a façade of anti-Reagan and anti-American rhetoric. This did not prevent some Soviet leaders worrying that hard-won Soviet weaponry might now be negotiated away, and that Chernenko might make excessive concessions to the United States in his all-consuming desire to restore the era of détente. When the Supreme Soviet convened in the Kremlin on 27 November, it approved a remarkable 12 per cent increase in the Soviet defence budget, the first official rise in military spending in five years. This was specifically linked to a Soviet challenge to American arms spending. Although the Soviet defence budget is to a large extent notional, since most of Russia's real defence spending is hidden under other headings, the move at the Supreme Soviet was intended to carry symbolic force.

As 1984 came to an end, doubts over whether Gorbachov had secured the succession as "Second General Secretary" began to be rapidly eroded. Gorbachov reappeared at the Supreme Soviet in the company of leading Politburo members, above all Gromyko, who was emerging as Gorbachov's firm friend and influential adviser. The cancellation of the November Plenum was explained away on the grounds that it was not obligatory to hold a Central Committee Plenum on the eve of the Supreme Soviet (constitutionally it is nowhere stated that the Central Committee must convene before the Supreme Soviet sessions). Boris Ponomaryov, candidate Politburo member and head of the Party's international department, told me that the decision not to hold a Plenum was due to Chernenko's desire to enhance the role of government bodies (as opposed to Party bodies) and to "encourage broader discussion of economic issues in the structure of Soviets". This was not, it has to be said, a particularly convincing explanation. But any lingering suspicions about Gorbachov's true position were soon swept away by his remarkably successful high profile visit to London, and the deliberate creation of what was to become the Gorbachov persona for the benefit of Western public opinion.

Despite the machinations and intrigues, with Gorbachov's enemies (including Romanov and Grishin) doing their best to trip him up, by December 1984 Gorbachov appeared to have achieved an almost unassailable position both at home and abroad. The London visit produced Mrs Thatcher's memorable phrase: "I like Mr Gorbachov, I can do business with him", and it showed British and Western public opinion a man who was young, able, sophisticated, well-dressed and willing to engage in debate and dialogue. By his side—no less of a revelation—was his wife, Raisa Maximovna, whose elegance and stylish fashions were as much discussed in London as Gorbachov's refreshing political approach. They made, it seemed, the ideal modern Russian couple, and posed an extraordinary contrast with the geriatric leaders to whom the West had become so accustomed over the recent years. Gorbachov was a man who could make jokes, when visiting the British Museum, about the origins of Marxism, and who could decide, apparently on impulse, to abandon the obligatory visit to Karl Marx's grave in Highgate Cemetery and go shopping instead. He could admire the stained glass in Westminster Abbey, and with the help of his wife, discuss art, philosophy and his hopes for East-West relations, as well as commerce and trade. Gorbachov's stature and confidence were underlined dramatically when at the very end of his visit, while he was preparing to make a tour of Scotland and had just arrived in Edinburgh, the news reached him from Moscow that Marshal Ustinov had finally died. Gorbachov announced the news to the world before there was any official statement on Ustinov's death in Russia itself—a most unusual departure from Kremlin protocol.

The death of Ustinov, described by both Chernenko and Gorbachov as a great and tragic loss, served to underline the passing of the old generation. Medical bulletins proved that Ustinov had died of a heart attack after liver and kidney failure arising from pneumonia contracted in late October. Once again, all the ailments which afflicted most members of the leadership were publicized, and once again the Kremlin had attempted to disguise what had been obvious to most of us in Moscow, namely that Ustinov had been in decline for several months.

Chernenko, perhaps wisely, decided to stay away from Ustinov's funeral on Red Square, held in bitterly cold temperatures of minus 7 degrees Centigrade. Death and dismissal had wrought havoc in the Kremlin leadership, to the benefit of the younger generation. Of Politburo members who attended Ustinov's funeral, only one, Viktor Grishin, had been also at the funeral, eight years previously, of Ustinov's predecessor, Marshal Grechko. Brezhnev, Andropov, Kosygin, Podgorny, Kulakov, Suslov were all dead: Kirilenko and Mazurov were living in obscurity and disgrace. Gorbachov's rival for the succession, Grigory Romanov, by now 61, was named to head the funeral commission for Marshal Ustinov, giving rise to immediate speculation that the Kremlin might appoint a civilian defence minister. This might have resolved the Gorbachov-Romanov rivalry, since Ministers of Defence rarely aspire to become General Secretaries of the Party. But in the event the leadership once again opted for a military man, choosing Marshal Sokolov, aged 73, the man who had stood in for Ustinov when reviewing the Red Square parade on 7 November.

A capable professional soldier, who had joined the army in 1932 and had made his way up through the ranks in tanks and heavy armour divisions, Sokolov did not have the stature of Ustinov—nor, at 73, was he ever likely to acquire it. He had been head of the Moscow military district in 1969, and head of the equivalent body in Leningrad four years later before becoming a First Deputy Defence Minister in 1967. Sokolov was a safe choice, and by replacing Ustinov with one of his long-serving deputies the leadership—still at this stage principally Chernenko himself—had decided to go for an option which would cause the least political disruption possible.

It was an interim move on the part of a leadership which was not quite sure what the political future held. It could only be a matter of time before Ustinov was followed into the grave by Chernenko, a thought which must have passed through Chernenko's mind as shortly before Christmas 1984 he stood once again in the Hall of Columns for the lying-in-state with other members of the Politburo, including Gorbachov. The Hall of Columns, so often used for this morbid purpose, had been taken over as the venue of the World Chess Championship between Anatoly Karpov and Gary Kasparov. But the two great chess contenders had to evacuate the building temporarily so that it could once again be used for a lying-in-state, and the huge sign on the front of the building, advertising the chess championship, was replaced by a giant portrait of Ustinov on a red background edged with black.

There were few other signs of public mourning, and most Muscovites seemed impatient for the struggle between the two titans of chess to be resumed. High level deaths in the Kremlin were becoming all too common, and were holding up other business. It was about time Russia got back to normal.

CHAPTER TWENTY-THREE

Gorbachov Takes Over

THE BEGINNING OF 1985 epitomized the central paradox of the Chernenko era, with Andrei Gromyko as Foreign Minister finally bringing about Chernenko's long-sought resumption of dialogue with the United States just as the Soviet leader went into final decline. After fifteen gruelling hours of talks at Geneva with George Shultz, Gromyko emerged to tell the world that while the abandoned Geneva missile talks "as such" were not being resumed, the superpowers had agreed on a framework for "new" arms talks covering three areas: space weapons, strategic missiles, and medium range missiles in Europe. This included the controversial issue of "Star Wars". The Geneva framework agreement marked the beginning of a new détente process which Gorbachov was to inherit ten months later, when he met President Reagan in the same Swiss city for the famous "fireside summit".

The Shultz-Gromyko agreement came at a time when Chernenko, until then artificially bolstered by drugs and the skills of the Kremlin doctors, no longer had the strength to reap the rewards. The first tell-tale clue came only days after Shultz and Gromyko had met. Greek diplomats revealed that a visit to Moscow by Andreas Papandreou, the Greek Prime Minister, was in jeopardy. After hectic behind-the-scenes contacts it was agreed that Papandreou would come to Moscow, but would not see the Soviet leader, a compromise which if anything made things worse rather than better. Once again the Kremlin resorted to a subterfuge to try and prove that Chernenko was well and active, sending a message in Chernenko's name to an eighteen-year-old Canadian girl who had written to him about world peace. A promised Warsaw pact summit in Sofia to discuss the results of the Shultz-Gromyko meeting failed to materialize. Chernenko messages to President Assad of Syria and a peace conference in Moscow provided no reassurance, and neither did the preface to the French edition of Chernenko's collected works, carried across five columns on *Pravda*'s front page.

Senior Soviet officials began to drop hints that Chernenko might do what Brezhnev had failed to do before him and become the first Soviet leader to retire honourably in office. The Politburo discussed several options on the leadership question, including an arrangement, short of retirement, under which Chernenko would take a back seat while the burdens of high office fell on others, principally Mikhail Gorbachov. None of this appeared in the published Politburo agenda. Chernenko had not been seen for a month, and his political and physical come-back the previous autumn was a fading memory. Some officials maintained that Chernenko had merely contracted influenza with bronchial complications, and although this turned out later to be true, it was far from reassuring, since at this stage any such setback was likely to prove fatal.

In this atmosphere factional struggles within the Politburo began to intensify, just as they had in the autumn of 1983 during Andropov's decline. Although most officials did their best to pretend that no such struggle was taking place, younger informants made clear that one faction strongly favoured the idea of a young and energetic Party leader after a series of temporary geriatric incumbents. Another faction, on the other hand, emphasized the value of age and experience. In what was to be a politically crucial turn of events, Andrei Gromyko swung his weight, at the beginning of February, behind Gorbachov and the youth faction, even though he was himself of the older generation. Romanov, on the other hand, began to ally himself with Viktor Grishin, the 70-year-old Moscow city Party boss, even though at 61 Romanov was held to be a member of the "younger" generation. It was not, in other words, a straight fight between the "young Turks" and the Old Guard. The hopes of the Grishin-Romanov faction partly rested on the fact that the Central Committee which would have to elect the next General Secretary was the same one which had chosen Chernenko rather than Gorbachov after the death of Andropov. But this left out of account the fact that Gorbachov, Vorotnikov, Ligachov and others in the Gorbachov faction had had time in which to gather support at all levels throughout the Party and to give the impression, not least to Central Committee members, that their time had come. Future political patronage would depend on them rather than on a "has been" such as Grishin.

To all appearances Chernenko was still in charge, giving a widely-publicized written interview to American television asserting that the Star Wars project was indefensible and that Moscow would match it if necessary. Soviet television made much of an article in the February issue of the magazine *Soviet Union* in which Chernenko marked the impending fortieth anniversary of the end of the Second World War by urging the other superpower to join him in preventing any such conflagration in the future. But all this was a smokescreen, and at the beginning of February a Soviet official offered a clue to the real state of affairs. Over lunch, he confided that Gorbachov was so sure the succession crisis was imminent that he had decided to stay in Moscow rather than travel to France, as planned, as the Kremlin's delegate to the annual congress of the French Communist Party. Coming at a time when Chernenko had not been seen in public for over a month and a half, and was reliably said to have had a stroke and to be in intensive care, this was a key indication that Gorbachov's instincts were correct and the crisis was not far off. His place in Paris was taken by Mikhail Solomentsev, 71, a lacklustre member of the Politburo who carried very little weight in the factional fighting.

Soviet officials admitted publicly that Chernenko was "resting" near Moscow—an obvious reference to the Politburo hospital—and that the preface to the French edition of his speeches had in fact been written the previous November. No one talked of celebrating the first anniversary of Chernenko's accession to power. Viktor Afanasyev played his now traditional role by telling reporters that Chernenko was indeed ill but nonetheless in charge of the country's affairs. A report on the front page of *Pravda* claiming that Chernenko had spoken on agricultural matters—notably the spring sowing campaign—at the weekly Politburo meeting in early February did nothing to allay mounting anxieties; suggesting that Chernenko had addressed the meeting, without evidence that he did so, was not much better than printing messages in his name. Rather absurdly, the reference to Chernenko was made in laconic fashion half way through the Politburo report, as if to suggest that his alleged reappearance was in no way remarkable. On closer inspection, indeed, the wording appeared to be ambiguous and could have meant that Chernenko's views were taken into account while giving the misleading impression that he was active. The real state of affairs was confirmed when Papandreou duly arrived in Moscow and was received by Nikolai Tikhonov, the Soviet Prime Minister, and not by the ailing Chernenko.

At this point *Pravda*, which under Afanasyev was unquestionably sympathetic to Gorbachov and the Andropovites, published an astonishing front page editorial marking the anniversary of the death of Yuri Andropov which talked openly of the problem of political succession. Transitions in the Kremlin, and the way in which they come about, are virtually taboo subjects in Russia; and yet here was *Pravda* talking of the way in which the Party had "skilfully used its accumulation of experience" after the death of Andropov to "ensure the succession of the leadership, implementing both domestic and foreign policy". What counted in Kremlin leadership, *Pravda* said, was "the human factor". Although much had been achieved since the change at the top since

February the previous year, the Party still had to do away with outdated leadership methods, including "all these commissions, instructions and declarations". This contrasted strangely with the massive attempt by other parts of the mass media, particularly television, to keep Chernenko's name and image in the public eye, for example by making great play with the cover photograph on the jacket of yet another edition of his speeches. Two of Chernenko's supporters, Dinmuhammed Kunayev of Kazakhstan and Vladimir Shcherbitsky of the Ukraine, made televised speeches as candidates for the forthcoming Soviet elections containing extravagant praise for the dying leader.

In his speech at Dniepropetrovsk, Brezhnev's former power base, Shcherbitsky went so far as to claim that he had just had a conversation with Chernenko. This could only have been by telephone, since at this stage Chernenko had suffered a series of strokes and was partially paralysed and practically immobile. On 14 February Dr Chazov cut short a lecture tour of the United States and hurried back to Moscow several days early. Romanov, with inept timing, joined Kunayev and Shcherbitsky in excessive praise of Chernenko in his election speech in Leningrad, which duly became the lead item on the evening television news.

Gorbachov, who significantly had been given a constituency in Moscow rather than the provinces, used his election speech to stake out yet more ground as Russia's future leader, offering a thoughtful analysis of international affairs and declaring that the United States was not the only focus of Soviet interest in East-West relations—a clear hint that if he succeeded Chernenko, Gorbachov would follow up his visit to Britain by concentrating on Russian links with Western Europe. "We note with satisfaction the striving of many West European states for political dialogue", Gorbachov said, noting that Europe was "our common home". Even more significant than the content of Gorbachov's speech was the fact that it came almost last in the list of Politburo electoral appearances, with only Tikhonov and Chernenko himself left to speak. This meant that Gorbachov had successfully manoeuvred himself into an almost unchallengeable position as heir apparent. The question on all minds in Moscow as Tikhonov made a routine penultimate speech in the election campaign was: would Chernenko reappear after two months out of the limelight, or would the doctors decide that a staged appearance was even worse than continued absence?

Whatever the doctors may have advised, the group around Chernenko decided that he had to appear—and the results were truly disastrous. On 22 February, on the eve of the poll, Chernenko failed to make an

appearance at the election meeting in the Kremlin, with his speech read
out at the meeting on his behalf. The speech laid down a three point
approach to the forthcoming arms talks in Geneva, and called on
President Reagan to reaffirm the spirit of détente. But once again the
message was lost because of Chernenko's absence. Viktor Grishin,
briefly taking on Chernenko's mantle, chaired the Kremlin rally as head
of the Party organization in Moscow and revealed that the Soviet leader
had stayed away "on doctor's recommendation". But the Kremlin had
decided that Chernenko, ill as he was, could not afford to miss the vote
itself. Officials therefore staged an embarrassing visit to the polling
station for the benefit of the state controlled television cameras. Not a
single foreign reporter was invited to watch Chernenko placing his ballot
unsteadily in the ballot box. Instead the foreign press were all asked to go
to the snow-bound polling station at the Architects' Club on Shchusev
Street, opposite a heavily-guarded Politburo residential block of flats. A
number of prominent personalities appeared to vote, including Aliyev.
But the main event, to the accompaniment of flash bulbs and the whirr of
television cameras, was the arrival of Gorbachov and his elegant wife
Raisa, glamorously swathed for the occasion in black fur and suede. Even
the Gorbachovs' granddaughter, Oksana, (a colloquial form of Xenia),
was produced. It was as if a Presidential contender and his photogenic
family were appearing in the United States. Despite the official fiction
that Chernenko was in charge, Gorbachov was being presented to us as
Russia's acting leader. He came across the floor of the hall to engage in
light hearted banter with reporters and photographers, much as Brezhnev
had done in Soviet elections at the height of his power.

The contrast with Chernenko's one minute television appearance
could scarcely have been greater. It was not even certain that the film
had been shot at the polling station, or indeed any polling station. No
other voters were shown as Chernenko moved stiffly from his seat to the
ballot box a few yards away, wheezing audibly with the effort, his face set
and unsmiling. Unlike Gorbachov, whom we had seen coming in from
the snow-covered street outside, Chernenko was not wearing an
overcoat and was surrounded by officials, with Viktor Grishin, again
leading the group, jollying the Soviet leader along. On the other hand,
while the attention of the world was on Gorbachov and his family, Soviet
television viewers and readers of *Pravda* remained unaware that
Gorbachov was being promoted as the future leader, and were only
shown old guard leaders like Chernenko and Tikhonov. Clearly there
was one message for opinion abroad and another for domestic consumption. The Soviet press made much of Chernenko's "meeting with his

'constituents'" at the Kremlin, even though he had not in fact been there at all, and reported at length Grishin's sycophantic eulogy of the absent Chernenko's "wisdom, modesty and vision". Russians were not allowed to see Gorbachov joking with photographers, who asked him to pose a second time for the benefit of the cameras, or to hear him remarking with a broad grin, "I feel fine", when asked about his health.

By this stage however it was impossible to hide from even the most apolitical Soviet citizen that Chernenko's time was limited and Gorbachov's hour was approaching. Romanov's position had slipped since he came low down in the list of Politburo members making election speeches. His strongest card was his relationship with the military, a point he emphasized by taking a prominent part in celebrations marking Red Army Day, and by dwelling at length in his speech to Leningrad constituents on the need to strengthen Russian defences against imperialism. On the surface, normality prevailed: Gromyko went to Italy and Shcherbitsky began an eleven-day tour of the United States, both apparent indications that a crisis was not necessarily imminent. Tass reported that Chernenko had made a further public appearance at a ceremony at which he was presented with his new credentials as a deputy to the Supreme Soviet. Roland Dumas, the French Foreign Minister, was to come to Moscow to see Chernenko on the eve of the resumption of the Geneva arms talks. Even Chernenko's failure to attend a gala meeting at the Bolshoi Theatre, marking International Women's Day, failed to arouse immediate concern. The world was becoming used to seeing Gorbachov leading the Politburo on to public platforms.

As we have seen, it tends to be one of the rules of Soviet succession that the fiction is elaborately maintained that the dying or politically weakened incumbent is still in full command of all his faculties and actively running the country from the General Secretary's Office. The transition struggle behind the scenes ensures that his successor is effectively chosen, or rather defeats all rivals, long before death or retirement at the top actually takes place. To some extent, indeed, the new leader holds the reins of power before he takes over. Thus Stalin had begun to place his hands on the levers of power before Lenin's death in 1924; Khrushchev's power was whittled away by the anti-Khrushchev conspirators before he was formally toppled; and Andropov used his power base in the KGB and the army to acquire control of the decision making process before Brezhnev ceased to breathe. The death of Stalin was an exception: so great was his hold over the machinery of state, and so great the fear and trembling of Politburo members in his shadow, that neither Khrushchev nor Malenkov dared to take control before the dictator was dead. Even then Stalin's successors could not quite believe he had truly proved mortal. In all cases, the overriding consideration is that the image of the State and those in charge of its destinies must not in any way be damaged, either in the eyes of the world or in the eyes of Russians themselves. This partly reflects the well developed Russian sense of propriety and observance of formalities, but above all has to do with the Russian horror of allowing the chaotic and often unpleasant details of political struggle to come to the surface.

To all intents and purposes therefore, Gorbachov had been running the country for three months by the time Chernenko finally died, on Sunday 10 March, of complications of chronic emphysema aggravated by long-standing heart deficiencies, chronic hepatitis and cyrrhosis of the liver. Previous successions had worked themselves out over a period of time, and, in the case of Chernenko, had taken four or five days after the death of Andropov. If there was one outstanding feature of the transition to Gorbachov, it was its speed and its smooth, ruthless efficiency. To some the succession smacked of indecent haste. To others it was a case of the by now well-oiled succession machinery clicking into place, with less need than before to pretend that the formalities of transition required a decent interval.

Gorbachov was an impatient man who had already been twice passed over for the leadership, and could scarcely wait to carry out the plans he had nurtured while watching the gerontocracy fade away with agonizing slowness. Already one precious year had been lost under Chernenko's less than inspiring leadership. None of this was stated openly, but it could hardly have been plainer if Gorbachov had put it on the front page of *Pravda*. On Monday 11 March, Tass and Soviet television announced for the third time in as many years that the Soviet leader had died. By the same afternoon—the fastest transition in Soviet history—Gorbachov was installed. Correspondents and diplomats were still compiling their list of contenders for power when the Gorbachov appointment rendered all such speculation instantly obsolete. The Central Committee convened with such haste that Shcherbitsky did not have time to return from the United States, to Gorbachov's advantage. Gromyko, on the other hand, had returned from Italy, and it was he, as one of the most authoritative members of the Old Guard, who quashed any remaining doubts in the minds of older Politburo members by nominating Gorbachov for the post of General Secretary and praising Gorbachov's outstanding qualities in a frank and impassioned nomination speech.

Gromyko's firm intervention was decisive. Though Gorbachov had been in charge of key policy areas for months, even he could not ascend the final rungs in the ladder entirely unopposed, and ran into stiff resistance in the Politburo from both Romanov and Grishin. Romanov, according to reports in Party circles, had hoped to the last that he himself would be put forward as a candidate for the leadership. When it became clear that he lacked the necessary support Romanov, in a desperate move, proposed Viktor Grishin as Chernenko's legitimate successor. But the Romanov-Grishin manoeuvre was doomed to failure and Gorbachov won a majority, not least thanks to Gromyko's firm recommendation of Gorbachov as a man of conviction and principle as well as plain speaking. Gromyko indirectly acknowledged the split in the Politburo by denying that there were divisions within the Soviet leadership—again a reflection of the fear that foreigners, and possibly internal opponents, might take advantage of differences within the Kremlin. But Gromyko's praise of Gorbachov's "brilliant analysis and decision making in both domestic and foreign policy" settled the issue even before Chernenko's lying-in-state at the Hall of Columns was over. "Comrades," Gromyko remarked in a phrase which was to resound around the world, "Mikhail Sergeevich has a nice smile, but he also has iron teeth."

The reaction of most Russians was one of overwhelming relief at the passing of a man who during his last, ill-fated appearance at the polling station had scarcely been able to wheeze his thanks when presented with the traditional bunch of red carnations by solicitous officials, or even to hold the flowers in his shaking hands. "We are tired of invisible presidents", one young Russian friend said quite openly to me.

In his acceptance speech to the Central Committee, Gorbachov said Moscow wanted agreement with the United States at the Geneva arms talks, which opened on the same day. "The peoples of the world will sigh with relief," he said, adding that the Gorbachov administration would pursue détente while "defending the interests of the Russian mother-land". There was, as in previous successions, an address to the Soviet people from the Soviet leadership—the Central Committee, the Council of Ministers and the Praesidium of the Supreme Soviet—calling on Russians to "rally round the Party in its hour of grave loss". But few Russians felt any sense of loss at all, and few needed any persuading to rally around a man who symbolized their hopes of change.

Gorbachov himself paid due respect to Chernenko in his acceptance speech, calling him a man with "a responsive heart and organizational talent". But rather more significant was his remark that Russia now had to make a "decisive turn" towards economic and technological achieve-ment by means of "the perfection of the economic system and the entire management", the phrase used time and again by Andropov as a code for reform. The spirit of Andropov, the most important and innovative Soviet leader since Lenin himself, had returned to the Kremlin, almost as if the Chernenko era had never been. Assuming that Gorbachov, Andropov's main protégé, remained as healthy and as active during his tenure of power as he was on taking office at the age of 54, the next succession crisis in the Kremlin would probably not take place for ten, fifteen or perhaps twenty years.

CHAPTER TWENTY-FOUR

The Gorbachov Era Begins

ONE SEPTEMBER EVENING in 1978 a train carrying President Brezhnev stopped at the spa town of Mineralnye Vody, in the Caucasus. At Brezhnev's side was Konstantin Chernenko, head of his private office, and on the station platform to meet them was the tall, stooping figure of Yuri Andropov, head of the KGB, who was taking a rest cure in the mountains nearby. At Andropov's side was a young man called Mikhail Gorbachov, First Secretary of the Stavropol region in the Caucasus, and about to make the breakthrough to the high ground of Kremlin politics after a swift rise up the provincial Party ladder. At the time, Brezhnev, Chernenko and Andropov were all powerful men in the hierarchy; and yet looking back, it is they who appear the transitional figures. They may even have sensed that the younger man would eventually succeed them all and come to power young enough to rule the Soviet Union for decades, perhaps rivalling or even outstripping Brezhnev's own eighteen years in power after the fall of Khrushchev.

The Gorbachov the world has seen since then is a product of a new generation, with a style which marks him out from his predecessors. The man who goes on walkabout tours in far flung Soviet provinces and is shown on television chatting with the workers and housewives, the man who handles the foreign press with aplomb during talks with Western leaders is clearly in a different mould from Brezhnev, Andropov or Chernenko. During his trip to Paris in October 1985, and again in talks with President Reagan, Gorbachov appeared to be an updated and polished version of Khrushchev, the man who was in power in the Kremlin while Gorbachov was beginning his political career in Stavropol, trudging through the mud of the collective farms as the man responsible for local agricultural policy. The relaxed and sophisticated image is reinforced by Gorbachov's mastery of public relations and image making. He is aware that it helps the Soviet image in the world if the Kremlin leader wears well-fitting suits, smiles at the cameras, and has a smart and attractive wife who can make speeches of her own while visiting art galleries or fashion houses.

But the comparison with Khrushchev is telling on another level. Just as much as his predecessors, Gorbachov is the product of the Soviet system. Although the system and the men who run it have adapted to meet the challenges of changing times, the essence of the system, and the essential thinking of Kremlin bureaucrats themselves, remains in many ways the same. Gorbachov is not a liberal, as some Western commentators mistakenly assumed when he came to power. He is a reformer—but so too was Khrushchev, so to some extent was Brezhnev, and so above all was Andropov. Gorbachov is the best-educated Soviet leader since Lenin, with two university degrees and an outlook shaped by the events of the 1950s and 1960s rather than by the Second World War and the years of hardship which preceded it in the 1920s and 1930s. But he is not about to overthrow or even radically overhaul the system which produced him. His attitudes on human rights, censorship of literature and the arts, minority questions and Russia's right to intervene in Afghanistan are those of a man who joined the Komsomol at Moscow University and who used both orthodox ideology and the Soviet Party system of patronage and political infighting to reach the very pinnacle of power. In the 1980s the ascent to the top does not require the kind of terror and paranoia which prevailed during the dark days of Stalin's rule. But the struggle is still utterly ruthless, and depends as it did in the days of Lenin, Stalin and Khrushchev on willingness to accept and exploit the Communist Party's monopoly of power.

Gorbachov's career so far underlines this. He was born on 2 March, 1931, in the village of Privolnoye in the Red Guard district of Stavropol in the Northern Caucasus to what official Soviet biographers describe as a peasant family (how well off is not known). Gorbachov's grandfather was the founder and chairman of a Stavropol collective farm and is described in official biographies as a "hard working and respected man".

The fact that Gorbachov did not fight in the Second World War and was only ten at the time of the German invasion of Russia in 1941 is often taken to mean that he does not share the views of the Brezhnev generation, for whom the War was the central event of their lives. But the young Gorbachov did witness Nazism at first hand when the northern Caucasus came under German occupation in 1942. Gorbachov has told American visitors in Moscow that he vividly remembers his late father, Sergei Andreevich, an agricultural machine operator, being taken away and questioned by the Nazi occupiers. And when the fortieth anniversary of the end of the Second World War was celebrated in 1985, much of what Gorbachov had to say in messages to the leaders of other countries in the former anti-Nazi alliance had the ring of personally-felt experience. In any case, even today no boy of ten can escape the deluge of reminiscence about the war which pours out of Soviet television and the state publishing houses. Gorbachov has shown no sign that he dissents from the relentless Soviet attempt to keep memories of the Great Patriotic War, with its twenty million Russian dead and the consequent lessons for history, uppermost in the minds of modern Russians.

This entirely orthodox pattern continued when, at the age of fifteen, Gorbachov worked as a combine-harvester operator at a machine and tractor station (a now defunct part of the Soviet agriculture system) during his school holidays, Many schoolchildren in the Soviet country-side were expected to help with the all-important harvest (and indeed still are). By all accounts, Gorbachov was no rebel when he left Stavropol region (where his mother, Maria, is still living, aged 75 in 1986) in 1950 to go to Moscow University to study law. To go to the capital as a student from the provinces was (and is) a major achievement, not to be thrown away lightly by any suggestion of unorthodox thinking. Gorbachov joined the Komsomol and the Party as soon as he got to University, and according to fellow students took a cautious line over the political issues of the day: the death of Stalin, the Malenkov-Khrushchev succession, and Khrushchev's attempts to de-Stalinize Russia and expose the former dictator's crimes.

Zdenek Mlynar, a fellow student and later a leading figure in the Prague Spring, recalls that Gorbachov was highly intelligent, honest, and a good listener. Yet Gorbachov praised Stalin and talked of the need for brute force to ensure discipline in the countryside. Many years later, when Mlynar visited Gorbachov in Stavropol after the fall of Khrushchev, Gorbachov showed no regret at Khrushchev's fate, criticizing the ousted leader for having acted autocratically and unpredictably. At the same time, Gorbachov had "a lot of the reformer in his make-up", according to Mlynar, and hoped Brezhnev would give more autonomy to local leaders and managers. Some of his reformist ideas came from his wife, Raisa Maximovna, a pretty philosophy student whom he met during his Moscow University years. Raisa, who still influences his thinking, was a bright and attractive partner for a politically ambitious man. Like her husband, she was and is conventional in her adherence to Marxism-Leninism; but her doctoral thesis, a sociological investigation into everyday conditions on Stavropol collective farms, gave an unusually frank account of rural realities, including low incomes, sub-standard housing with no sanitation, and backward cultural and educational standards—the legacy Gorbachov is now trying to tackle with his wife's backing.

The bare bones of the official record do not reveal the way in which Gorbachov astutely grasped the principles of the Soviet power structure, in particular the way in which a Party official's fortunes depend on the patronage of those likely to rise in the hierarchy. Gorbachov, having joined the Party in 1952, worked steadily as a Party functionary in Stavropol District (Krai), First Secretary of the Stavropol Komsomol City Committee, Deputy Head of the Department of Party Propaganda, Second, then First Secretary of the Komsomol Regional Committee, Party organizer for Stavropol Collective and State Farms (March 1962); head of Party Organization in the region (December 1962); First Secretary of the Stavropol City Party Committee (September 1966); and Second Secretary of the Stavropol Regional Committee (August 1968). In 1967 he had taken his second degree in agronomy at Stavropol Agriculture Institute. The ultimate aim of this tedious climb was First Secretaryship of the Stavropol Regional Committee, achieved in April 1970, followed by membership of the Central Committee the following year. This might seem the record of a man destined for ever to hold petty office in an agrarian backwater. But Stavropol is no ordinary region. It is a particularly rich agricultural area of European Russia; but, more importantly for Gorbachov's career, it has traditionally been associated with prominent political figures who made it their base. In the early 1960s the head of the Stavropol Regional Committee was Kulakov. After Kulakov's elevation to Moscow in 1964, Gorbachov's superior (until 1968) was Leonid Efremov, formerly a close associate of Khrushchev. Although Gorbachov took a cautious line during de-Stalinization, rather than enthusiastically espousing Khrushchev's cause, he was nonetheless influenced by the extraordinary events of the Khrushchev years, from the madcap agricultural schemes to the publication of *One Day in the Life of Ivan Denisovich*. Efremov was head of the Central Committee department in charge of the Russian Federated Republic under Khrushchev, and after the fall of Khrushchev was demoted to First Secretary of the Stavropol Region, a post in which he served for six years and in which he influenced Gorbachov, at that time in his thirties.

More importantly for Gorbachov's ambition to make the leap to Moscow politics, two prominent members of the post-Khrushchev régime were also associated with Stavropol: Mikhail Suslov and Yuri Andropov. It was Suslov as much as Andropov who spotted Gorbachov's potential. Suslov, the chief Kremlin ideologist, was instrumental in bringing Gorbachov to Moscow as a Central Committee Secretary in 1978. Suslov had commanded partisan forces against the Nazis in the Stavropol region during the war, and still kept an eye on rising officials there, as did Andropov, who favoured the northern Caucasus as a place to take rest cures. Between them Andropov and Suslov were responsible for Gorbachov's Central Committee appointment, giving him responsibility for agriculture. This had been the fief of yet another Kremlin figure associated with Stavropol: Feodor Kulakov, a specialist on agriculture under Khrushchev and First Secretary of the Stavropol Krai from 1960, when Gorbachov was in charge of the local collective farms. The mysterious death of Kulakov in 1978, shortly after the meeting in the Caucasus mountains with Brezhnev, Andropov and Chernenko, gave Gorbachov his chance to step into Kulakov's shoes.

Gorbachov was a member of the funeral commission for Kulakov, and spoke during the burial on Red Square. In 1979 he became a Candidate Member of the Politburo, and a Full Member the following year. It was an astonishing rise for a man who had not yet reached fifty. This partly reflected his undoubted merits as an administrator, and was partly due to politicking on the part of Andropov and Suslov, who were keen to bring in fresh blood during Brezhnev's last years. Even so, it was more usual for a senior Party official to have to wait several years between promotions: Chernenko was perhaps one of the few comparable cases, having become a Central Committee Secretary in 1967, a candidate Politburo member in 1977 and a full Politburo member two years after that. Again this was due to direct patronage, in the case of Chernenko patronage from Brezhnev himself, the Party leader and President.

In 1981, at Brezhnev's last Party Congress (the Twenty-Sixth), Gorbachov was listed after Chernenko in the Central Committee Secretariat. The following year he rose to Number Three in the Secretariat pecking order, after Brezhnev and Suslov had died and Kirilenko had been removed by Andropov. As we have seen, under Andropov Gorbachov gradually widened his powers to include the economy as a whole, an element of foreign affairs and Party personnel (cadres). After the death of Andropov he acquired ideology (once Suslov's province) as well, thus moving into the Number Two slot. When he told an Indian reporter in Moscow in May 1985 that the secret of his political success lay in the Soviet way of life rather than "some kind of patronage", Gorbachov was clearly being disingenuous. He is genuinely proud of the fact that he was able to work his way up from humble origins to the leadership of one of the world's two superpowers, and genuinely believes that this demonstrates the ability of the Communist system "to find and exploit human potential". But the fact remains that he sits in the General Secretary's office because he understood and exploited the way in which the Soviet power structure actually works.

When Gromyko proposed him for the leadership at the Central

Committee Plenum on 11 March 1985 he stressed that Gorbachov possessed "the priceless gift of Party experience" and was a man of broad erudition and education who took "a Party approach to people" and knew how to find a common language with them. The common language includes shared assumptions about the world with Party officials of all generations, and a ruthlessness which lies behind the affability and willingness to listen and to take part in give and take discussions which led to Mrs Thatcher's remark, quoted earlier, during his visit to London in December 1984. But, "You govern your society and leave us to govern ours", was his revealingly terse response in London when challenged over human rights. The man the British popular press dubbed "the Gucci Comrade" has the kind of distorted Soviet view of the world which led him to accuse Britain of persecuting "entire communities, entire nationalities in Northern Ireland."

On the other hand, this is to see Gorbachov very largely in Western terms and from a Western perspective, rather than as the man who has given the Russians themselves a breath of fresh air. For Russians he represents new hope that the Soviet system may yet redeem itself by living up to the promises it has so dismally failed to fulfil over the last seventy years. "A bold creative search, freshness of thought and an energetic struggle against everything hypocritical and obsolete", was Gorbachov's theme in the speeches he made in the autumn of 1984 while manoeuvring to take over from Chernenko. He had, after all, been responsible for a partly successful agricultural policy in Stavropol at a time when the Soviet harvest was failing year after year. Much of this success was due to his introduction of the contract system of agriculture management, under which teams of workers on the farms were paid according to results, and divided the profits among themselves on a productivity basis. This was and is very far from private enterprise, but it is an attempt to make the centralized Soviet system more responsive by introducing an element of initiative and reward, which is probably the most that can be expected of any leader who adheres to Soviet ideology.

A similar interpretation can be put on Gorbachov's attitude to the West, which again has its roots in his political career. When he visited Canada in May 1983, when he was still an aspiring Politburo member under Andropov, Gorbachov displayed the same inflexible attitudes on human rights, Afghanistan and Jewish immigration that he was to reveal when in power, even accusing the United States of whipping up "spy mania" against Russia and using ideological sabotage to discredit the Soviet Union and strike at her prestige. "Do you really think we are such simpletons?" Gorbachov said angrily when Canadian parliamentarians raised awkward subjects. His accusation that they were simply trying to "ruin the atmosphere" was a typical Soviet point of view.

On the other hand, unlike many other Soviet politicians he was willing to discuss East-West affairs openly, and in his speeches between 1980 and 1985 laid genuine stress on the need to restore détente. One of his most important themes, which has come to the fore since he succeeded Chernenko, was that Russia has to catch up with the West economically and technologically at all costs, and that part of the cost is diverting resources from military expenditure to domestic needs.

Gorbachov's record in the period since he came to power has been dominated by this determination to modernize the country and to tackle the legacy of the Brezhnev and Chernenko periods by removing Old Guard bureaucrats from the power structure and reversing their policies. "Now we'll see Russia move," a young Russian friend said as Gorbachov passed swiftly into the Kremlin in March 1985. "Chernenko was not the man for the times. We need someone dynamic and technology minded who is willing to take risks rather than make safe choices." This optimism was widely shared, and for the most part completely genuine. A fresh-faced fur-hatted policeman I talked to on a snow lined avenue near our office raised his fist in a crude gesture denoting virility, and said, "What we need is a young and vigorous boss, and we've got one, thank God."

The Chernenko lying-in-state at the Hall of Columns, the last replay of this all too familiar routine, symbolized the passing of the Stalin generation. While Russians paid their respects to the prostrate white-haired figure of Chernenko, there was almost indecent impatience to have done with the ritual and get on with the Gorbachov programme. In contrast with the deaths of Brezhnev and Andropov, Chernenko's black edged portrait was on an inside page of *Pravda* as foreign leaders arrived for the Chernenko funeral, and the front page was dominated by the face of the new leader. Gorbachov did not yet have an absolute majority in the Politburo, but he had enough support to accomplish a swift transition, with the additional backing of the KGB and economic technocrats. His first speech as leader was low key, but conveyed the urgency he felt about economic reform and détente with the West. Overtures from the West came swiftly: Vice President Bush, making his third and last appearance at a Kremlin funeral, conveyed a proposal from Reagan for a summit meeting, and although the initial Russian response was cautious, this was to bear fruit in November at the Reagan-Gorbachov "fireside summit" at Geneva.

In his funeral oration on Red Square, delivered from the top of the Lenin mausoleum in a clear, decisive voice, Gorbachov reaffirmed Russia's readiness for détente, and made the bold claim that Communism would prove its advantages "not by force of arms, but by force of example in all fields of life—economic, political and moral." He also revived Andropov's anti-corruption programme by warning Russians to expect strict discipline, and a crackdown on "idle talk, swagger and irresponsibility, in fact anything which contradicts socialist norms"—a foretaste of Gorbachov's austere anti-alcohol campaign.

The funeral itself, held in chilly temperatures under cloudy skies, was a polished spectacle, with the ritual refined to the last degree by repetition. It symbolized the new era, with Gorbachov leading the Politburo on to the mausoleum, Tikhonov to his left, and Grishin on his right, two members of the Old Guard who were to be ousted before long. Like Andropov before him, Gorbachov used the funeral reception to send signals in foreign affairs, warning President Zia of Pakistan over the Afghan situation while seeking rapprochement with Peking in talks with the Chinese. On arms control, the Kremlin entered the newly-opened Geneva talks with avowals of good intent while trying to persuade the West Europeans to freeze deployment of medium range missiles. Gorbachov also began to forge his own relationship with the military, seeking allies among younger generation officers and future senior commanders. It was striking that not a single Marshal or General appeared alongside him on top of the mausoleum during the funeral ceremonies, an unprecedented break with previous practice.

The first full Politburo meeting after the change-over in the Kremlin laid down a clear policy of détente abroad coupled with reform and discipline at home, although Gorbachov's aides were at pains to stress that this meant neither market socialism nor political pluralism. That would mean "giving up the socialist foundations of our society", commented Vadim Zagladin of the Party's International Department. Russia's "false well wishers" hoped for radical reforms whose real aim would be "to put an end to socialism and wipe it off the face of the earth". At the end of March came the first moves in a growing Party purge, with the replacement of the First Secretary of the Kirov region, the dismissal of the 74-year-old Minister for Power and Electrification, and the sacking of the First Secretary at Bratsk in Siberia. All were replaced by younger (and more honest) men. A series of local Party meetings began in towns from Ufa to Irkutsk at which local officials were reprimanded in tough language for corruption and inefficiency.

In *Izvestiya*, Professor Aganbegyan, who had been giving Gorbachov discreet and informal economics tutorials in the Kremlin, called for Western-style business schools in Russia. "Times have changed," he said. "We are living in the century of technological change." At the Russian Republic Supreme Soviet on 26 March, Tikhonov, who was two months short of 80 and had appeared unsteady during the Chernenko funeral, failed to appear, the first sign that he might be about to step down. The same information machine which had presented an instant image of Andropov after Brezhnev's death now presented Gorbachov to Russian and world opinion as a modest, brisk, no-nonsense leader of the new generation, whose aim was efficiency and reform, not self-glorification. At *Pravda*, Viktor Afanasyev related with relish the way in which Gorbachov had telephoned him from the Kremlin to ask if he kept the works of Lenin in his office. "Certainly," Afanasyev had replied. "Then be so good in future as to quote him and not me," the new leader commanded.

Gorbachov, the optimists said, was not only a child of the Khrushchev era, but had also made a close study of Lenin's New Economic Policy (NEP) in the 1920s. Where Andropov had been an old man in a hurry, Gorbachov was a young man in a hurry. The local Party purges continued apace, with the sacking of the First Secretary at Minsk, three senior officials in Kirghizia and a regional Secretary in Azerbaijan. Even the chief of police in Gori, Stalin's birthplace, was singled out for dismissal. In the new Politburo line-up the average age had dropped from 70 to 67, and the average age of the four younger generation members was 59. At the beginning of April Gorbachov unveiled his stern if Quixotic anti-alcohol programme, designed to eradicate the "ugly phenomenon" of alcoholism and to "remove this evil from our society". He also took up where Chernenko had left off on the question of computer education, launching a comprehensive programme to instil computer literacy in secondary schools and universities (although the campaign was and remains hampered by Russia's lack of up to date desktop computers).

The dominant worry, however, as the Gorbachov era got off the ground, was arms control, just as it had been for Gorbachov's predecessors. On 8 April Gorbachov declared a Soviet freeze of missile deployment in Europe, dismissed the argument that Star Wars amounted to harmless research as "fraudulent", and at the same time called for a "serious impulse" to East-West relations "at a high political level", the clearest hint so far that Gorbachov was willing to reverse Soviet policy at last and meet the much vilified Reagan face to face. "Will the real Mikhail Gorbachov please stand up," one exasperated Western diplomat said in May, when Gorbachov used celebrations marking the fortieth anniversary of the end of the Second World War not only to launch a vociferous attack on the Western powers as the "imperialist heirs of Nazism", but simultaneously to send conciliatory V.E. Day telegrams to Reagan and Thatcher calling for joint efforts towards peace in the spirit of the wartime anti-Hitler coalition. Gorbachov was merely reflecting the ambiguity of all Soviet policy toward the West. When Gromyko and Shultz met once again in Vienna in mid-May, superpower dialogue was high on the agenda. It was Gromyko's final contribution to the launching of Gorbachov as a world statesman. Within two months, Gromyko had agreed to move out of the Foreign Ministry and into the office of Head of State, to enable Gorbachov to continue his re-invigoration of the Kremlin team, a process which reached its culmination in the Twenty-Seventh Party Congress in February 1986.

CHAPTER TWENTY-FIVE

Gorbachov's Russia

THE RUSSIANS ARE on the whole a conservative people and dislike change. There was rejoicing in the Party structure when Brezhnev discarded Khrushchev's policy of keeping *apparatchiks* on their toes by regularly replacing them. It is a mark of Gorbachov's achievement so far that he has revived Khrushchev's turnover of cadres without at the same time making the apparatus feel insecure or arousing the fear of unpredictable upheaval. In the government structure he has very largely replaced ministers with their deputies, merely insisting that the new ministers should be as efficient and honest as possible. Changes in the Party structure have been more radical: approximately a third of the OBKOM (provincial) regional and district Party secretaries have been replaced since March 1985 by a number of Central Committee officials (often at inspector level) loyal to Gorbachov and Ligachov, sent out from Moscow to ensure that the Gorbachov reforms reach down to the grass roots. The Politburo itself has changed almost out of recognition, with the watershed Party Congress in February 1986 setting the seal on this changeover.

The process began almost as soon as Gorbachov had taken over. In April 1985 he astonished and delighted Russians by going on the first of his Western style walkabouts to get his modernizing message across directly. He began in Moscow, where he visited a truck factory, a hospital, a school and a housing estate where he took tea with a flattered if disconcerted young working class couple. The walkabout was stage-managed for maximum PR effect, but Gorbachov nonetheless managed to inject an air of spontaneity into his televised chats with ordinary people. He used the same technique in subsequent "meet the people" exercises in Leningrad, the Ukraine, Siberia and other regions.

This revelation of the new Gorbachov style was immediately followed on 23 April by a Central Committee Plenum at which three of Gorbachov's key supporters—Yegor Ligachov, Nikolai Ryzhkov, and Viktor Chebrikov, the head of the KGB—were promoted to full Politburo membership. Ligachov, 64, and Ryzhkov, 55, had not even previously been candidate Politburo members, although both were Central Committee Secretaries. At the same Plenum Marshal Sokolov, the Defence Minister, became a candidate Politburo member, a move which did not reflect Sokolov's political weight (he was no Ustinov) so much as the post-1973 tradition of giving the military a Politburo representative. The agriculture portfolio in the Secretariat was taken by Viktor Nikonov, 56, another member of the Gorbachov generation, and a former Agriculture Minister of the Russian Federation (which includes Stavropol). The instant promotion of Ryzhkov and Ligachov was highly significant, since both were efficiency-minded technocrats who entirely shared Gorbachov's goals. Ryzhkov, a former director (at the age of 41) of the giant Uralmash Engineering complex in the Urals and the Deputy Head of GOSPLAN, had been spotted by Andropov as the kind of "hands on" manager Russia needed. He was moved to Moscow as a Central Committee Secretary in 1982, to streamline the economic department. Ligachov, also an engineer (in aviation) had personnel experience on the Central Committee before being sent to Tomsk as First Secretary in 1965. He was brought back from obscurity by Andropov in 1983 to take over from his former boss, Ivan Kapitonov, as head of cadres policy.

At the end of April the Kremlin announced that Chernenko, like Brezhnev and Andropov before him, was to escape complete political oblivion: the small town of Sharypovo, in his native Siberian region of Krasnoyarsk, was renamed Chernenko, and passenger liners, grain harvesters and streets were also to bear his name. Even the celebrated frontier post in which he had served as a border guard was rechristened. But to all intents and purposes the Chernenko legacy was forgotten. On May Day 1985, both Gorbachov and his fashionably-dressed wife received genuine rather than purely orchestrated applause from the marchers on Red Square, and it was a relief for Russians and foreign diplomats alike not to have to examine the leader closely for signs of ill health or decrepitude. The grandiose march-past, a few days later, marking the Fortieth Anniversary of the Soviet victory over Nazism, was an unashamed display of might and pride, similarly presided over by a confident and beaming Gorbachov. Unusually, television showed us close-ups of Raisa and of Gorbachov's daughter, Irina, which brought the new first family well into the limelight.

However, it would be wrong to suppose that Gorbachov acquired immediate total mastery of the Kremlin. On the contrary, he still had opposition, not least from his defeated rival for the leadership, Grigory Romanov, as well as from the Old Guard members such as Grishin. It was not accidental that Gorbachov chose Leningrad, Romanov's former fief, for his second populist walkabout in mid-May, impressing on shop floor workers at the Kirov engineering plant the need to master new technology. Behind the scenes, Gorbachov was preparing the way for the vital July Central Committee and Supreme Soviet sessions. His speeches on the need for efficiency ("We cannot expect manna from heaven") and on the damage to both health and labour productivity caused by alcoholism were only the public face of fast moving shifts in the apparatus. Ligachov was replaced in June as head of Organizational Affairs by Georgy Razumovsky, former Party leader in Krasnodar on the Black Sea, and a firm Gorbachov supporter. Razumovsky was also closely associated with Vorotnikov, who had also been First Secretary in Krasnodar. Ligachov, meanwhile, was making pronouncements on ideology, a clear sign that at the Plenum he would take over the ideology portfolio and thus move into the Number Two slot in the hierarchy.

The main talking point on the eve of the Supreme Soviet was Gorbachov's remarkable off-the-cuff speech to Party activists in Leningrad in May, an impassioned attack on incompetence. The speech made a belated impact in Moscow because it caught the propaganda machine off-guard, and was not reported in full for several weeks. The version circulated subsequently portrayed Gorbachov, his jacket off and his glasses at the end of his nose, warning officials that Russia could not afford to relax merely because it had begun to enter the modern era after "seventy years of strain and suffering since the Revolution". It was an impressive tour de force. Gorbachov spoke without notes and, on the whole, without Party clichés, deploring the fact that Russia's huge natural resources had made Russia "lazy and corrupt" and warning all those who opposed his programme of change that they would have to "get out of the road".

A few days later, at a special Party conference on science and technology, Gorbachov launched an equally devastating and detailed attack on Russia's ills, demanding a complete overhaul of industry, a measure of decentralization, material incentives, a role for scientists in planning and management and the drastic streamlining of overmanned ministries. "There must be no delay, no waiting, there is no time left for warming up, it has been exhausted by the past," Gorbachov declared. "We can only move forward, and at an even greater speed." Without mentioning Brezhnev by name, Gorbachov blamed many of Russia's problems on the Kremlin's failure to take the necessary measures from the early 1970s onwards. He sarcastically lambasted incompetent managers, and stressed the close connection between performance and remuneration, as well as the need to re-equip and update plants rather than build new ones. The result of this remorseless catalogue of failure was an unprecedented rejection of the draft Five Year Plan for 1986–90, a severe jolt to the bureaucrats of the state planning agency. Even Andropov had not moved so fast. The new economic drive coincided with the release in Moscow cinemas of a new film on Andropov's life which used rare footage and photographs to trace Andropov's career from his student days on the Volga to supreme power in the Kremlin, portraying him as a man of humanity and wisdom in a manner reminiscent of hagiographical films about Lenin.

The fall of Romanov, when it finally came, at the Central Committee Plenum on 1 July, caused very little surprise and a great deal of approval, not to say glee. A small, dapper figure, Romanov had made numerous enemies because of his overbearing manner and crudity, and his growing dependence on alcohol (excessive even by Russian standards) aroused distaste. All the anti-Romanov jokes and rumours which had circulated in secret came out into the open: he had borrowed a priceless Sèvres Catherine the Great dinner service from the Leningrad Hermitage for his daughter's wedding reception, and had smashed it to pieces like a peasant. He had entertained his mistress, a Leningrad pop singer, in the Politburo box at the opera, and had taken her in his yacht outside Soviet territorial waters on the Bay of Finland, nearly causing an embarrassing international incident. He was a liability to the Party, not only because of his personal habits but also because of his name, which recalled the overthrown Tsarist dynasty. All this overlooked Romanov's genuine contribution to economic efficiency in the Leningrad region, especially in engineering. But he had to go, and his fall proved once again that Leningrad was the wrong power base from which to make a bid for the leadership, as Grigory Zinoviev, Sergei Kirov and Andrei Zhdanov had found before him.

But the real surprise came at the Supreme Soviet the following day. At the Plenum Eduard Shevardnadze, the 57-year-old Georgian Party leader, was promoted from candidate to full Politburo membership, to fill the gap left by Romanov. Few anticipated that this was the penultimate move in Gorbachov's strategy for removing Gromyko from the Foreign Ministry, after nearly thirty years in the post, and replacing him with a younger man. This plan had been devised with Gromyko's consent, another aspect of the pivotal Gromyko-Gorbachov partnership. The condition of the deal was that Gromyko should be given the ceremonial but nonetheless prestigious title of Chairman of the Praesidium of the Supreme Soviet, or Head of State. Although all his predecessors, except Lenin, had combined Party leadership with either the Presidency or the Premiership, Gorbachov walked to the Supreme

Soviet podium on 2 July to nominate Gromyko as the new Head of State, to general astonishment. Combining the Party leadership with the Presidency had been justified "in the conditions of the time", Gorbachov said, but times had changed. The Party leader now had to concentrate to the maximum on "new tasks in both Party and economic spheres". He praised Gromyko, evidently sincerely, as an eminent politician of deep knowledge and experience. Gromyko, inscrutable as ever, thanked his young ally for his kind words, and said he was deeply moved by the trust placed in him. He gave no indication of how he felt about being pushed upstairs to make way for a relatively unknown Georgian, who had no foreign policy experience worthy of the name and who as Interior Minister and Party leader in Tbilisi specialized in exposing corruption and the Georgian Mafia—not particularly relevant training for dealing with arms control and East-West relations (although the appointment of a politician from an ethnic minority was likely to find favour in the Third World). Gromyko, by contrast, had been appointed Foreign Minister in 1957, at a time when Khrushchev had just rounded on the anti-Party group, the Sputnik was about to be launched, and an American actor called Ronald Reagan was starring in a film called *Hellcats of the Navy*. But Gromyko, now almost 76 was increasingly willing to take a secondary role on the diplomatic stage he had occupied since 1943 when he was Stalin's ambassador to Roosevelt's Washington. The Kremlin's hope was that as a result of Gorbachov's piece of political theatre at the July Supreme Soviet, the Soviet Union would be able to field a new foreign policy team at the superpower summit in November and outclass the Reagan administration.

As the Kremlin's traditional summer break approached, Gorbachov's purge of the Party and the government continued—and so, no less significantly, did a shake-up in the Soviet military structure. The elderly Minister for Light Industry, 74-year-old Nikolai Tarasov, jocularly known as the Minister for Queues, was replaced, in an attempt to improve consumer supplies. The ministers of electrical engineering, transport construction and ferrous metals, among others, were also axed. Doubts grew about Tikhonov, who had been notably unenthusiastic when nominating Shevardnadze for Foreign Minister at the Supreme Soviet, merely observing that the Georgian's background gave "grounds for believing" that he was qualified for the job. Romanov's place as Leningrad Party leader was taken initially by Lev Zaikov, and then Yuri Solovyov, the former Minister of Industrial Construction. Zaikov moved up the ladder to become one of the powerful Central Committee Secretaries at the July Plenum. So too did Boris Yeltsin, yet another technocrat from the Urals region, who was to replace the decrepit Grishin as Moscow city Party boss towards the end of the year.

Zaikov was at Gorbachov's side when the new leader made yet another provincial tour, this time at Minsk, where he met military commanders of the Byelorussian military district, a meeting attended by Marshal Ogarkov. In a speech to local citizens Gorbachov vowed "this year" to remove barriers to technological change, to raise productivity and give managers greater responsibility in a more flexible and up to date system. *Pravda* echoed him by asserting that Russian workers who failed to move with the times should not hope to keep their jobs, an unusual reference to possible unemployment for the incompetent and inefficient. In mid-July, having delivered this message, Gorbachov left for a holiday by the Black Sea, just as Reagan was undergoing surgery in Washington—a neat reversal of the superpower leaders' usual states of health.

Even with Gorbachov resting at the Politburo summer resort, the shake-up continued. The Party purge claimed victims in Kazakhstan, including the First Secretary of the huge Chimkent region, who was accused of building himself hunting lodges and race tracks and diverting funds from more worthy projects such as childrens' homes and hospitals. This augured badly for Kunayev, the Kazakh Party leader. Alexander Yakovlev, Director of the Institute for World Economics and International Affairs (IMEMO) took over the Central Committee Propaganda Department from Boris Stukalin (sent to Budapest as Ambassador), part of Gorbachov's and Ligachov's increasingly successful attempt to revamp and revitalize the Kremlin propaganda machinery.

But the most intriguing moves came in the military hierarchy, as Gorbachov created his own links with senior army commanders. Following the meeting at Minsk there were widespread reports that Ogarkov had retrieved his position and was to be appointed Commander in Chief of the Warsaw Pact in place of his former rival, Marshal Viktor Kulikov. This was denied, or at least not confirmed, by the Ministry of Defence. But Kremlin officials insisted the appointment had been discussed at a high level, although it had yet to be approved by the Warsaw Pact as a whole. This might have been seen as an isolated incident, except that it coincided with a whole series of new military appointments. Marshal Alexei Yepishev, 77, was replaced as head of armed forces Political Directorate—the channel for Party control over the Army—by General Alexei Lizichov, 25 years his junior. Lizichov had formally served under the astute General Mikhail Zaitsev, commander of Soviet troops in East Germany, who was now recalled to Moscow. Marshal

Vladimir Tolubko, the highly-regarded but ageing Commander of Strategic Rocket Forces, gave way to 61-year-old General Yuri Maximov, a former regional commander in Central Asia. Even *Red Star*, the army newspaper, acquired a new editor for the first time in thirty years.

The world of diplomacy was not immune either. Anatoly Dobrynin, the veteran ambassador to Washington, was the most prominent of a number of senior diplomats who packed their bags in the wake of Gromyko's departure from the Stalin-Gothic Foreign Ministry on the Moscow river. The Washington post was taken by 56-year-old Yuli Vorontsov, a man with long experience at more junior levels in the Washington embassy, and more recently Ambassador to France (in which post he had delicate diplomatic contacts with the Israelis at the home of the pianist, Daniel Barenboim). Dobrynin was able to give Gorbachov valuable advice on how to handle the Americans (and more particularly the American press) at the Geneva superpower summit. As the summit approached, Gorbachov allowed the first faint hints of a personality cult to appear in the Soviet press, an indication that he is as much attracted by the idolatry conferred by Kremlin power as were his predecessors. The press published the first photographs of the Gorbachov family, showing Gorbachov with his wife, daughter and granddaughter in an informal pose at the Artek pioneer holiday camp in the Crimea, with Gorbachov himself wearing a pioneer's red hand-kerchief.

As Gorbachov returned from holiday in mid-August, a debate between liberals and hardliners surfaced over the extent of permissible economic change. Vsevolod Ovchinnikov, the *Pravda* commentator, returned to China after a gap of thirty years and concluded that Chinese concessions to private enterprise under Deng had proved "fraught with negative and social and political consequences". But simultaneously, Dr Tamara Zaslavskaya of the Novosibirsk Economic Institute, who had caused such a stir under Andropov by leaking her report condemning the Soviet system as antiquated and inflexible, kept up liberal pressure on Gorbachov. She wrote in the Institute's journal *Eko* that vital economic reforms were being held up by obsolete methods of administration which imposed unnecessary limits on "freedom of choice". A series of articles in *Izvestiya* floated the idea of legalizing moonlighting and the black economy in the service sector, citing Estonian experience as an example. Gorbachov disappointed the liberals by using the anniversary of the Stakhanovite movement in the 1930s to suggest that the "shock brigade" methods used by Stakhanov under Stalin to achieve big production had relevance even in the age of new technology. But on yet another walkabout, this time in the Tyumen oil fields of Siberia, he drove home his message about efficiency as if he was a Western politician campaigning for office, and seemed only momentarily disconcerted when the workers responded by telling him a few home truths about the shoddy equipment they had to use.

Gorbachov, in other words, was and is faced with the dilemma of all reforming leaders in Russia: how far to go without upsetting vested interests and encouraging the kind of criticism which might eventually lead to unacceptable challenge to the Party's conduct of political, social and economic affairs.

Foreign policy is part of this dilemma, as Gorbachov's successful visit to Paris in October 1985 and his Geneva fireside summit with Reagan the following month demonstrate. On the eve of the Paris visit, Gorbachov astonished and delighted Soviet television viewers by answering publicly hard-hitting questions from French journalists on subjects previously taboo in the Soviet Union, including the number of political prisoners in Russia, and the persecution of Russian Jews. This frankness did not spill over to the Soviet media, but nonetheless disconcerted and alarmed hardliners in the Party who strongly disapproved of Gorbachov's decision to air matters which had been forbidden territory under all previous Soviet leaders.

The Geneva summit with Reagan proved a phenomenal public relations success for both Gorbachov and Raisa. Gorbachov's offer to reduce medium range missiles by balancing them against both American and British and French nuclear missiles, and his subsequent programme for a fifteen year phased reduction of weapons leading to a nuclear free world, won him widespread praise. But it was not lost on either Party hardliners or the military hierarchy that for all the smiles and bonhomie Gorbachov left Geneva empty-handed, with no American undertaking to abandon the Strategic Defence Initiative. His disarmament programme, announced in January, to the year 2000, necessarily involves large-scale reductions in both strategic and intermediate missiles which the generals and marshals must regard with apprehension. In his relaxed and even humorous interview with *Time* magazine in September 1985, which made such an impact on the West, Gorbachov said he hoped God on High would give Russia and America the wisdom to achieve peace. But this remark (admittedly made outside the formal framework of questions submitted beforehand) was censored from the *Pravda* version. In terms of domestic policy, which is what matters most to ordinary Russians, the key passage in his *Time* interview was that Russia needed disarmament abroad because he, Gorbachov, was embarking on such challenging reform programmes at home.

The completion of the Gorbachov team may help him to square the circle and embark on reform and disarmament while containing criticism and challenges. In late September, without waiting for the next Supreme Soviet session, Gorbachov retired Nikolai Tikhonov as Prime Minister and moved Nikolai Ryzhkov into the Premier's office at the age of 56. At a Central Committee Plenum on 15 October Tikhonov was dropped from the Politburo, and Nikolai Baibakov, the geriatric head of GOSPLAN, made way for 56-year-old Nikolai Talyzin, formerly in charge of relations with COMECON. In December came more changes in the military, with the retirement of 75-year-old Admiral Sergei Gorshkov, as Commander in Chief of the Soviet Navy after nearly thirty years, and his replacement by a man almost twenty years younger, Admiral Vladimir Chernavin, former Commander of the Northern Fleet and a pioneer of nuclear submarine warfare training in the 1960s. At the end of 1985 Viktor Grishin, by now 71, finally lost his grip on the Moscow city Party leadership and was succeeded by Boris Yeltsin. Only 54, Yeltsin had risen from political obscurity to become head of the Central Committee construction department in April 1985 and then a Central Committee Secretary only three months later. As the Twenty-Seventh Party Congress approached, in February 1986, with a reshuffle of both the Politburo and the Central Committee, Yeltsin gave the Party a taste of the Gorbachov style by delivering a blistering attack on the mismanagement of Moscow under both Grishin and the disgraced Moscow mayor, 77-year-old Vladimir Promyslov. Six out of the seven city Party Secretaries were sacked, as Grishin listened in humiliation. In January 1986 General Fedorchuk, who had succeeded Andropov as head of the KGB but had also been associated with Brezhnev, was removed as Interior Minister and replaced by 54-year-old Alexander Vlasov, a former regional First Secretary with no police background.

It is one thing to sack, disgrace and humiliate the Brezhnev generation, and another to face the problems it created and propose innovatory solutions likely to take Russia forward. Can Gorbachov do this? The best hints of his approach so far come from the new draft Party programme, endorsed at the October Party Plenum for adoption at the Party Congress. It avoids Khrushchev-style boasting about the future triumph of Communism, emphasizes Gorbachov's leitmotifs of modern management and technological change, and urges the country to double economic output over the next fifteen years, a target which would require an annual growth rate of nearly 5 per cent. But the programme only indirectly tackles the Brezhnev legacy, referring obliquely and faintheartedly to "certain unfavourable trends and difficulties in the seventies and early eighties" and accusing the former leadership of failing to assess "in due time and proper manner" the need for profound change in all spheres of Russian life. The *ancien régime*, the Gorbachov programme declares, also failed to "persist in making such changes". The next generation will judge whether Gorbachov is able to live up to his own analysis and succeed where his predecessors failed, or whether his successors will eventually lay the same charges at his door.

The most important question for Russians living under the rule of Soviet Russia's seventh leader is whether the frankness and flexibility of Gorbachov abroad will extend to Gorbachov at home. The Soviet failure to admit that there had been a disastrous accident at a nuclear power station at Chernobyl in the Ukraine in April 1986, with the facts only emerging because of radioactive fallout over Scandinavia, is certainly not an encouraging sign. In the long run, the expectations aroused by Gorbachov's performances, from Geneva and Paris to the oil fields of Siberia, could rebound on him—unless, that is, he is able to fulfil them.

CONCLUSION

Soviet Succession and Generational Change

THE SIX SOVIET succession crises since the Revolution have all taken place in different circumstances. In 1924 the struggle involved the generation of Bolsheviks who had only recently emerged from the conspiratorial anti-Tsarist underground and were still creating the new Soviet state. By the time Stalin died in 1953 many of the old Bolsheviks had perished, and Stalin's heirs had to restore the Party structure and deal with the dictator's terrible legacy while fighting it out for succession. To use Ralph Miliband's terms, Stalin's successors substituted an oligarchical collectivism for his "tyrannical collectivism". The third crisis, the fall of Khrushchev in 1964, occurred in still different circumstances, with the Soviet Union challenging the United States as a modern superpower and Brezhnev rising from the grey mass of Party bureaucrats to embody the managerial politics of the sixties and seventies.

The fourth, fifth and sixth succession crises between 1982 and 1985, which can be seen as one continuous process of transition, were a test of the Soviet political system's ability to produce a leader for the circumstances of the late twentieth century, with the Soviet Union under pressure as never before to meet the challenges of Western technology and ideas. The succession struggle eventually produced such a figure in Mikhail Gorbachov, but not before two members of the preceding generation, Andropov and Chernenko, had taken their turn at the top, a process which lost Russia valuable time after the Brezhnev generation had already had a stranglehold on Soviet policy for over two decades.

Despite the changing circumstances, and the fact that the first three successions were spread over forty years and the last three condensed into four years, common patterns can be discerned in the process of transition. The transition from Brezhnev to Gorbachov has shown that the selection of a new General Secretary, and the associated power struggle throughout the structure, need not be traumatic, and can become almost routine. As *Pravda* noted on the eve of Chernenko's death, the Party has by now "accumulated enough experience" to "ensure the succession". The hysterical scenes which greeted Stalin's death, with Russians dying in the crush at the lying-in-state at the Hall of

Columns, are presumably a thing of the past. On the other hand the mechanism for succession is no more firmly established or defined in 1986 than it was in 1924. Although the Party rules lay down clear procedures for the Central Committee, the Politburo, the Central Control Commission, the Party Congress and the Secretariat, there is no provision for the election of a leader. The stock Soviet response—that this is of no consequence because the Kremlin leadership is "collective"—has been proved to be spurious. The last three successions demonstrate conclusively that the personality and outlook of the leader are decisive in setting the tone for the Soviet domestic and foreign policy, and ultimately govern the pace and quality of Russian life in all spheres.

Secondly, the six successions show that the Communist Party remains the only source of real power in the Soviet Union, even if this power is sometimes shared with, and modified by, the parallel government structure, the armed forces, and other interest groups such as the security services, the scientific community and economic and industrial managers. The rise to power of Andropov was a partial exception to this rule, since more than any other contender he had the clear backing of the KGB and the military. But even Andropov was a product of the Party system. The history of Soviet successions is littered with abortive attempts by both secret police and military figures to overreach themselves and interfere in the exclusive preserve of the Party: supreme power. The fate of Beria after Stalin's death, and of Marshal Zhukov under Khrushchev's rule, underline this message, as by all accounts does the fall of Marshal Ogarkov during the Chernenko period. The Party leader rules, and does not relinquish power voluntarily. There is still no precedent for honourable retirement.

Thirdly, it is not the case, as might be supposed, that the struggle for power only occurs when the incumbent leader is either dead or in the final stages of decline. On the contrary, the nature of the Soviet system is such that jostling for position at all levels in the hierarchy never ceases. Even in the case of Stalin, both Khrushchev and Malenkov manoeuvred for advantage before the tyrant was dead, although they did so in fear and trembling lest they be accused of daring to presume to take his place. In other cases manoeuvring has been even more open, a mark of the fact that the succession process is no longer overshadowed by terror, and that although officials' careers depend on the outcome, their lives do not. Thus, as the Brezhnev era dragged painfully to a close, it was obvious that Andropov was seeking to outmanoeuvre Chernenko by becoming a Central Committee Secretary in order to make a bid for the leadership. Similarly, during the Andropov era supporters of Gorbachov, Chernenko, Romanov and other contenders used the media—including the Western press—to advance their cause.

It follows from this that if the power struggle precedes the moment of leadership crisis, it also continues after it, with factions—often revolving around geographical power bases as well as interest groups—struggling for influence. Even now, with Gorbachov firmly established in the Kremlin from the word go, the struggle for power goes on in his shadow. One large and influential group—including his Number Two, Yegor Ligachov, his Prime Minister, Nikolai Ryzhkov, and the new Moscow Party boss, Boris Yeltsin—consists of men of engineering and technocratic backgrounds drawn from Siberia and the Urals region. Gorbachov himself was a beneficiary of the pre-eminence under previous régimes of figures drawn from his native Stavropol, such as Suslov, Kulakov and Andropov. Similarly, the Brezhnev mafia was centred on the Ukraine.

This illustrates the fourth constant principle of the succession process: that political success depends on the right choice of political patron. Gorbachov has specifically denied that he is a product of the patronage system, claiming instead that the Party is able to spot and exploit talent to the full wherever it may be found. But this is disingenuous. Khrushchev rose through the ranks by coming to the attention of Stalin and then serving his dictatorship, even though he was later to repudiate it when he was in power himself. Brezhnev in turn was Khrushchev's protégé (and overthrew him) and Chernenko was Brezhnev's Number Two and his personal choice for successor (although he was initially passed over in favour of Andropov). Gorbachov was without question the man Andropov wished to see put into practice the reform programme Andropov himself was unable to realize. To be second in command does not on the other hand guarantee the succession, and a number of aspiring Party politicians such as Kirov or (in different circumstances) Kirilenko have used the patronage system to rise high, only to fall later on.

Fifthly, issues of both domestic and foreign policy are clearly used by contenders in the power struggle. The two salient policy issues of the past seventy years (and no doubt of the next seventy) have been the running of the Soviet economy (which directly touches on sensitive ideological questions), and Soviet relations with the West. All aspiring Soviet leaders have taken their stands on questions such as decentralization, consumer needs, the demands of heavy industry and agriculture, and openings to the West or China with a view to gaining an upper hand over their rivals, quite often adopting the very policies advocated by their defeated opponents once in power. Gorbachov has neatly combined the

questions of reform at home and détente abroad by saying that he needs
the latter in order to achieve the former, although whether the
difficulties he encounters will be exploited by potential critics in the
Politburo remains to be seen. The pressure is on Russia to avoid a costly
arms race over SDI and reform the domestic economy, and the sharp
drop in oil prices in the spring of 1986 has added to the squeeze by cutting
precious foreign currency revenue by a third. Moscow has its own
strategic defence programme, which it maintains is for peaceful rather
than military purposes, but will find it difficult to compete with the West,
especially as the European allies join Washington in Star Wars
research. Gorbachov, having presided triumphantly over the Twenty-
Seventh Congress, commands an unchallenged majority in the Politburo. But his fireside summit in Geneva with President Reagan aroused
some adverse comment behind the scenes in Russia, since having made
concessions (not least by agreeing to meet Reagan in the first place)
Gorbachov emerged with a new East-West climate of bonhomie and
hand shakes, but with no American undertaking to back down over "Star
Wars" or other arms issues. Similarly, Gorbachov's ambitious fifteen-
year programme for nuclear disarmament is said to have caused anxiety
in the Soviet military.

On the other hand the Gorbachov succession differs from previous
successions in one vital respect: there was no question, from the moment
he was appointed in March 1985, that he was the *vozhd*, the Russian
term for "boss". Partly because Gorbachov had had three years in which
to prepare his ground, relatively little lip service was paid in Party
literature or the mass media after Gorbachov's accession to the principle
of collective leadership. There were no reminders, as there had been for
Brezhnev after the fall of Khrushchev and for Andropov after the death
of Brezhnev, that the Party leader is the servant of the Party and a
humble member of the Kremlin team rather than its *nachalnik* (another
word for "boss"). As we have seen, the Brezhnev-Kosygin-Podgorny
troika was a genuine collective leadership for many years. For that
matter, Andropov can be said to have ruled together with two of his most
powerful colleagues, Ustinov and Gromyko, although arguably this was
largely because he was a sick man and would otherwise have been
"boss". In this as in other matters Gorbachov has emulated Andropov,
but with the vigour of a man in his fifties. Possibly senior members of the
Gorbachov team such as Ligachov and Ryzhkov will come to acquire
Kosygin-like status as the Gorbachov era progresses (although on
present showing no military figure is likely to do so). Gorbachov has also
broken with recent precedent by not combining the Party leadership

with the post of President. This does not preclude him from doing so in the future, once Gromyko leaves the stage, or from combining the Party leadership with the premiership, as Stalin and Khrushchev did.

The Gorbachov era will also show whether the change of generation in the Kremlin, so frustratingly delayed by Brezhnev's slow decline and the consequent hiatus, has produced a leadership with a new outlook which will enable it to tackle Russia's endemic problems and forge a new relationship with the West. One prominent representative of the Gorbachov generation is the poet Yevgeny Yevtushenko, also now in his early fifties. In his *Precocious Autobiography* Yevtushenko recalls his Communist upbringing and the impact on his generation of Khrushchev's revelations about Stalin. Thirty years on, Yevtushenko sometimes sounds like the court poet of Gorbachov's Kremlin, taking up Gorbachov's fight against corruption and hypocrisy and lambasting the "no-risk takers" who refuse to roll up their sleeves, and prefer a life of ease at the expense of the state system. "I long for the time when the no-risk takers will be chucked head over heels out of their armchairs", Yevtushenko wrote in a poem published in *Pravda* in September 1985. "Great motherland of ours, push them out of their offices, and give them some fresh air."

But on the evidence so far there are limits to the reforms Gorbachov has in mind. Like others of his generation, he is constrained by Soviet ideology. No less than the Brezhnev generation, the new team in the Kremlin runs the risk of falling victim to its own propaganda.

Bringing about the change of generations throughout the structure after so many years of immobility is in any case no easy matter. Despite all the talk of change, and despite the replacement by Gorbachov, and Ligachov, of officials from top to bottom of the structure, the new leadership has stopped short of a Khrushchev-style permanent turnover of officials. The new Party rules (Rule 25) adopted at the February 1986 Congress lay down a system of "systematic renewal" without insisting on regular and obligatory rotation. Republican level Party meetings during February, in the run up to the Party Congress, produced confessions of corruption and incompetence from Uzbekistan to Azerbaijan as part of Gorbachov's undeclared programme of "de-Brezhnevization". But on the other hand Gorbachov was obliged to allow the Party organizations in Kazakhstan and the Ukraine to re-elect Kunayev and Shcherbitsky respectively as republican First Secretaries. Both are indelibly associated with the Brezhnev years, as earlier chapters on Brezhnev have shown. Gorbachov's Russia is a country with an advanced space programme and mighty armed forces, but still women draw water from wells only a few miles from Moscow and many basic goods are in short supply or unavailable. In arms control, too, Gorbachov has inherited the problems his predecessors faced over strategic and medium range arsenals, and has to contend with a defence budget of 15–17 per cent of Soviety GNP (according to both the Pentagon and the CIA). Russia's international problems remain formidable, not least in the Middle East, after recent setbacks in the Yemen. Russia and America still have to seek to control unpredictable troublespots, for fear that regional conflicts will spill over into superpower confrontation. The appointment of former UN envoy Oleg Troyanovsky as Ambassador to Peking upgrades the post, but does not make Sino-Soviet differences easier to resolve.

It is an error to suppose that the new generation is much less conditioned in its thinking by the experiences of the Revolution, Civil War and Second World War than were previous generations in the Kremlin. The generation which witnessed the Revolution and the 1920s has died out; the generation for which Stalin and the war against Nazism were the formative experiences is growing old and being swiftly edged out of office. The Gorbachov leadership was brought up in the post-Stalin period: Gorbachov himself was only ten when war broke out. But the national myths of revolution and war are so powerful in Russia that they mould the outlook of all generations. Coupled with the indoctrination of Marxist-Leninist ideology and the constraints of the educational system, these myths ensure that while political style and economic methods change, the Soviet view of the outside world does not. Under Gorbachov, as under previous leaders, Russia is ever ready to expand its power and exploit Western weaknesses while at the same time remaining suspicious and fearful of encirclement and invasion. As Reagan appears to have learned, to patronize or antagonize the Soviet Union merely arouses Russian defensiveness and aggression. Yet Moscow is perfectly capable of restrained and responsible behaviour, as Gorbachov showed by his understated reaction to the American attacks on Libya in April 1986.

In 1972, T. H. Rigby observed of the Brezhnev generation that the typical senior Party official had begun his career as a manual worker and/ or Komsomol official, had taken a diploma at a technical institute and gone into industrial management before entering the Party machine and rising to be OBKOM or regional secretary before reaching Moscow.*

*Soviet Succession: Leadership in Transition, edited by Dimitri Simes, Georgetown Center for Strategic and International Studies, Washington 1978, p. 14).

But much the same could be said of the Gorbachov generation, fourteen years on. Ryzhkov graduated from the Urals Polytechnical Institute, and began work as an engineer in the Urals. Viktor Nikonov graduated from the Azov-Black Sea Agricultural Institute before heading a department of the Krasnoyarsk regional Party committee. Yegor Ligachov went to the Ordzhonikidze Aviation Institute in Moscow followed by engineering posts at an aircraft factory in Novosibirsk and Party officialdom in Novosibirsk and Tomsk. Yeltsin attended the same Urals Polytechnic as Ryzhkov before becoming first secretary of Sverdlovsk.

At the end of 1985, Ligachov made a stern call for ideological orthodoxy in the Soviet media and warned against excessive liberalization. This may have been aimed at the "liberal" Gorbachov: but it also reflects the fact that the Gorbachov generation is the Brezhnev generation with smarter suits, more up-to-date technology and smoother public relations. Hardline warnings to Hungary, in *Pravda* in January 1986, not to take liberalism too far, carry the same message. In the end however, allowance must be made for the unpredictable. Gorbachov's interaction with the Western world and his refreshing new style are bound to have an impact on Russians' thinking and expectations. The system will not alter fundamentally; but Russians may be able to test its limits more boldly, and thus alter it in small but significant ways. Gorbachov himself may yet surprise us: the succession process produced, in Khrushchev and Andropov, two leaders whose background would hardly have led analysts to forecast their actions when in power. Gorbachov spent his favourite years under Khrushchev's rule, and learnt his mastery of Kremlin politics at Andropov's feet. Gorbachov's marathon five hour speech to the Twenty-Seventh Party Congress in February–March 1986 was disappointing for those who hoped for what *Sovietskaya Rossiya* described on the eve of the Congress as "drastic changes". The Congress took place thirty years almost to the day after Khrushchev's denunciation of Stalin at the 1956 Party Congress; Gorbachov himself attended the 1961 Congress, when Khrushchev's de-Stalinization programme was taken further. When he rose in the Palace of Congresses as leader, Gorbachov (who earlier in his career had praised Brezhnev's leadership) launched an attack on the "inertia and rigidity" of the Brezhnev years, without once mentioning Brezhnev or his associates by name. The 5000 delegates heard an incisive diagnosis of Russia's malaise, including bribery, the decline of dynamism and the escalation of bureaucracy. But the system Gorbachov now heads, and through which he has to work to achieve change, is by its nature corrupt, un-dynamic and bureaucratic. The newly elected Central Committee contains many new faces, giving the long-frustrated generation of men in their fifties access to power at last and symbolizing the departure of the Brezhnev generation. But Gorbachov stopped short of a wholesale cleansing of the apparatus. "Some comrades have suggested a purge", he said. "I do not think there is any need for a special campaign to purge the ranks. Our party is a healthy organism."

But is it? Gorbachov is a product of the Soviet system, and is not about to overthrow it—on the contrary, he hopes to make it work better. There are distinct echoes in his reforms of ideas which have been tried before, such as the Kosygin reforms of 1965–66—although Gorbachov is more determined to carry them through. Despite the record of Soviet history, Gorbachov passionately believes that the system he has inherited can fulfil the promises of Marxism-Leninism. The cards are stacked against him, and much will depend on whether the refreshing and innovative Gorbachov style, which at the moment baffles unimaginative Soviet officials, proves infectious and comes to permeate the apparatus. In Gorbachov's first year in power we watched him trying to conduct a dialogue with people—including his own officials—who obviously preferred to pass on instructions from the top and avoid taking responsibility for their actions. Gorbachov, when in Stavropol, used to take motoring holidays in Italy and France with Raisa, and is still at ease in the Western world. But he is operating in a manner reminiscent of a Western politician in a context—the Soviet system—which has not yet changed fundamentally. He has moved ahead, but the system has not. "He has never been a cynic", Zdenek Mlynar observed in his article "My Fellow Student Mikhail Gorbachov".* "He is in character a reformer who considers politics as a means to an end, its objective being to meet the needs of the people." In Stavropol, Gorbachov used to walk to his office from his single-storey home rather than take the officially-provided limousine. A quarter of a century later, the same man—part *apparatchik*, part idealist, part populist—warned the Twenty-Seventh Party Congress against the "peculiar psychology" of those who want "to improve things without actually changing anything".

The evidence so far is that his approach is inherently contradictory, with Gorbachov the reformer at odds with Gorbachov the *apparatchik*. This schizophrenia is reflected in the leadership as a whole, where the struggle for power continues in Gorbachov's shadow. As in previous Politburos, there are powerful secondary figures—Yeltsin, Ryzhkov, Ligachov—who have their own power bases, their own protégés and

L'Unita, 9 April, 1985.

their own policy directions. At the Party Congress Ryzhkov called for radical reforms—within the "fundamental principles" of Communism—and like Gorbachov catalogued the "intolerable deterioration" of discipline and responsibility during the Brezhnev years, holding up the Andropov era and 1983 as the new beginning. Yeltsin spoke in similar terms of the previous generation's failure to root out bureaucracy and abuse of power, and admitted that he and others had lacked the "courage and experience" to speak up at the Brezhnev Congress of 1981. Ligachov, by contrast, emphasized orthodox, hardline ideology, and appeared most unhappy with the proposed pace of reform, reprimanding *Pravda* for having gone too far on the eve of the Congress by printing letters from old Bolsheviks critical of the hidden privileges of the élite. Hardliners in the arts such as Alexander Chakovsky, editor of the *Literary Gazette*, and Georgy Markov, head of the Writers' Union, dashed hopes of a cultural thaw under Gorbachov. Markov said Pasternak's *Doctor Zhivago* could still not be published even though the press had praised Pasternak before the Congress.

Markov and Chakovsky are survivors from the *ancien régime*, and Politburo and Secretariat changes at the Congress also reflected a political balancing act rather than radical change. Boris Ponomaryov finally stepped down at 85 as candidate Politburo member (never having made it to full membership), and Alexandra Biryukova entered the secretariat (expanded from ten to eleven) to become at the age of 57 the first woman at the top in Russia since Ekaterina Furtseva, Khrushchev's Minister of Culture. But the only new full Politburo member was Lev Zaikov, with Boris Yeltsin, Yuri Solovyov and Nikolai Slyunkov—Party First Secretaries in Moscow, Leningrad and Byelorussia—becoming candidate members (in Yeltsin's case just before the Congress). Marshal Sokolov did not gain full membership of the Politburo, thus still leaving the top Party body with no military representative. The appointment of Anatoly Dobrynin as a Central Committee Secretary at the age of 66, after 24 years as ambassador to Washington, was an unusual move from diplomacy to Party apparatus and reassuring for East-West relations—but it was scarcely a break with the past. The average Politburo age has dropped to 63, but Gorbachov—who turned 55 during the Congress—still has to balance the new against the old, fresh blood against the old guard, innovation and reform against rigid ideology and conservatism. His exhortation to Congress delegates to take home the message of "radical transformations" in Soviet life is in practice tempered by caution, realism and the narrowness of Soviet thinking.

To implement his changes, Gorbachov has not only to overcome the inertia of the system but also to rise above the limitations of the ideology in which he believes. He is no Stalinist (even though he joined the Party the year before Stalin's death); both he and Raisa Maximovna believe that reform and the constraints of Communism are compatible. "The way out, as we see it, lies in a thorough modernization of the national economy", Gorbachov told the Congress. This Andropovian recipe involves autonomy for farm and factory managers, computerization, and capital investment, with showcase plants like the Togliatti car factory able to keep 40 per cent of its profits, including foreign currency—but the central planning apparatus remains firmly in place. There are hints that illegal dealers (*shabashniki*) might be legalized, and at the Congress Gorbachov referred to the private enterprise tolerated under Lenin's New Economic Policy (NEP). Gorbachov even used Lenin and WEP as a precedent to justify his proposal for allowing state and collective farms to dispose of a third of their fruit and vegetable output as they wished. But he also made it clear that concessions to capitalism were out of the question. The release of the Jewish human rights activist Anatoly Shcharansky on the eve of the Congress, in a dramatic "spy swap" on a Berlin bridge, coincided with stern reminders to the Soviet people that their first duty was to the Communist state and dissidents would be punished. Gorbachov referred to Afghanistan as a "bleeding wound", but put all the blame for the Afghan war on "imperialist interference". His anti-American rhetoric at the Congress, and his dismissal of the American position on nuclear disarmament and a freeze on nuclear testing, appeared not to have been softened by the bonhomie of the first Reagan-Gorbachov summit, giving rise to fears that the second super-power summit might founder. Unless the new Gorbachov style alters the *substance* of Soviet policy at home and abroad, it may yet be said of Gorbachov—as he himself once said of Khrushchev—that he started out a reformer and decentralizer but became an autocrat as inherited problems proved intractable, blunting the edge of the drive for change. Can Gorbachov avoid this fate by learning from the record of his six predecessors in the Kremlin?

He has made the forging of links between Russia and Western Europe one of his main aims, and the formal contacts between COMECON and the EEC which Gorbachov proposed during his Paris visit have led to exploratory talks. But the Western Powers are fully aware that Gorbachov hopes, as his predecessors hoped, to divide the Western Alliance by wooing Europe. For both Europe and America the Soviet failure to act responsibly over the meltdown of the graphite-moderated lightwater reactor at Chernobyl in the Ukraine has already dented Gorbachov's polished image and undermined his new "openness" (*glasnost'*) at an early stage although Moscow sought to regain the propaganda advantage by accusing the West of exaggeration. Chernobyl, with its echoes of the earlier mishandling of the Korean airline disaster under Andropov, has underlined the Kremlin's continuing obsession with secrecy, underlining at the same time that Gorbachov is a man of the East as much if not more than a man of the West. The tough and blunt Boris Yeltsin said in West Germany that the catastrophe was due to human error ("subjective factors") and admitted radiation problems in the Kiev area—but none of this filtered back home, where *Pravda* presented instead a rosy picture of May in the Ukraine and television took eight days to show pictures of Chernobyl. For NATO the incident once again raises the question of Soviet trustworthiness, and brings to the fore the importance of verification in arms control agreements. It casts grave doubt on Gorbachov's repeated assertion, in the course of his 15 January disarmament speech, that verification presented no major obstacles. There will also be profound long-term implications for Gorbachov's ambitious plans for both Soviet technology and the future of agriculture.

At home, Gorbachov's attempt to appear a modern European-style leader clashes not only with traditional controls of society and the Russians' belief that the authorities know what is best for them, but also with ethnic trends. The increasingly Asian nature of Soviet society is illustrated by the high birth-rate in the Southern Muslim Republics such as Uzbekistan, making it inevitable that by the year 2000 there will have been a demographic shift toward the Central Asian and other non-Russian populations, putting the European population in a minority. Gorbachov and his generation will have to face up to the challenges this poses for industry, the armed forces, and nationalist tensions in the Soviet system.

As the Brezhnev era drew to a close it was a common joke (or *anekdot* as the Russians say) in Moscow that Brezhnev had been given three envelopes by Khrushchev when he took over, and was told to open one whenever a crisis arose. When the first crisis broke out Brezhnev (so the *anekdot* went) opened the first envelope, and the note inside said: "Blame me for everything, and carry on"—which Brezhnev did. When the second crisis arrived, the Soviet leader opened the second envelope and read: "Re-shuffle the Politburo and carry on"—which he duly did. When the third and final crisis broke, Brezhnev tore open the third envelope, desperate to find the solution to the problems of supreme power in the Kremlin. The message read: "Start writing three envelopes". This *anekdot* was repeated under Andropov, and again under Chernenko after Andropov's death. It has not, so far, been told about Gorbachov.

SELECT BIBLIOGRAPHY AND SOURCES

1. General

BIALER, SEWERYN: *Stalin's Successors; Leadership, Stability and Change in the Soviet Union*, Cambridge and New York 1980.

BROWN, ARCHIE, and GRAY, JACK (eds): *Political Culture and Political Change in Communist States*, London 1977.

BRZEZINSKI, ZBIGNIEW: *Dilemmas of Change in Soviet Politics*, New York 1969.

CARR, E. H.: *A History of Soviet Russia*, ten volumes, London and New York 1952–1978.

COATES, KEN (ed): *Detente and Socialist Democracy, A Discussion with Roy Medvedev*, Nottingham 1975. (Essays by Ralph Miliband, Ernest Mandel, E. P. Thompson and others.)

CONQUEST, ROBERT: *Power and Policy in the USSR, A Study of Soviet Dynastics*, London and New York 1961.

HOLLOWAY, DAVID: *The Soviet Union and the Arms Race*, Yale 1984.

HOUGH, JERRY F.: *Soviet Leadership in Transition*, Washington 1980.

MCNEAL, ROBERT: *The Bolshevik Tradition; Lenin, Stalin, Khrushchev and Brezhnev*, second edition, Englewood Cliffs, N.J. 1975.

RIGBY, T. H.: *Communist Party Membership in the USSR 1971–1967*, Princeton 1968.

RUSH, MYRON: *Political Succession in the USSR*, New York 1968.

SCHAPIRO, LEONARD: *The Government and Politics of the Soviet Union*, London and New York 1979.

SCHAPIRO, LEONARD: *The Communist Party of the Soviet Union*, second edition, London and New York 1971.

SIMES, DIMITRI (ed): *Soviet Succession; Leadership in Transition*, Center For Strategic and International Studies, Georgetown University, Washington D.C. 1978. Washington Papers No. 59.

SIMIS, KONSTANTIN: *USSR, Secrets of a Corrupt Society*, London and New York 1982.

VOSLENSKY, MICHAEL: *Nomenklatura: Anatomy of the Soviet Ruling Class*, New York and London 1984. (By a former Soviet history professor.)

YEVTUSHENKO, YEVGENY: *A Precocious Autobiography*, London 1963.

2. Lenin

LEWIN, MOSHE: *Lenin's Last Struggle*, New York 1968.

SCHAPIRO, LEONARD, and REDDAWAY, PETER (eds): *Lenin: the Man, the Theorist, the Leader*. London and New York 1967.

SHUB, DAVID: *Lenin*, London and New York 1966.

ULAM, ADAM B.: *Lenin and the Bolsheviks*, New York and London 1966.

3. Stalin

ALLILUYEVA, SVETLANA: *Twenty Letters to a Friend*, London and New York 1967, and *Only One Year*, London and New York 1969. (Both valuable despite her return to Russia and "repudiation" of these works.)

BORTOLI, GEORGES: *The Death of Stalin*, London 1975. (By a former French TV correspondent in Moscow.)

DEUTSCHER, ISAAC: *Stalin: A Political Biography*, London and New York 1970.

HINGLEY, RONALD: *Joseph Stalin, Man and Legend*, London 1974.

KHRUSHCHEV, N. S.: *Khrushchev Remembers*, translated and edited by Strobe Talbott, New York 1970. Also: *The Last Testament*, 1974.

MEDVEDEV, ROY: *All Stalin's Men*, Oxford 1983 (Biographical sketches of Voroshilov, Mikoyan, Suslov, Molotov, Kaganovich and Malenkov.)

RIGBY, T. H. (ed): *Stalin*, Englewood Cliffs, N.J. 1966.

SOUVARINE, BORIS: *Stalin: A Critical Survey of Bolshevism*, New York 1939.

4. Khrushchev

BRESLAUER, GEORGE: *Khrushchev and Brezhnev as Leaders*, London 1982.

CRANKSHAW, EDWARD: *Khrushchev*, London and New York 1966.

FRANKLAND, MARK: *Khrushchev*, London 1966.

MEDVEDEV, ROY: *Khrushchev*, Oxford 1982.

TATU, MICHEL: *Power in the Kremlin*, London 1969 (on Khrushchev and Kosygin, and Khrushchev's fall).

TUCKER, ROBERT C.: *The Soviet Political Mind: Studies in Stalinism and post-Stalin Change*, London 1963.

5. Brezhnev

DORNBERG, JOHN: *Brezhnev: the Masks of Power*, London 1974.

EDMONDS, ROBIN: *Soviet Foreign Policy—The Brezhnev Years*, Oxford 1983.

KISSINGER, HENRY: *Years of Upheaval*, New York and London 1979. (Memoirs.)

6. Andropov, Chernenko and Gorbachov

ANDROPOV, Y. V.: *Selected Speeches and Writings*, Oxford 1983. Also: *Izbrannye rechi i stati*, Moscow 1979.

BYRNES, ROBERT (ed): *After Brezhnev—Sources of Soviet Conduct in the 1980s*, Washington 1983 (general essays).

CHERNENKO, K. U.: *Selected Speeches and Writings*, Oxford 1984.

GORBACHOV, M. S.: *A Time For Peace*, New York 1985 (speeches and interviews).

HALLIDAY, FRED: *The Making of the Second Cold War*, London 1983.

MEDVEDEV, ZHORES: *Andropov*, Oxford 1983.

OGARKOV, N. V.: *V interesakh povysheniya boyevoi gotovnosti*, in Kommunist Vooruzhenikh Sil' No 14 (July) 1980.

SHEVCHENKO, ARKADY: *Breaking with Moscow*, London 1985 (useful insight into Gromyko and the Soviet foreign service).

SCHMIDT-HÄUER, CHRISTIAN: *Gorbachov: The Path to Power*, translated by Ewald Osers and Chris Romberg, London 1986 (By a former West German correspondent in Moscow).

STEELE, JONATHAN, and ABRAHAM, ERIC: *Andropov in Power*, New York 1984.

7. Selected Articles

Much of this book draws on my own reports for *The Times* between 1982 and 1985–6. Accounts of Central Committee Plenums and Supreme Soviet sessions are based on *Pravda* and Tass. In addition I am indebted to research papers by Radio Liberty and to articles in *Problems of Communism*, including Archie Brown's "Gorbachov—New Man in the Kremlin" in No 3, 1985. Useful issues of *Newsweek* were 12 April 1982 ("Brezhnev's Final Days"), 14 October 1985 ("Gorbachov in Paris") and 2 December 1985 ("The Geneva Summit: What They Said Behind Closed Doors"). Also useful: *Time Magazine* 22 November 1982 ("After Brezhnev: Andropov Takes Command"), 27 February 1984 ("Chernenko: The Kremlin's New Master"), 25 March 1985 ("Gorbachov, Moscow's New Boss—Younger, Smoother and Probably Formidable") and 9 November 1985 ("Interview with Gorbachov"). *International Business Week* of 11 November 1985 surveys the economic future ("Gorbachov's Russia: Can He Revive the Soviet Economy?"). This book draws on a wide range of Soviet publications including *Kommunist*, the theoretical journal of the CPSU, *Literaturnaya Gazeta* and other daily newspapers.

INDEX